D1807521

The Political Economy of Celebrity Activism

This edited collection brings together scholarly works of both a theoretical and empirical nature to critically analyse the forms and functions of the contemporary celebrity activist and to examine how these intersect with the political economic structures in which celebrity activists operate.

Collectively, the volume illuminates some of the inherent tensions between the ethos of solidarity and compassion that the celebrity activist works to generate on the one hand and the processes of corporate sponsorship and discourses of individualism upon which the celebrity often depends, on the other. By offering empirical case studies that situate instances of celebrity activism within specific political contexts, the collection highlights how celebrity activism intersects with some of the underlying structures of gender politics and political discourses such as neoliberalism. In addition, the volume discusses how the tensions between, for example, individualism and solidarity can raise important questions about the authenticity of individual celebrity activists and how individual celebrity activists work, with varying degrees of success, to obfuscate such tensions and obscure the potential contradictions of their work.

This book will be of great interest to students and academics within the fields of politics, international development, political communication, social movements, activism studies, and celebrity culture.

Nathan Farrell is Senior Lecturer in Media and Communication at Bournemouth University, UK. His research interests include celebrity activism, corporate social responsibility, and popular culture. His work on celebrity activism has been published in a number of international journals.

Popular Culture and World Politics

Edited by Matt Davies
Newcastle University

Kyle Grayson
Newcastle University

Simon Philpott
Newcastle University

Christina Rowley
University of Bristol

Jutta Weldes
University of Bristol

The *Popular Culture and World Politics* (PCWP) book series is the forum for leading interdisciplinary research that explores the profound and diverse interconnections between popular culture and world politics. It aims to bring further innovation, rigor, and recognition to this emerging subfield of international relations.

To these ends, the PCWP series is interested in various themes, from the juxtaposition of cultural artefacts that are increasingly global in scope and regional, local, and domestic forms of production, distribution, and consumption; to the confrontations between cultural life and global political, social, and economic forces; and to the new or emergent forms of politics that result from the rescaling or internationalization of popular culture.

Similarly, the series provides a venue for work that explores the effects of new technologies and new media on established practices of representation and the making of political meaning. It encourages engagement with popular culture as a means for contesting powerful narratives of particular events and political settlements as well as explorations of the ways that popular culture informs mainstream political discourse. The series promotes investigation into how popular culture contributes to changing perceptions of time, space, scale, identity, and participation while establishing the outer limits of what is popularly understood as 'political' or 'cultural'.

In addition to film, television, literature, and art, the series actively encourages research into diverse artefacts including sound, music, food cultures, gaming, design, architecture, programming, leisure, sport, fandom, and celebrity. The series is fiercely pluralist in its approaches to the study of popular culture and world politics and is interested in the past, present, and future cultural dimensions of hegemony, resistance, and power.

The Political Economy of Celebrity Activism

Edited by Nathan Farrell

For more information about this series, please visit: www.routledge.com/Popular-Culture-and-World-Politics/book-series/PCWP

The Political Economy of Celebrity Activism

Edited by Nathan Farrell

Routledge
Taylor & Francis Group

LONDON AND NEW YORK

First published 2020
by Routledge
2 Park Square, Milton Park, Abingdon, Oxon OX14 4RN

and by Routledge
52 Vanderbilt Avenue, New York, NY 10017

Routledge is an imprint of the Taylor & Francis Group, an informa business

© 2020 selection and editorial matter, Nathan Farrell; individual chapters, the contributors

The right of Nathan Farrell to be identified as the author of the editorial material, and of the authors for their individual chapters, has been asserted in accordance with sections 77 and 78 of the Copyright, Designs and Patents Act 1988.

All rights reserved. No part of this book may be reprinted or reproduced or utilised in any form or by any electronic, mechanical, or other means, now known or hereafter invented, including photocopying and recording, or in any information storage or retrieval system, without permission in writing from the publishers.

Trademark notice: Product or corporate names may be trademarks or registered trademarks, and are used only for identification and explanation without intent to infringe.

British Library Cataloguing-in-Publication Data
A catalogue record for this book is available from the British Library

Library of Congress Cataloging-in-Publication Data
A catalog record for this book has been requested

ISBN: 978-1-138-67568-1 (hbk)
ISBN: 978-1-315-56051-9 (ebk)

Typeset in Times New Roman
by Apex CoVantage, LLC

Contents

Figure

Contributors

Annika Bergman Rosamond is Associate Professor in International Relations at the Department of Political Science, Lund University. She is also the Director of the MA in Global Studies, Faculty of Social Sciences. She is the current chair of the Feminist Theory and Gender Studies section of ISA. Her main research interests include cosmopolitan thought; feminism and IR/security studies including feminist foreign policy; celebrity humanitarianism and politics. She has published widely on feminist foreign policy, international ethics, gender cosmopolitanism and celebrity humanitarianism in a range of journals and books.

Bruno Campanella is Associate Professor in the Department of Media and Cultural Studies at Universidade Federal Fluminense, Brazil. He is the author of the book 'Os Olhos do Grande Irmão: Uma etnografia dos fãs do Big Brother Brasil', and has recently published on media practices, and processes of media recognition.

Nathan Farrell is a Senior Lecturer in Media and Communication at Bournemouth University, UK. His research interests include celebrity activism, corporate social responsibility, and popular culture. His work on celebrity activism has been published in *The British Journal of Politics and International Relations* and *M/C* journal.

Catia Gregoratti is Lecturer in Politics and Development at Lund University, Sweden. Her research is situated in the field of feminist international political economy. She has written and published on UN-business partnerships, corporate social responsibility, and more recently on the corporatisation of feminism and its contestation.

Joshua Gulam is a Lecturer in Media and Communication at Liverpool Hope University. His PhD, completed at University of Manchester in January 2017, focused on the charitable and political campaigning of contemporary Hollywood films stars, including Angelina Jolie and George Clooney. Publications include chapters in Lasting Screen Stars: Images that Fade and Personas that Endure (2016) and Make America Hate Again: Trump-Era Horror and the Politics of Fear (2019), as well as a journal article on film star campaigning in Celebrity Studies (forthcoming 2020).

Susan Hopkins is a senior lecturer within the Open Access College of the University of Southern Queensland, Australia. Her research interests include sociological approaches to the education of marginalised groups including LSES youth and incarcerated students as well as critical cultural studies and media representations of gender, feminism and empowerment.

Panos Kompatsiaris (PhD, University of Edinburgh, 2015) is assistant professor in art and media at the National Research University Higher School of Economics in Moscow. He works at the intersection of contemporary art theory, cultural studies and ethnography, focusing on the broader politics of culture under capitalist relations of production.

Eric Louw is a Professor in the School of Communication and Arts at the University of Queensland. He has previously worked for a number of South African universities, and run an NGO engaged in development work. Louw currently serves on the editorial boards of five journals and is a research Fellow at the University of South Africa. He has published widely in the fields of political communication, South African media and South African political discourse.

Samita Nandy holds a doctoral degree from the School of Media, Culture and Creative Arts (MCCA) at Curtin University in Australia. Her research focuses on celebrity activism and nationalism, and has been sponsored by international and national grants in Australia and Canada. Dr. Nandy has taught at the University of Toronto, Ryerson University, and Curtin University. She is now the founding director of the Center for Media and Celebrity Studies (CMCS).

Jackie Raphael teaches at Curtin University. Her research predominantly focuses on celebrity culture, social media, endorsements, branding, iconic status and bromances. Dr. Raphael is on the Editorial Board of Waterhill Publishing and on the Advisory Board of Centre for Media and Celebrity Studies. Dr. Raphael has organised and chaired conferences globally and is the creator/producer of Celebrity Chat. Furthermore, she has published various books including *Building Bridges in Celebrity Studies* (2016) and *Becoming Brands: Celebrity, Activism and Politics* (2017).

Lukasz Swiatek lectures and researches in communication and media studies in the Faculty of Arts and Social Sciences at the University of New South Wales, Sydney. His research interests include strategic communication, including digital developments affecting professional communicators and organisations, and the changing shapes and roles of different types of rewards. He has published extensive research on public relations, communications and creativity and his teaching and learning blog regularly receives visitors from around the world.

Dr Hilary Wheaton is a member of the Editorial and Advisory Board for the Centre for Media and Celebrity Studies (CMCS), Editorial Board Member for Water Hill Publishing, and Executive Committee Member of Open & Distance Learning Association Australia (ODLAA). Her research interests include sexuality and embodiment, persona and celebrity, and learning and teaching in higher education. She currently works at RMIT Australia, as the Lead Learning Design and Technology.

Series editors' preface

The contemporary political power of celebrity cannot be denied. Celebrities sell us products and beliefs, advocate causes, get us to donate money, and run for and sometimes win political office. Celebrity can even, in the absence of experience, expertise, skills, or knowledge, catapult a candidate into the American presidency.

In the contemporary Western world, celebrity activism fits well with neoliberal practices, as this volume attests. Celebrity activism relies on and reproduces an individualist ethos while reproducing corporate power and corporate legitimacy. The contemporary culture of celerity spans the symbolic and the economic, the cultural and the political, relations that are interrogated and exposed in this volume.

More specifically, this volume focuses on a central dimension of the wider topic of celebrity and celebrity activism. It explores how, in an era in Western society of rampant celebrity endorsements and celebrity advocacy, 'celebrity activism' in particular, generates symbolic capital – whether conceptualised as 'social capital', 'solidarity capital', or 'emotional capital' – and how these different forms of symbolic capital relate to, can be transformed into, or rely upon economic capital. It thus highlights diverse links between celebrity and the structures of contemporary neoliberal capitalism. Hence the volume's title, *The 'Political Economy' of Celebrity Activism*.

The volume draws on a diverse set of sometimes unexpected cases. It's not all Bono and Band Aid. An early chapter examines how Nobel laureates transform their visible symbolic capital into ongoing capital accumulation; another conversely examines how entertainment celebrities were able to use their celebrity personas to carry out child abuse while hiding it in plain sight. Celebrity brands are investigated. One chapter investigates the DiCaprio celebrity brand and its effects on environmental activism; another highlights the subsumption of Russell Brand's rebellious brand back into the neoliberal structures he critiques. The focus is not exclusively on the West. Limitations on solidarity imposed by Western discourses of celebrity female empowerment are exposed through an analysis of the Nigerian 'Bring Back Our Girls' campaign, and an analysis of George Clooney's celebrity endorsement for Nestlé highlights tensions with the goals of activists in Africa, specifically in Sudan. In investigating these and other empirical cases of celebrity activism, the volume collectively investigates how celebrity activism relates to – draws on, reproduces, contests, and is sometimes subsumed by – wider social discourses, from patriarchy to neoliberalism.

Jutta Weldes

1 Introduction

"Getting busy with the fizzy" – Johansson, SodaStream, and Oxfam: exploring the political economics of celebrity activism

Nathan Farrell

In January 2014, Hollywood actor Scarlett Johansson found herself embroiled in something of a public relations difficulty. The controversy that enveloped her was caused by insurmountable tensions between different components of her public persona: her performances as an actor, her social activism, and her role as a commercial brand endorser. In terms of her acting career, Johansson had demonstrated her ability in more critically acclaimed, independent productions such as Christopher Nolan's *The Prestige* (2006) and Woody Allen's *Vicky Cristina Barcelona* (2008), as well as more art house films such as Jonathan Glazer's *Under the Skin* (2013). In addition, she is also an integral member of the ensemble cast within the Marvel Cinematic Universe that, at the time, was being developed into a lucrative, ongoing film franchise. With a bankable box office appeal, Johansson had established herself as a noteworthy actor of her generation. At the same time, she was serving as a global ambassador for the aid agency, Oxfam. Beginning her association with the NGO in 2005, Johansson was a suitable celebrity spokesperson for Oxfam, as she presented a fresh-faced image that resonated well with a young demographic. More importantly, her value as an asset to Oxfam was projected to increase as her acting career prospered and her celebrity status rose. With Oxfam, Johansson embarked on campaigns concerning topics such as the education of girls in Sri Lanka and India, in which she raised publicity by visiting schools whose reconstruction, following the 2004 Asian Tsunami, Oxfam had funded. She also helped raise money for the charity by taking part in an auction for the opportunity to meet with her at the premier of one of her films (BBC 2008). In addition, she has lent her support to a range of other causes, charitable foundations, and not-for-profit campaigns and has publicly supported Democratic presidential nominees in the 2004, 2008, and 2016 US presidential elections.

While Johansson makes regular public appearances to support social causes, she also engages in commercial endorsements. Some of the more notable include her work for Dolce and Gabbana perfume and SodaStream, manufacturers of domestic soft drinks machines. It is this latter commercial relationship that proved to be difficult. Oxfam, along with a range of other NGOs, opposes the colonisation by Israel of Palestinian land in the West Bank, believing Israeli 'settlements' there to be illegal and that they 'further the ongoing poverty and denial of rights of the Palestinian communities that we [Oxfam] work to support' (Oxfam 2014). Consequently, Oxfam opposes trade with companies operating from occupied Palestinian territory. However, SodaStream operated a factory within this location, and this, understandably, created a conflict of interest for Johansson. Within public discourse, she was said to have 'attract[ed] the wrath of activists' (Child 2014), and among the more vocal Palestinian human rights campaigners, she was dubbed Oxfam's 'Ambassador of Oppression' (Abunimah 2014). As her simultaneous relationships with both institutions were seemingly untenable, Johansson decided to end her ambassadorship with Oxfam, tendering her resignation from the role, which the organisation duly accepted.

The example of Johansson, Oxfam, and SodaStream reveals some very important aspects of celebrity in contemporary Western society, insomuch that it draws attention to the potential dangers facing the socially active celebrity and highlights some of the possible tensions between the different components from which celebrity is derived.[1] The potential for such problems to impact the ways that activist campaigns are conceived and practiced, as well as the successes or failures they might produce is quite significant, particularly when one considers how widespread the inclusion of celebrities in these campaigns has become. Indeed, as Jo Littler astutely observes 'offering support for global charities has become both practically part of the contemporary celebrity job description and a hallmark of the established star' (Littler 2008, 238).

There is something about celebrity and the very condition of fame in late modernity that lends itself to the potential problems that Johansson's example demonstrates. Understanding what that 'something' is and the ways in which it might be problematic is one of the aims of this collection. As such, this introductory chapter first outlines how celebrities have come to be seen by some as legitimate political spokespeople, how the structures of the Western media landscape have facilitated this, and how the nature of contemporary celebrity has, in some ways, necessitated it. This, in turn, warrants unpacking the concept of 'celebrity' and the political economy of celebrity before the chapter explores how this can inform celebrity activism and create the type of predicament in which Johansson found herself.

The power and legitimacy of the celebrity activist

As noted above, the appearance of entertainment celebrities within activist campaigns is increasingly common. In addition, such individuals, as Mark Wheeler (2013, 114) notes, may engage in numerous different roles with these organisations. Where some act as *patrons* who lend their name to an organisation, for example, David Attenborough's work with the World Land Trust, others are more readily identifiable as *spokespeople* who create visibility for an organisation by publicly speaking on its behalf, such as Joanna Lumley's work with the Gurkha Justice Campaign. Some celebrities function as fundraisers for causes by prompting the public to donate funds, for example, Tom Hiddleston's work with UNICEF, while others take a more central role in the *governance* of organisations, as evidenced by the Leonardo DiCaprio's work with his self-named foundation.[2] The idea of celebrities – that is, individuals who are 'highly visible through the media' due to activities or achievements within the sports or entertainment industries (Turner 2013, 3) – enjoying such positions within campaigns might seem singularly peculiar. Indeed, many of them lack even the most rudimentary qualifications or experience in, for example, politics, diplomacy, or conservation science. However, looked at another way, there is something expected and, one might even proffer, inevitable about the alignment of the worlds of celebrity and activism within Western democracies. This is not merely an outcome of the seeming ubiquity of celebrity. Instead it is indicative, first, of the ways in which celebrity reflects and reinforces some of the overarching political and economic discourses that shape contemporary Western societies, and, second, how celebrity is intertwined with the ways in which the media functions as the key arena of politics.

The social prominence of celebrity is, in part, an outcome of its relations to some of the core tenets of contemporary Western societies, namely democracy and consumer capitalism. Both democracy and consumer capitalism, which P. David Marshall cites as the 'twinned discourses of modernity' (2006, 635), place significant value on the individual, conceived as the citizen and consumer, respectively. Individualism, as Marshall argues, is both 'one of the ideological mainstays of consumer capitalism and one of the ideological mainstays of how democracy is conceived' (2006, 635). Accordingly, in a society that valorises individualism, a space is created for the celebrity, as a form of hyper-individual, to become a key cultural focus. Celebrities represent individual agency writ large. They are, as Marshall suggests, 'given greater presence and a wider scope of activity and agency than are those who make up the rest of the population. They are allowed to move on the public stage while the rest of us watch' (Marshall 2014, xlvii). Through their movements on the public stage, celebrities can exert influence by performing as role models 'represent[ing] typical ways of behaving, feeling and thinking in contemporary society' (Dyer 2004 [1986], 18). Simultaneously, celebrities reflect aspects of the majority from whom they seemingly stand in distinction. This is because, on a practical level, the successful celebrity must in some way reflect the interests of their public to sustain their audience's attention and maintain their position of fame. However, deeper than this, Marshall points towards an affective function of celebrity manifested in the ways celebrities 'embody the sentiments of an audience' (Marshall 2014, 203). This begins to outline the contours of the *power* of celebrity in terms of its 'capacity to house conceptions of individuality and simultaneously to embody or help embody "collective configurations" [such as audiences] of the social world' (Marshall 2014, xlix–l). This power can be mobilised for political ends, particularly when considering celebrities' capacity to embody their audience's concerns about political, social, or environmental problems and their desire that appropriate solutions to such problems are enacted.

The political mobilisation of celebrities is also underpinned by a concurrent decline in public trust of, and interest in, traditional political figures and institutions (McAllister 2009; Siaroff 2009). John Corner and Dick Pels describe a movement away from 'the entrenched oppositions of between traditional "isms" and their institutionalisation in the form of party politics [. . . and towards] more eclectic, fluid, issue specific and personality-bound forms of political recognition' (Corner and Pels 2003, 7). Rather than institutions and organisations as the prime vehicles for organising and mobilising mass political sentiment, individuals pronouncing on single cause issues offer a key means of embodying the concerns of mass publics. Of course, the latter have not supplanted the former as, for example, membership of traditional political parties still exists. Importantly, '[i]n a world where entangling alliances are the rule, these individuals [celebrity activists] are as close to free agents as one can find' (West 2008, 81), and this contributes to them potentially being 'considered more trustworthy and less partisan' (West 2008, 79). The perceived legitimacy of celebrity activists by their audience rests on the celebrity's ability to assume the appearance of outsiders to formal politics who manage to infiltrate elite political institutions. They are, as Andrew Cooper says of Bono, 'outsider[s] who moved inside' (Cooper 2008, 42). Despite their mingling with the upper echelons of elite politics, they are not *of* such institutions. Instead, such celebrities act on behalf of their audience, giving form to their political sentiments and potentially speaking truth to power.

The prominence and legitimacy afforded to celebrity activists is also an outcome of the forms and structures of the media in which they operate. The media – particularly broadcast, print, and, more recently, social media – have become key arenas in which democratic politics is enacted (Dahlgren 2009). Such media provide important platforms for reaching the electorate and for politicians, political candidates, and social campaigners to secure public favour. If one considers the speed of the twenty-four-hour news cycle and the instantaneous nature of social media, it is evident that the political commentator has less time available to contribute to political discourse and less time to react to ongoing political events. Moreover, as social media has effectively widened access to public debates, there is an increasing amount of media content, and accordingly, this has heightened the competition for audience attention (van Krieken 2012). Within this attention economy (Davenport and Beck 2001), less time is afforded to spell out complex policy platforms, for example, and consequently political pronouncements are more frequently packaged as soundbites (Franklin 2004).

It is in this environment that the personality of the individual political speaker and their political style – that is, the aesthetic qualities they present – become paramount (Pels 2003). This is, in part, because these personal qualities can stand in as a proxy for political sentiments. For example, a political candidate being seen with their family can suggest to the electorate an adherence to family values (Street 2004). Such developments, in part, facilitate the emergence of what can be thought of as the personalisation of politics (McAllister 2009) and explain the incentives on offer to the politician that uses 'the forms and associations of celebrity culture' as a means of political self-promotion (Street 2004, 437).

This is not to say that political personalities did not exist prior to the emergence of modern democracy or the mass media, nor that they are a phenomenon exclusive to democratic systems, particularly if one considers the cult of personality evident in authoritarian regimes. Instead it highlights how certain technologies and structures of the media have helped to centralise personality within political discourse. Moreover, it creates a political environment in which it is advantageous for a politician, candidate, or activist to possess some form of stage presence, personal charisma, or mediacentric appearance. That celebrities such as musicians and actors are trained in such skills helps to cement their position as political agents and legitimise their role as activists.

Activism is broadly understood here as socially, politically, or environmentally minded actions that, to borrow from Alastair Fuad-Luke, seeks to 'catalyse, encourage or bring about change, in order to elicit social, cultural and/or political transformations' (Fuad-Luke 2009, 6).[3] The discussion of celebrity activism above has the potential to paint the celebrity as an important component within activist campaigns and a key agent of activist causes, a function that prompts Mark Wheeler to ask if 'celebrities can use their reputations and charisma to invigorate politics with new ideas' (Wheeler 2013, 12). However, things are not quite so simple. The possibilities of the celebrity activist are rendered more complicated – indeed more precarious – when one considers the commodified nature of celebrities.

Celebrity is an outcome of an industrial process. As Milly Williamson concisely puts it, it 'is a form of fame commensurate with capitalist society' (Williamson 2016, 1). Celebrities are, of course, real people.[4] However, a celebrity – as they exist in the media – is the result of a process of selection by media industry agents from the multitude of potential applicants, followed by careful training and grooming by various media professionals. In other words, celebrities are the outcome of an investment of labour that creates a tradeable commodity. More than this, the celebrity represents a unique form of self-actualising commodity, as the celebrity plays a part in their own rendering as a tradeable object. What Turner refers to as the 'celebrity-commodity' (2013, 37) is, simultaneously, an individual with a degree of agency, a cultural worker who is paid for their labour, and the entity upon which that labour is exerted.

A celebrity must somehow negotiate a balance between their own individuality and interests, the interests of their audience, those of the industrial networks of which they form a part, and the political causes they might represent. These interests may not necessarily be congruous – as Johansson's example suggests – and this points towards the precarious position of some celebrities. In addition, it goes some way towards explaining the short-lived nature of specific celebrity careers (Redmond 2014, 69). It also illuminates why some celebrities choose to involve themselves with activist campaigns. It is certainly plausible that, given the public attention that celebrities can generate, they might feel obliged to direct this attention towards a worthy cause. The musician John Legend cited this as sense of obligation as a key motivator of his social activism (quoted in Scacchi 2011). At the same time, however, forms of activism are beneficial to celebrities because they provide a means to foster the approval of audiences, as the celebrity is seen to 'give something back'. In the attention-competitive environment described above, an association with a good cause becomes a key asset for a celebrity and suggests why the traditional work of celebrities (film, music, and television, for example) and appearances in the gossip columns no longer mark the boundaries of their profession.

Mobilizing the authentic celebrity activist

It is commonly understood that a successful celebrity's career is financially lucrative. That is, through a successful career, a celebrity can generate significant economic capital. On one hand, being rich and famous is an accepted part of the celebrity lifestyle and is a primary draw for those hopefuls who seek to acquire celebrity status for themselves (see Halpern 2007). On the other hand, if a celebrity's reserves of economic capital are seen by their audience as being undeserved or if a celebrity's deployment of their economic capital is seen as excessive, it may create an affective barrier between the audience and the celebrity in whom they are emotionally invested. This was evident in some commentaries about, for example, Paris Hilton. The socialite and heiress built a public persona upon her perceived excessive materialism and leaked sex tape, which caused many to question the sincerity of her claims to have turned over a philanthropic leaf following her release from prison for a DUI offence (Finn 2006).

While celebrities generate economic capital, they also generate forms of symbolic capital by connecting with audiences at the affective level. This comprises much of the 'emotional work' (Nunn and Biressi 2010) that celebrities carry out. There are clear ways in which symbolic capital, such as prestige, admiration, and authenticity, can translate into and generate economic capital. Being liked by one's audience provides a clear aid to box office revenue, album sales, or television ratings. Equally, an association with a financially lucrative media product – such as a hit movie – increases a celebrity's visibility with an audience, creating the potential to cultivate new audiences and generate greater symbolic capital. This, in turn, facilitates the generation of further economic capital (see Davis 2013, 119–123). More importantly, an association with a suitably worthy activist cause provides a clear location in which to generate symbolic capital. If successful, a celebrity activist can demonstrate to their audience that they care about (a) specific issue(s), embodies their audience's concerns, and cares enough to be motivated to act. If successful, the celebrity activist can appear 'authentic'.

Suggesting that a celebrity can 'appear' authentic is not to imply that a celebrity's authenticity is the result of some form of effort to be seen in a particular way that renders authenticity as artifice and, by extension, *in*authentic. Instead it highlights the aesthetic nature of authenticity; that authenticity is something that is read by audiences (see Lai 2006). Celebrities, as they appear in the media, are texts that can be read (Dyer 1979, 2004 [1986]), and authenticity is one among many potential aspects of their personality that can be inferred from an audience's reading. As Raphael (in this volume) contends, celebrity authenticity rests on the identification, by the audience, of consistencies between the celebrity's private and public personas, the different aspects of their public activities, and their stated beliefs and observable actions' (citation). The authentic celebrity activist then is one who is seen by their audience as motivated by genuine concerns; their activism is not seen as derived from some sort of commercial necessity or career requirement. Thinking about authenticity in these terms moves the concept away from it colloquial use as an expression of some pure 'inner self' in contrast to 'the outer self [which] is merely an expression, a performance, and is often corrupted by material things' (Banet-Weiser 2012, 10). Instead the authentic celebrity activist is one whose audience read them in this fashion, by making sense of the various components, images, practices, and performances from which the celebrity-commodity has been manufactured as a media text. As Sarah Banet-Weiser (2012, 14) suggests, 'the authentic and commodity self are intertwined' such that authenticity can be part of a celebrity's brand.

This is important for any consideration of celebrity activism because authenticity is a central aspect of a celebrity activist's persona. A recognised authentic celebrity activist can use their authenticity to generate both economic and symbolic capital for themselves and to advance the activist cause. This can be seen, for example, with Bono's work with Product (RED), a campaign he established in 2006 with Bobby Shriver. RED is a type of cause-related marketing scheme involving a collection of large multinational corporations that provides a sustainable revenue stream to the Global Fund to Fight Aids, TB and Malaria. The corporations join the campaign and pay 'a licensing fee in exchange for the right to append the RED label to a segment of their product line' (Dadush 2010, 1273). That is, the companies produce a RED version of their existing products, and a portion of the profits from the sale of these items is then donated to the Global Fund. The launch of the campaign was treated with much fanfare in the corporate media (Winfrey 2006; Vallely 2006). However, others were sceptical of the campaign and voiced their opinions in the comments sections of online publications. Such critics proposed that RED was a form of corporate PR and essentially whitewash for corporations. Importantly, RED partners exhibited an awareness of these arguments and justified their involvement in the campaign as '[p]eople could be sceptical [about (RED)] but this is about making a real contribution. With his record in this field, Bono would not be advocating this programme unless he felt we were doing the right thing' (quoted in Milmo 2006, 12). The key here is that the perceived authenticity of a celebrity activist, within some circles, is used to legitimise specific forms of partnerships between for- and non-profit agents. This demonstrates not only the usefulness of celebrity activists, but also their legitimising effect by mobilizing authenticity in this way. And yet criticisms of such campaigns persist, particularly within academic circles.

For Ilan Kapoor, celebrity activism typified by RED emphatically 'legitimates, and indeed promotes, neoliberal capitalism and global inequality' (Kapoor 2013, 1). Kapoor offers a critique of specific instances of neoliberal development policy that point not only to its failures to alleviate poverty, but also its role in exacerbating inequality. He then paints celebrity activism, more or less, as a component of neoliberal development policy. Celebrity activism, he argues, does not address the inherent nature of neoliberal capitalism to produce inequality, but instead seeks to address humanitarian crises by deferring to 'decaf capitalism', that is 'a sort of humanized capitalism that manages to hold together both enormous wealth accumulation and significant global inequality by attending to the worst manifestations of such inequality through charity' (2013, 2). The celebrity activist is a key figure in this so-called 'decaf capitalism' by effectively drawing attention away from the structural violence of neoliberal policies.

Stated with more nuance, Goodman (2013) argues that celebrity activists are represented as idealised role models for interventions into political, social, and environmental debates. Their activities are built on consumerist practices that normalise neoliberal, market-led actions as a remedy for development problems. For Goodman, celebrity activists 'have situated and also have worked to situate themselves as a stylised form of the neoliberalized governance of the problems of environment and development', and their work both reflects and contributes 'to the moral authority of a hegemonic market-led governance of sustainability' (Goodman 2013, 72–73). This is consistent with a comprehensive study by Lisa Ann Richey and Stefano Ponte that introduces and dissects the phenomenon of 'Brand Aid', which, to paraphrase, describes brands that give aid to activist causes through campaigns that give aid to brands (Richey and Ponte 2011, 10). As a sophisticated form of public relations, solutions to – in the case studies their work cites – global development are found in consumerist practices such as ethical shopping. Celebrity plays an important role in legitimising and validating such cause-related marketing initiatives as they work to 'guarantee the cool quotient' of campaigns concerning issues that might otherwise be unappealing to mass publics (Richey and Ponte 2011, 37). From the consumer's perspective, this gives rise to a form of activism founded on the capacity for populations in the global north to save a distant 'other' through their consumer activity. Indeed such campaigns often focus on a celebration of abundance in the global North and the supposed ability of consumer capitalism to bestow aid. This focus on the self as consumer and the distant other as a mediated spectacle promotes what Chouliaraki (2013) argues is a form of 'ironic spectatorship' of distant suffering, as opposed to more progressive forms of solidarity.

To summarise then, the prominence of celebrity activism is consistent with the rise of the personalisation of politics and the heightened role of the media to convey key political messages. In this environment, the celebrity activist becomes a key political voice whose success is dependent on, among other things, their perceived authenticity upon their successful performance as an accurate embodiment of the political sentiments of their audience. However, the economic structures and industrial processes that create celebrity and the political needs that they foster might not be consistently congruent with the media performances and surface-level appearances that celebrity activists must maintain. There may indeed be the possibility of tension between these two facets of celebrity activism, as the next section discusses.

Political economy and celebrity activism

When introducing his 2006 edited collection on the broad topic of celebrity, Marshall suggests that a 'useful way to theorize about celebrity is along two axes – surface and depth'. He goes on to offer that '[c]elebrity provides a *surface* through which contemporary culture produces significance and a *depth* of investment in particular identities, moments, and personalities' [emphasis added] (Marshall 2006, 1). While celebrity can easily be seen as an ultimately *shallow* cultural form, as evidenced by its routine characterisation as base and unworthy (Clarke 2003), which has seduced certain demographics (Halpern 2007; Twenge and Campbell 2009), celebrity – as noted above – is *deeply* entwined with contemporary Western cultures. For all its iconography of superficiality, celebrities can provide a focus of deep emotional attachment for some sections of an audience, and particular moments – such as a celebrity's wedding or death – provide a forum for social celebration or introspection. Marshall's perpendicular axes of celebrity also provide a useful means of unpacking important aspects of celebrity activism and interrogating some of its potential problems. For example, the presentation of a celebrity activist may suggest an altruistic individual, motivated by a sense of duty to mobilise the type of public attention they can garner to assist a political cause. However, a deeper dig – that is, a look behind the scenes at the economic and institutional structures that support the celebrity's activism – may provide a more substantial understanding of the celebrity's endeavours.

Sarah Dadush (2010), for instance, raises important concerns about the organisational structure of the RED campaign. While appearing as a charitable organisation, RED is not technically a charity but instead is a limited liability company. Consequently it is under no legal obligation to disclose the nature and content of its agreements with its commercial partners; nor is it mandated to divulge the exact amount that each purchase of a RED consumer product generates for the global fund.[5] More importantly, it is not required to reveal the salaries or other renumerations, if any, of the campaign's chief organisers. In short, by occupying a grey area between philanthropic venture and cause-related marketing, RED can forego the transparency requirements of a bona fide charitable organisation, while leveraging its image of doing good to circumvent criticism. This becomes problematic when one considers the vast economic capital that RED generates (RED n.d.), some of the unethical labour practices of RED corporate partners (De Haan and Vander Stichelede 2007; McDougall 2007a, 2007b, 2007c; McDougall and Watts 2009), and, more widely, that these types of for-profit and non-profit hybrid campaigns represent an emerging trend within political activism (Farrell 2015). Despite these concerns, a common theme within the media discourse surrounding RED is that ventures such as RED are legitimate by virtue of their association with 'authentic' celebrity activists; Bono was considered the 'reigning king of hope', no less (Winfrey *et al.* 2006). This suggests the importance of celebrity activists' legitimising presence within campaigns. More importantly, it reveals that, to return to Marshall's two axes, the *surface* of celebrity activists performing for campaigns has the potential to obscure some important political and economic *depths* of the campaigns with which they work. This is not to suggest that the surface of a campaign and the depth of its structure necessarily contradict each other, although tensions may exist between them as the case of RED exemplifies. It is also not to suggest the somewhat conspiratorial stance that celebrities provide a distraction from some ulterior motives of non-profit organisations. Instead it highlights that a consideration of the political and economic structures that underpin different celebrity activist campaigns, such as the commercial relationships between NGOs, celebrity activists, and corporate partners, can provide a more rounded appreciation of the implications of celebrity activism as a vehicle for contemporary Western political action, particularly as the public-facing components of the campaign diverge from the political and economic structures that facilitate it. This, therefore, provides a rationale to explore the political economy of celebrity activism.

The use of the term 'political economy' in this volume draws from the political economy of communication, a subdiscipline of media and communication studies. The term can be understood by drawing on perhaps the central text in this discipline, Vincent Mosco's (2009) *The Political Economy of Communication*. For Mosco, political economy consists of the 'study of the social relations, particularly the power relations, that mutually constitute the production, distribution and consumption of resources, including communication resources' (Mosco 2009, 24). Mosco's work draws together a tradition of inquiry that points towards a careful consideration of the relationships between the economic structures of the media industries, the political orientations of such organisations, and the cultural artefacts they produce. It is a critical approach that, Jonathan Hardy argues, begins with the central claim that

> different ways of organising and financing communications have implications for the range and nature of media content, and the ways in which this is consumed and used. Recognising that the goods produced by the media industries are at once economic and cultural, this approach calls for attention to the interplay between the symbolic and economic dimensions of the production of meaning.
>
> (Hardy 2014, 7)

Political economic approaches, as conceived within these disciplinary boundaries, are concerned primarily with the relationships between the ownerships of the media industries and the content they produce, often with a particular focus on the discursive links between the two. For example, Robert McChesney characterises the political economy of the media as a coin that on one side 'examine[s] the firms, owners, labor practices, market structures, policies, occupational codes, and subsidies that in combination provide the context for the production' of media content. The other side looks at how 'the media system as a whole interacts with broad social and economic relations in society' (McChesney 2008, 151).

By considering these two aspects of the media, and the ways they interrelate, the political economy of the media poses questions such as '[d]oes the media system tend to challenge or reinforce broader trends society?' (McChesney 2008, 151). Much scholarship within this area uncovers, for example, links between the ownership and economic imperatives of news organisations, the political positions and practices these foster, and the types of content consequently produced by news organisations (for example, Bagdikian 2004; Edwards and Cromwell 2006; Herman and Chomsky 1994). To summarise these works: the profit-oriented market system in which media firms operate and their individual dependence on commercial revenue creates an environment in which news media content is largely consistent with the ideological necessities of the overarching system and dissent from such positions is effectively weeded out from the ranks media staff.

The works cited above have done much to draw out the links between political discourses, economic structures, and the commodities (such as media content) produced by the media industries. When we consider, as noted above, that celebrities too are commodities created in part by the media industries, a space is created to question the potential for political economic considerations of celebrities. More to the point, a space is opened for political economic considerations of their activism because it is often through their activism – as noted by Goodman (2013), Kapoor (2013) and Richey and Ponte (2011) among many others – that celebrities address many of the social inequalities and environmental concerns that might be laid at the door of the very system of production on which they are dependent. Moreover, it is through their activism that celebrities create the necessary symbolic capital to maintain their career, as well as the affective connections with their audience, an audience that may include those disadvantaged by social inequalities. This is, in part, why activism can be difficult for a celebrity to successfully execute and why tensions between the commercial work of celebrities and their emotional work may arise.

To return to the beginning, a key problem for Johannsson was the contradiction between her efforts in these two areas, and her relationship with Oxfam actually worked to locate the domestic sphere, to which SodaStream's products are marketed, in an environment over which there has been a bitter struggle for over sixty years. The negative publicity received by Johansson could have damaged her persona and brand appeal had the two contradictory institutional relationships been allowed to continue. During that time, her value as an asset to both Oxfam and SodaStream would have been diminished. On one level, Johansson's example points to the inherent tensions between the celebratory narratives of self-realisation woven into the celebrity form and the harsh realities of neoliberal practices. At another level, it points to the complexity of relationships between the symbolic surface of celebrity and the deeper economic relationships from which they are produced. This is not to suggest that the symbolic is always superficial and the economic always deep; nor does it slyly point to some form of economic reductionism. Instead it argues that some of the successful instances of celebrity activism owe their success, in part, to the development of powerful symbolic relationships between celebrity, audience, NGOs, and beneficiaries that mask more complex and sometimes counterproductive economic structures.

This opens up much territory to explore, and so this volume aims to examine how celebrity activism works to create new forms of symbolic capital beyond the economic, such as 'social capital', 'solidarity capital', and 'emotional capital' and how these new types of capital relate to the economic. More specifically, the chapters offer theoretical contributions to understand how different types of symbolic capital can be transferred into, and can even create, economic capital. As such, this edited collection highlights some of the relationships between the symbolic and the economic, between the cultural and the political, and how these relationships are articulated through the celebrity activist. In addition, the volume will offer empirical case studies that situate instances of celebrity activism within specific political contexts. For example, the chapters analyse how celebrity activism – and the symbolic capital it generates – intersects with underlying structures of gender politics and political discourses such as neoliberalism. These chapters illuminate some of the inherent tensions between individualism, types of patriarchy, and processes of corporate sponsorship, commodification, and CSR on the one hand and the ethos of solidarity and compassion associated with the symbolic capital celebrity activism generates on the other. Moreover, the collection aims to advance current ideas regarding the authenticity of celebrity activists. It provides a discussion of how the tensions between the economic and the symbolic – for example, the tensions between individualism and solidarity – raise questions about the authenticity of celebrity activists and how the types of solidarity capital described above work, with varying degrees of success, to obfuscate such tensions.

The structure of this collection

Collectively, the chapters make theoretical and empirical contributions that critically analyse and scrutinise the forms, functions, and narratives of the contemporary celebrity activist, together with the political-economic structures in which they operate. As a whole, the collection serves to provide a platform for both thoughtful reflections on the interactions between political economy and popular culture, the implications of the migration of value between these two realms, and ways this can be used to serve particular discourses or ideological programmes.

To begin, **Bruno Campanella** explores the relationships between different forms of economic and symbolic capital generated by celebrities. In particular, his work demonstrates the ways in which a celebrity's activities for a social cause can help to generate symbolic capital and how this can be converted into economic capital. Campanella offers a theoretical framework that, drawing on Bourdieu's field theory, develops the concept of 'solidarity capital' as a specific form of symbolic capital, which can aid the perceived authenticity of the celebrity activist and help to foster affective connections with their audience. This, in turn, provides opportunities to develop further economic capital. Taking these ideas forward, **Lukasz Swiatek** demonstrates the relationships between symbolic and economic capital through the empirical case study of Nobel laureates. While winning a Nobel Prize awards the laureate a substantial sum of money, this newly acquired economic capital is accompanied by the symbolic capital of having been *recognised* by the Nobel Institute. This, in turn, affords the laureate a perceived authority, which Swiatek conceptualises as a form of soft power. Laureates can then put this power to work establishing foundations in their name in a manner that personalises their cause and allows them to embark on a continual process of capital accumulation. Swiatek's focus is on the generation of types of value, the result of a perceived socially beneficial behaviour worthy of a prize that can be exchanged between different social fields.

Inverting this completely, **Hilary Wheaton** and **Samita Nandy** provide an insightful discussion of the misuse of forms of symbolic capital through the case study of the historic child abuse perpetrated by entertainment celebrities. With a particular focus on Rolf Harris and Jimmy Savile, the chapter advances our understandings of the uses of persona. It analyses how the celebrity persona, as a commodity produced through the celebrity's labour and as something with an exchange value, can be used to facilitate a celebrity carrying out unspeakable crimes while effectively 'hiding in plain sight'. Wheaton and Nandy consider the effects of the revelations of scandal on the exchange value of the celebrity commodity and its associated commercial artefacts and material manifestations, the artworks by Harris, for example.

The next four chapters use a range of case studies to analyse the relationships between celebrity activism and prevalent political and economic discourses. **Susan Hopkins** and **Eric Louw** provide a meaningful and poignant analysis of a campaign to raise awareness of the plight of kidnapped Nigerian schoolgirls. They provide an account of how the campaign was subsumed into broader Western discourses of celebratory female empowerment in relation to marketised, neoliberal individualism. Their discussion of the Bring Back Our Girls campaign carefully demonstrates the limitations placed on 'solidarity' when it has been rendered in the commodified form of the selfie and articulated within populist post-feminist discourses. Their work points to the potential for ostensibly progressive celebrity activism to be appropriated by political economic discourses such as neoliberalism and points to some of the limitations of activism when celebrity and the political-economic structures that create celebrity become involved in campaigns. In a similar vein, **Joshua Gulam** also studies the possible tensions between the agendas of activists in Africa (in this case, Sudan) and the outcomes of the political activities of Western celebrities. Through the case study of George Clooney, Gulam considers the extent to which the spectacle of celebrity can draw public attention away from such tensions and align activist campaigns with the goals of Western capital. Beginning with an overview of Clooney's celebrity persona, his commercial endorsements, and his activism in Sudan, Gulam goes on to outline the ways in which Clooney attempts to negotiate the tensions between his work as a brand ambassador for Nestlé, a company that has been much criticised for questionable business practices, and his interventions in African politics. Taken together, Hopkins, Louw, and Gulam identify some of the limits of certain types of campaigns when celebrity activists become involved. In such instances, the political economy of celebrity influences the nature of celebrity involvement and the shape of the campaigns. This is particularly the case when the aims of the campaign do not align with the needs of capitalism.

Conversely, the next two chapters investigate case studies that represent neoliberal capitalism as the solution to the given social problem and the celebrity activist as the embodiment of particular neoliberal discourses. **Annika Bergman**

Rosamond and **Catia Gregoratti** discuss the relationships between celebrity, development, and neoliberal philanthropy. Through their study of Francine LeFrak's *Same Sky* initiative, Bergman Rosamond and Gregoratti critically analyse the forms of women's empowerment enacted by assemblages of public and private actors. Such actors work to neoliberalise feminist discourses and practices of activism, and the chapter problematizes the efforts to situate women's empowerment within market structures and represent the empowered woman as an entrepreneur. Their analysis pays particular attention to the role of LeFrak's public persona in narrativising and legitimising *Same Sky*'s business model. In doing so, they tease out some of the ways in which the individual entrepreneur has converged with traditional notions of celebrity and the links this draws between political economy and representation of the individual.

This critique of neoliberalised celebrity activism is expanded upon by **Nathan Farrell**. Through an analysis of the activism of Bob Geldof, it is shown that Geldof's specific symbolic capital is generated, in part, by his perceived status as an impartial outsider to institutions of elite political power. However, an historical analysis reveals that Geldof's activism has evolved in tandem specific iterations of neoliberal doctrine.

Collectively these four chapters present a variety of ways in which celebrity activism both relates to overarching social discourses – such as patriarchy, feminism, or neoliberalism – and how these campaigns can be subsumed by such discourses. In their different ways, these four chapters present some of the limitations of celebrity activism, which become evident when consideration is paid to the different political economic structures in which celebrity operates. Moreover, these chapters raise significant questions about the perceived authenticity of celebrity activists, particularly as the agendas of the campaigns with which the celebrities are involved may differ considerably from both the actions of the celebrity activists and the motivations of the industries in which they operate. **Jackie Raphael** directly addresses such questions of authenticity through a detailed analysis of the celebrity brand of Leonardo DiCaprio. This encompasses his film work, commercial endorsements, and the philanthropic and environmental activities of DiCaprio's self-named foundation. Raphael notes the synergies between these different facets of DiCaprio's public persona and how an effective meaning transfer can be created that enhances DiCaprio's brand. However, through an analysis of dissenting responses to DiCaprio's environmental, specifically climate change activism, Raphael draws out some of the inherent contradictions between the trappings of a celebrity lifestyle and the necessities of environmentalism and uses this to interrogate perceptions of DiCaprio's authenticity. This allows Raphael to pick out the potential limitations placed on the agency of a celebrity activist by the economic structures in which they operate and upon which they are dependent.

However, this relationship between celebrity activist and the political economy of celebrity becomes more complicated when consideration is given to the outspoken celebrity activist that explicitly challenges the overarching political-economic discourses in which the celebrity industry is dependent. **Panos Kompatsiaris** looks more closely at this idea through his analysis of the comedian and activist Russell Brand. Brand is an outspoken critic of neoliberal policies and, to some extent, seems to circumvent this conceptual obstacle in a way that other have not. However, on closer inspection, Kompatsiaris reveals the disjuncture's between Brand's advocacy of complete disobedience to the dominant economic system on the one hand and the ways in which his professional life and celebrity status can be read as a tacit assertion of the values of that system on the other. Using the Foucauldian concept of 'parrhesia', Kompatsiaris explores how the normalised and expected characteristics of the creative celebrity as an anti-conformist align with the archetype of the committed revolutionary. If Brand's persona as a creative nonconformist houses the conflicts, tensions, and discrepancies embodied by the contemporary celebrity activist, then efforts to highlight the gap between what he says and what he does can work to enable his status, for some audiences, as an anti-austerity activist and critic of neoliberal political-economy.

The works in this volume provide a number of ways of thinking about the inter-sections of politics and economics in relation to the forms and images of celebrity activism. Together, the chapters represent an effort to view behind the scenes of the spectacle of the socially conscious celebrity and consider the political economic forces that work to add sparkle and fizz – to return to the SodaStream example – to performances of social activism. The chapters that follow provide a means of thinking about how celebrity activism creates and mobilises symbolic and economic capital and how the efforts that produce these forms of capital relate to, align with, or oppose overarching political and economic discourses. Collectively, the volume's chapters trace some of the potentials and limitations of celebrity activism that emerge from the political economy of celebrity and consider how this influences the perceived authenticity and, perhaps, usefulness of the contemporary celebrity activist.

Lastly, the chapters in this collection represent the works of number of insightful and inspiring scholars, and I would like to express my gratitude for their invaluable contributions to this book, as well as their patience during the creation of this volume. I would also like to extend my sincere thanks to the Popular Culture and World Politics series editors and, in particular, Jutta Weldes, for her extremely valuable guidance. In addition, I would also like to thank Lydia de Cruz, Nicola Parkin, Lucy Frederick, and Robert Sorsby at Routledge for their help and, most of all, their unfaltering patience, which I have surely tested. As always, I am deeply indebted to Heather Savigny for her priceless intellectual input, her time, given without question, and her boundless optimism. I am also indebted to Mike Goodman and Julie Doyle for their wise words and all-too-regular pep talks. I am also grateful to Bruce Clackett and Cora Farrell, Jason Druce, Meeta Gargav, and Jeff Hofland.

Notes

1 It should be noted that the types of strained relationships between NGOs and celebrity spokespeople, as demonstrated by Oxfam and Johansson, can also work the other way around. This can be seen with the scandal surrounding Oxfam employee's conduct in post-earthquake Haiti, which led to numerous celebrities, such as Minnie Driver, terminating their associations with the charity (Parkinson 2018).

2 The activities of these celebrities are labelled with different monikers by scholarly studies, such 'celebrity diplomacy' (Cooper 2008), 'celebrity endorsement' (Wheeler 2013), 'celebrity humanitarianism' (Kapoor 2013; Richey and Ponte 2011), and 'celebrity advocacy' (Markham 2015). However, within this volume, such work is termed 'celebrity activism'.
3 The specific actions this encompasses vary. Where necessary, the individual chapters within this volume will tease out the specific characteristics that define particular instances of celebrity activism.
4 This is complicated by fictional characters that are treated in all other respects as celebrities.
5 Although it does provide such information as an aggregate.

References

Abunimah, A. (2014) 'Signs of Disarray at Oxfam over "Ambassador of Oppression" Scarlett Johansson', *Electronic Intifada*, 27 January [online] Available: https://electronicintifada.net/blogs/ali-abunimah/signs-disarray-oxfam-over-ambassador-oppression-scarlett-johansson [accessed 15 May 2016].

Bagdikian, B. (2004) *The Media Monopoly*, Boston: Beacon Press.

Banet-Weiser, S. (2012) *Authentic TM: The Politics of Ambivalence in a Brand Culture*, New York: New York University Press.

BBC (2008) 'Fan Pays 20,000 to Date Scarlett', *BBC News*, 14 March [online] Available: http://news.bbc.co.uk/1/hi/entertainment/7295871.stm [accessed 15 May 2016].

Child, B. (2014) 'Scarlett Johansson Steps Down from Oxfam Ambassador Role', *The Guardian*, 30 January [online] Available: www.theguardian.com/film/2014/jan/30/scarlett-johansson-oxfam-quits-sodastream [accessed 15 May 2016].

Chouliaraki, L. (2013) *The Ironic Spectator: Solidarity in the Age of Post-Humanitarianism*, Cambridge: Polity Press.

Clarke, N. (2003) *Shadow of a Nation: How Celebrity Destroyed Britain*, London: Phoenix.

Cooper, A.F. (2008) *Celebrity Diplomacy*, Colorado: Paradigm Publishers.

Corner, J. and Pels, D. (2003) 'The Restyling of Politics', in J. Corner and D. Pels (eds.) *Media and the Restyling of Politics*, London: Sage Publications: 1–18.

Dadush, S. (2010) 'Profiting un (RED): The Need for Enhanced Transparency in Cause-Related Marketing', *New York University Journal of International Law and Politics*, 42: 1269–1335.

Dahlgren, P. (2009) *Media and Political Engagement: Citizens, Communication and Democracy*, New York: Cambridge University Press.

Davenport, T. and Beck, J. (2001) *The Attention Economy: Understanding the New Currency of Business*, Boston: Harvard Business School Press.

Davis, A. (2013) *Promotional Cultures*, Cambridge: Polity Press.

de Haan, E. and Vander Stichelede, M. (2007) *Footloose Investors: Investing in the Garment Industry in Africa*, Amsterdam: Centre for Research on Multinational Corporations.

Dyer, R. (1998 [1979]) *Stars*, London: BFI.

Dyer, R. (2004 [1986]) *Heavenly Bodies*, London: Routledge.

Edwards, D. and Cromwell, D. (2006) *Guardians of Power: The Myth of the Liberal Media*, London: Pluto Press.

Farrell, N. (2015) '"Conscience Capitalism" and the Neoliberalisation of the Non-Profit Sector', *New Political Economy*, 20 (2): 254–272.

Finn, N. (2006) 'Paris Hilton's Traumatic Trip to Jail Was 10 Years Ago: How She Revamped Her Life after the Celebutantes Gone Wild Era', *Enews*, [online] Available: www.eonline.com/news/846325/paris-hilton-s-traumatic-trip-to-jail-was-10-years-ago-how-she-revamped-her-life-after-the-celebutantes-gone-wild-era [accessed 10 February 2010].

Franklin, B. (2004) *Packaging Politics Political Communications in Britain's Media Democracy* (2nd ed.), London: Arnold.

Fuad-Luke, A. (2009) *Design Activism: Beautiful Strangeness for a Sustainable World*, London: Earthscan.

Goodman, M.K. (2013) '*Celebritus Politicus*, Neoliberal Sustainabilities and the Terrains of Care', in G. Fridell and M. Konings (eds.) *Age of Icons: Exploring Philanthrocapitalism in the Contemporary World*, Toronto: University of Toronto Press: 72–92.

Halpern, J. (2007) *Fame Junkies: The Hidden Truths Behind America's Favorite Addiction*, New York: Houghton Mifflin.

Hardy, J. (2014) *Critical Political Economy of the Media: An Introduction*, Oxon: Routledge.

Herman, E.S. and Chomsky, N. (1994) *Manufacturing Consent: The Political Economy of the Mass Media*, London: Vintage.

Kapoor, I. (2013) *Celebrity Humanitarianism: The Ideology of Global Charity*, Oxon: Routledge.

Lai, A. (2006) 'Aura and Authenticity in the Celebrity Photographs of Juergen Teller', in S. Holmes and S. Redmond (eds.) *Framing Celebrity: New Directions in Celebrity Culture*, Oxon: Routledge: 215–230.

Littler, J. (2008) '"I Feel Your Pain": Cosmopolitan Charity and the Public Fashioning of the Celebrity Soul', *Social Semiotics*, 18 (2): 237–251.

Markham, T. (2015) 'Celebrity Advocacy and Public Engagement: The Divergent Uses of Celebrity', *International Journal of Cultural Studies*, 18 (4): 467–480.

Marshall, P.D. (2006) 'New Media: New Self: The Changing Power of Celebrity', in P.D. (ed.) *The Celebrity Culture Reader*, Oxon: Routledge: 634–644.

Marshall, P.D. (2014) *Celebrity and Power* (2nd ed.), Minneapolis: University of Minnesota Press.

McAllister, I. (2009) 'The Personalization of Politics', *The Oxford Handbook of Political Behaviour*, [online] Available: www.oxfordhandbooks.com/view/10.1093/oxfordhb/9780199270125.001.0001/oxfordhb-9780199270125-e-030 [accessed 21 July 2012].

McChesney, R.W. (2008) *The Political Economy of Media: Enduring Issues, Emerging Dilemmas*, New York: Monthly Review.

McDougall, D. (2007a) 'GAP Slave Kids', *The News of the World* [London], 28 October: 6.

McDougall, D. (2007b) 'Indian "Slave" Children Making Low-Cost Clothes Destined for GAP', *The Observer* [London], 28 October: 3.

McDougall, D. (2007c) 'Special Report: Child Sweatshop Shame Threatens Gap's Ethical Image', *The Observer* [London], 28 October: 36.

McDougall, D. and Watts, D. (2009) 'Gap Factory Danger to African Children?', *The [London] Times*, 1 August [online] Available: www.timesonline.co.uk/tol/news/world/africa/article6736290.ece [accessed 19 October 2009].

Milmo, C. (2006) 'The Red Revolution: Irish Rock Star Bono Launched a New Weapon in the Battle against Global Poverty Yesterday: A Guilt-Free Brand to Harness Conspicuous Consumption for the Cause', *The Independent* [London]: 12.

Mosco, V. (2009) *The Political Economy of Communication* (2nd ed.), London: Sage Publications.

Nunn, H. and Biressi, A. (2010) 'A Trust Betrayed: Celebrity and the Work of Emotion', *Celebrity Studies*, 1 (1): 49–64.

Oxfam (2014) 'Oxfam Accepts Resignation of Scarlett Johansson', *Oxfam*, 30 January [online] Available: www.oxfam.org/en/pressroom/reactions/oxfam-accepts-resignation-scarlett-johansson [accessed 15 May 2016].

Parkinson, H.J. (2018) 'Minnie Driver: Oxfam Bosses "Knew What Was Going on and Did Nothing"', *The Guardian*, 21 February [online] Available: www.theguardian.com/film/2018/feb/21/minnie-driver-oxfam-bosses-knew-what-was-going-on-and-did-nothing [accessed 21 February 2018].

Pels, D. (2003) 'Aesthetic Representation and Political Style: Re-Balancing Identity and Difference in Media Democracy', in J. Corner and D. Pels (eds.) *Media and the Restyling of Politics*, London: Sage Publications: 41–66.

Prestige, The (2006) [Film] Directed by Christopher Nolan. USA: Touchstone Pictures, Warner Bros.

RED (n.d.) 'How RED Works' [online] Available: https://www.red.org/how-red-works [accessed 1 November 2018].

Richey, L.A. and Ponte, S. (2011) *Brand Aid: Shopping Well to Save the World*, Minneapolis: University of Minnesota Press.

Redmond, S. (2014) *Celebrity and the Media*, Basingstoke: Palgrave.

Scacchi, G. (2011) *Celebrity Activists*, BBC Radio 4 [UK] Radio Broadcast, 6 February 13:30–14:00.

Siaroff, A. (2009) 'The Decline of Political Participation: An Empirical Overview of Voter Turnout and Party Membership', in J. DeBardeleben and J.H. Pammett (eds.) *Activating the Citizen*, Basingstoke: Palgrave Macmillan: 41–59.

Street, J. (2004) 'Celebrity Politicians: Popular Culture and Political Representation', *The British Journal of Politics & International Relations*, 6 (4): 435–452.

Turner, G. (2013) *Understanding Celebrity* (2nd ed.), London: Sage Publications.

Twenge, J.M. and Campbell, W.K. (2009) *The Narcissism Epidemic: Living in the Age of Entitlement*, New York: Atria.

Under the Skin (2013) [Film] Directed by Jonathan Glazer. UK: Film4, British Film Institute.

Vallely, P. (2006) 'A Red Revolution on the High Street: Tomorrow "the Independent" Joins a Growing Number of Companies to go RED: The Campaign Pioneered by Bono Combines the Muscle of Big Business and the Power of the Consumer to Open a New Front in the Battle against AIDS', *The Independent* [London], 15 May: 10.

van Krieken, R. (2012) *Celebrity Society*, Oxon: Routledge.

Vicky Cristina Barcelona (2008) [Film] Directed by Woody Allen. USA: The Weinstein Company.

West, D.M. (2008) 'Angelina, Mia, and Bono: Celebrities and International Development', in L. Brainard and D. Chollet (eds.) *Global Development 2.0*, Washington: The Brookings Institute: 74–84.

Wheeler, M. (2013) *Celebrity Politics*, Cambridge: Polity Press.

Williamson, M. (2016) *Celebrity, Capitalism and the Making of Fame*, Cambridge: Polity.

Winfrey, O. *et al.* (2006) *Oprah and Bono Paint the Town "RED"*, Harpo Productions Inc. Broadcast: 13 October.

2 Celebrity activism and the making of solidarity capital

Bruno Campanella

The influence of economic factors in the popularization of celebrity has been a key preoccupation since the first works investigating the phenomenon were published. Lowenthal (2006 [1944]), for example, reflects on the importance of the culture industry in the proliferation of biographies in newspapers and magazines revealing details of the private lives of actors and other members of the entertainment business during the first half of the twentieth century. In *The Triumph of Mass Idols*, the German sociologist suggests that the shrinking number of biographies of "idols of production",[1] preponderant during the early 1900s, and the concomitant increase in biographies of "idols of consumption"[2] a few decades later marks the consolidation of an industry interested in transforming the lifestyles of sport and film stars into models for consumption.[3] In this sense, Lowenthal's seminal work has often been taken as an important reference in debates investigating the role of the culture industry in the growing attention given to the private lives of celebrities, who profit with their prominent media visibility (Dyer 1998; Marshall 1997, 2006).

The present chapter is an attempt to develop a distinctive facet of this phenomenon by analysing the emergence of a dynamic that further complicates the relationship among celebrity, visibility, and economic interests. There is a certain consensus that the exposure of the private life of actors, singers, and idols in general has intensified with the expansion of social media (Baym 2013; Marwick and Boyd 2011). Nevertheless, more than just offering moments of their everyday life via Facebook or Instagram, contemporary celebrities are often engaging in activism in an attempt to use their visibility positively. Support for campaigns to help communities in need, victims of natural disasters, or even participation in initiatives against global warming have become part of the job description of entertainment industry stars.

Much has been researched and written about this issue. Cooper (2008), for example, has a positive take on what he calls *celebrity diplomacy*. He recognizes that although personalities such as Bono Vox and Angelina Jolie sometimes deflect the focus from well-structured and informed diplomatic efforts to solve complex humanitarian crises, they usually play an instrumental role in giving wide visibility to the causes they support. Taking a similar stance, Lucy Bennett conducts an analysis of Lady Gaga's use of social media to mobilise her fans in philanthropist and activist causes to conclude that celebrities can now speak directly to the public without the filters of large news outlets (Bennett 2014, 149). As a consequence, there is a dislocation in communication structure, from vertical to horizontal, which allows for freer dispersion of calls for action.

Other academics, however, look at this phenomenon with some reservations. Brockington (2014), for example, provides evidence for the argument that *celebrity advocacy* does not mobilize general audiences in a meaningful way as it has often been presumed. Celebrity advocacy, suggests Brockington (2014, 9), is "by and for elites". Moreover, similarly to Couldry and Markham (2007), he proposes that the participation of high-profile media personalities marks a disconnection between public and civil society.

Chouliaraki (2013) sees contemporary engagement in humanitarian causes from a different angle. She is interested in understanding the moral transformations underlying the participation of stars in mass campaigns meant to generate solidarity towards distant sufferers. Chouliaraki describes the involvement of celebrities such as Angelina Jolie in humanitarian projects as a utilitarian strategy of self-transformation. In other words, in Chouliaraki's view, Jolie's engagement in celebrity activism involves a mirror structure engaging a self-reflexive Western individual who wants to be transformed by getting in touch with her own emotions. Therefore, such campaigns should be understood not as a form of ethical-ization of the persona via the identification with a universal condition of suffering, but rather as a key experience for the autonomous individuals of our contemporary world. It is a self-growth experience in a post-humanitarian context.

From an ideological perspective, Campanella (2012), Kapoor (2013), Nash (2008), Rajagopal (1999), Richey and Ponte (2008), and Rojek (2013) argue that the participation of celebrities in solidarity[4] campaigns often help disseminate the improbable idea that fragmented individual actions, within the structures of the neoliberal capitalist system, are able to shift contemporary social and environmental imbalances. A good example is the case of Product RED, a trademark adopted by big corporations wanting to draw attention to and raise donations for the Global Fund, which supports the fight against AIDS, tuberculosis, and malaria. The campaign successfully contributed to improving the ethical credentials of companies such as Apple and Gap, and, at the same time, drew a lot of positive media visibility to rock star Bono Vox and other personalities involved in the project. Richey and Ponte (2008), nevertheless, argue that the revenue derived from RED Products during the initial years of the campaign represented less than 0.6 percent of donations made by governments to the Global Fund. Jo Littler (2008) also draws attention to the financial inequality when it comes to the benefits resulting from such campaigns. In many cases, the symbolic or material profits accrued by celebrities who participate in societal causes far exceed the gains directed to the deprived beneficiaries (*ibid.* p, 242). This inequality is particularly evident in initiatives involving the marketing of products destined to raise funds for a "good cause", as in the case of Product RED.

The arguments above, however, should not be taken as a simple condemnation of celebrity activism. Despite its contradictions, celebrity activism is a growing and complex phenomenon that often generates positive results regarding the issues at stake. One of the ignored aspects, nevertheless, has to do with the implications that taking part in these campaigns has on the celebrities themselves. They are frequently portrayed as selfless people whose only motivation is to "make a difference" in the world[5] (Leal 2017). Although this might be the case in some situations, it is important to get a broader picture of all the explicit and implicit forces at work and outcomes that are at stake.

With this in mind, the present chapter attempts to examine the economic benefits that accrue to celebrities participating in activism. It argues that celebrity participation in environmental, social, and humanitarian actions is able to produce a kind of symbolic capital, hereby denominated *solidarity capital*, which can be accumulated and later converted into economic capital. As is the case for other forms of immaterial capital described by Bourdieu (1986, 2000), *solidarity capital* may provide privileged access to certain jobs that are inaccessible to those who do not hold it. In an increasingly connected world, the consuming public's demand for socially engaged celebrities has never been greater, whether in terms of product endorsements or artistic productions.

From an economic perspective, celebrity involvement in humanitarian and environmental activism helps to widen and qualify the media exposure they enjoy over the course of their careers. This is to say that solidarity engagement provides artists and personalities with a new qualitative source of support not encountered in other forms of celebrity-related capital.

Olivier Driessens, for example, works with the concept of *celebrity capital* as a way of redefining celebrity. Using Bourdieu's field theory, he develops a framework capable of analysing the conversion of celebrity into other types of capital, which for him is a key to understanding its very nature. For Driessens (2013, 551), celebrity capital is recognisability that works across social fields, as opposed to field-specific symbolic capital. In other words, it is an accumulated media visibility that can be transformed into political or economic resources. Heinich (2012) works with a similar concept, *visibility capital*, which is largely related to the quantitative dimension of visibility that can be cumulative, measured, and converted into economic capital. Solidarity capital shares this capacity of conversion into materiality, in the economic sense; nonetheless, it is distinguished from visibility and celebrity capital by its connection to the moral field. It is produced throughout the participation of celebrities in media actions based on very clearly defined principles of social awareness, humanitarianism, and altruism.

Celebrity civic engagement

Celebrity participation in civically engaged campaigns is far from a new phenomenon (Bardia 2010). One can trace its origins back to the mid twentieth century, when radio and film stars were invited to participate in a media crusade to persuade the US population to buy war bonds, important for the stabilization of the national economy during the Second World War. In spite of the fact that personalities like Kate Smith and Bette Davis were acting on behalf of US government, and not 'distant sufferers' in need, this was probably one of the first times celebrities participated in a media push directed at major challenges facing society. Cooper Lawrence argues that radio star Kate Smith's effort was crucial in persuading the public to donate over $600 million for the campaign, a huge sum even by contemporary standards (Lawrence 2009, 148). In *Mass Persuasion*, Robert Merton suggests that Smith's evident commitment to the cause was demonstrated by her tireless effort in answering phone calls from radio listeners. Perhaps even more importantly was the perception that she was not doing it for money, but for patriotism. She built a reputation for sincerity and as a doer of good that worked in a virtuous cycle (2004 [1946], 100).

Since then, several initiatives have taken advantage of the voluntary participation of music and film stars to tackle different societal challenges. But it was in the 1980s that celebrity activism reached new heights. Bob Geldof's *Live Aid* is probably the most significant example. *Live Aid* was a series of concerts organised in 1985 to fight the famine that was affecting millions of people in Ethiopia. It represented unprecedented international cooperation that brought together some of the most important rock and pop artists of the 1980s. In a dual-venue concert taking place in London and New York, Madonna, Paul McCartney, Mick Jagger, U2, Queen, and Led Zeppelin played with other international music stars in order to raise funds to help that African nation. It was watched by about two billion people and fetched over $150 million (Richey and Ponte 2008, 61). *Live Aid* changed the rationality of independent efforts to tackle humanitarian and environmental challenges. From that moment on, this type of campaign would be closely connected to the participation of celebrities.

More recently, the phenomenon of celebrity activism has begun to include the support of big corporations, 'clicktivism' – based on weak-ties engagement – and the endorsement of 'ethical' products marketed to fund good causes. *Live 8*, *Make Poverty History*, and *Product RED*, for example, relied partially on the idea that there is today a market for people who want to use T-shirts, bracelets, and other products that provide consumers with the self-image of people who stand on high moral ground (Nash 2008).

Using a postcolonial perspective, however, Yrjölä (2012) problematizes celebrity discourses and representations in relation to humanitarianism in order to confront this very idea of a Western high moral ground. She reminds us that fictional colonial narratives helped to justify the Western presence and intervention in Africa. Through the accounts of missionaries, explorers, and writers, Africa was frequently portrayed as dark, savage, and wild country, as opposed to the rational, safe, and civilized West (Said 2003 [1978]). For Yrjölä (2012, 369), the participation of Bono Vox, Bob Geldof, and others serves to update the colonial discourse, depicting them as protectors and promoters of justice, guided by the civilized values of the west. They are characterized as idealistic, altruistic, and self-sacrificing citizens who represent Western ethics and morals and promote empathy for Africans. Such discourses reinforce mythical Western values of moral supremacy, whilst locating Africa outside modernity, freedom, and civilization. With a similar view, Ilan Kapoor suggests that African subject is usually portrayed as passive and voiceless and treated as a victim who needs guidance from enlightened Western celebrities (2013, 42).

These perspectives incorporate a shared notion that celebrity activism cannot be fully grasped if it is analysed without taking the multiple political and economic interests behind the phenomenon into account. An illustration is the involvement of North American actor George Clooney, the 'global ambassador' for the sophisticated Swiss brand Nespresso, in a media stunt conceived to draw the attention to the reproachable actions of the Sudanese government (see Gulam, in this volume). On March 2012, Clooney was handcuffed and arrested by Washington D.C Police Department after blocking the entrance to the Sudanese embassy.[6] The spectacular event organized by the actor included the presence of activists and members of the international press and was meant to draw attention to the massacre of the mountain population of Nuba that was being perpetrated by the central government of Khartoum[7] (*The Guardian* 2012). Despite the humanitarian intentions of such action, which the actor described as an attempt to 'stop rapes and deaths by hunger', Clooney was criticized by many specialist analysts who considered his depiction[8] of the Sudanese situation to be erroneous and decontextualized[8] (*The Guardian* 2012). Even the largest Sudanese oppositional movement published an open letter against Clooney's declarations arguing that

> Portraying the regional conflicts in the country as a simplified war between Arabs and African concerns us. It does not fully capture the historical and political aspects of the conflict [. . .] The regional conflicts in Sudan are not simple and are highly political with a strong basis on economic gains such as oil and other resources.
>
> (Sudan Tribune 2012)[9]

Controversies aside, George Clooney's humanitarian and political engagement has earned him awards and considerable visibility. In 2010 the actor won the Ripple of Hope Awards offered by the Robert F. Kennedy Center for Justice and Human Rights. The award is granted annually during a gala ceremony in New York City and is a way to publicize the individual work of influential people who show concern for global challenges. Often granted to widely known celebrities, in 2012 the award was given to the young country singer Taylor Swift. Swift, who turned twenty-seven years old in 2016, is described by Kerry Kennedy, niece of the assassinated former president and founder of the entity, as an example of engaged artist who 'is not afraid to publicly demonstrate her opinions' and is 'the type of woman we want our daughters to be: authentic and powerful'. Furthermore, Kennedy claims that society needs brave people like Swift who 'are capable of confronting tyrants, whether school bully or powerful dictator'[10] (Cision *PR Newswire*). For Kennedy, Swift's supposedly authentic style shown in her lyrics and her engagement with 'solidarity and charity campaigns' has the capacity to positively influence complex political problems in faraway countries. Despite the limitations of this kind of argument, the contemporary understanding that celebrities can (and should) play a part in humanitarian, social, or environmental consciousness – often conflated with their entertainment industry professions – has resulted in the recent creation of many awards that aim to bring attention to this type of initiative.

Perhaps more surprising in Swift's young career than all the Grammy awards she has received or all the platinum albums she has accumulated are the many awards she was granted in recognition of her involvement in humanitarian causes. The Do Something Awards (received four times in a row, including 2015), The Big Help Award, Ripple of Hope Awards, and The Giving Back Award are examples of awards given to Taylor Swift in recent years, which are concrete markers of solidarity capital.

Perhaps even more revealing is that this type of recognition has virtually been offered, in differing degrees, to so many major pop culture artists. Whether through awards, nominations, or public lists of celebrities engaged in issues that affect the planet, artists such as Miley Cyrus, One Direction, Katy Perry, Madonna, Lady Gaga, Oprah Winfrey, Bono Vox, Angelina Jolie, and Justin Bieber, among many others, often reinforce their own civically engaged credentials in the public eye. The speed with which the entertainment industry has welcomed the growing number of spectacular humanitarian and environmental initiatives in recent decades seems to indicate that support for such causes can be quite advantageous.

Some authors have even suggested that it would be almost impossible today to find well-established celebrities who do not publicly demonstrate some kind of activism (Littler 2008; Panis 2012). In other words, it seems that Boorstin's acclaimed definition of celebrity (1992 [1961], 57) in the beginning of the 1960s – 'a person who is known for his (sic) well-knownness' – does not encompass the full complexity of the phenomenon. Nowadays celebrities are known for the causes they support.

Although the creation of an image as someone who is politically concerned about the world's problems may reflect the sincere sentiments of many contemporary celebrities, the phenomenon also responds to the demands of a society that seems to increasingly enjoy the idea that consumerism, 'media people', and the entertainment industry can solve major contemporary challenges without endangering the structures of the neoliberal capitalist system. Consciously or not, celebrities who take part in this type of arrangement are rewarded with a kind of visibility that is valorised in present consumer market.

In other words, being an actor or a musician who participates in civic campaigns may accrue tangible economical benefits over the course of that person's career. This is to say that the person accumulates solidarity capital. This observation is crucial for a deeper understanding of all the variables involved in celebrity activism.

Solidarity capital formation

Throughout his career, Pierre Bourdieu developed many studies that became key references in our understanding of the way culture and current social and economic structures are articulated. One of his main concerns was the study of the influence of the immanent structures of the social world over probabilities for individual economic success. Bourdieu was sceptical about the notion of a 'roulette' of social opportunities, that is, the belief in a world free of inertia in which the accumulation of financial chances is equally available to everyone.

Noneconomic forms of exchange that apparently do not correspond to personal interests – that is, forms that are apparently 'disinterested' – were analysed by the French scholar in terms of their ability to reproduce hierarchies and power structures. Through extensive empirical research, he described the transubstantiation process in which 'the most material types of capital- those which are economic in the restricted sense – may be present themselves in the immaterial form of cultural capital or social capital and vice versa' (Bourdieu 1986, 242).

Cultural capital, for example, is a concept created by Bourdieu to describe specific types of knowledge, modes of behaviour, tastes, and lifestyles responsible for the opportunities and access to specific job markets, professions, or occupations. In *Distinction*, the sociologist suggests that a taste for certain genres of music and cultural expression, such as classical music or Renaissance art – most widespread in the upper classes – constructs a symbolic hierarchy responsible for the perpetuation of social inequalities (Bourdieu 2000). This is to say that cultural choices not only reflect the socio-economic origins of individuals but also help to reproduce the social structure in which they meet.

In addition to initiation in artistic tendencies or the appreciation of sophisticated types of cuisine, the bearer of cultural capital is also expected to act naturally and confidently in expressing them. The appreciation of the work of an artist such as Mozart should not seem contrived. It should be the result of personal experiences acquired since childhood through visits to concert halls, trips, school, family record album collections, and so on. In other words, cultural capital is acquired through long-term exposure to different environments that, in many cases, are inaccessible to other social classes.

What makes cultural capital a type of capital in itself is its capacity to be converted into other concrete types of capitals, particularly the economic. The highest positions in big corporations and institutions, for example, demand that those who occupy them are familiar with the tastes and cultural references of their peers. Knowing how to behave in restaurants, choosing the best wines, and taking part in appropriate cultural events are abilities that are constantly put to test in the routine of this social group. Professions related to the arts, curatorial practices, or the luxury market are also examples of careers that require expertise related to socially exclusive symbolic references (McRobbie 2005). In conclusion, the kinds of knowledge that constitute cultural capital are convertible into economic benefits since they are needed in order to access better wages or specific types of work.

In describing the process of reproduction of social hierarchies through noneconomic forms of exchange, Bourdieu also developed the concept of social capital. This concept is more centred on someone's social network than on the knowledge or taste that this person has developed throughout their lifetime. Although this concept often carries positive connotations, connected to association and cooperation capacities in society (Putnam 2000), Bourdieu emphasized social capital's ability to generate personal benefits for its bearer. Equally convertible into financial benefits, social capital may be acquired through prolonged access to exclusive social spaces such as expensive clubs, elite schools, or trade associations (Bourdieu 1977, 183–184). In these spaces, the individual cultivates selective social networks that may be used as a resource for building economic prosperity. Accepting a job offer, meeting potential clients, or obtaining the personal support needed in order to develop a specific project are ways to convert social capital into an economic form. According to Bourdieu, people with important family names or titles of nobility are the privileged targets of those who want to accumulate social capital because 'they are known by more people than they know, and their work of sociability, when it is exerted, is highly productive' (Bourdieu 1986, 249).

Nathalie Heinich evokes the concept of social capital developed by Bourdieu as well as the issue of asymmetry in personal visibility to talk about today's celebrities. According to Heinich, the high visibility celebrities enjoy is a specific kind of social capital. In other words, the social advantages of belonging to an important family or the possession of a title of nobility may be replicated by the individual who becomes visible, that is, who knows how to build a reputation through the media (Heinich 2012, 45). The kind of social capital that defines the celebrity, baptized by the author as *visibility capital*, may be perceived as a typically contemporary way to accumulate social relations that are convertible into economic gains. According to Heinich, visibility capital

> has all the characteristics of a capital in the classical sense – economic – of the term: it effectively represents a measurable, cumulative, transferrable resource that refers to interests and that can be converted.
>
> (ibid, 46)[11]

Heinich analyses the changes responsible for the crystallization of this kind of capital that have occurred since the early twentieth century. Among such transformations, she emphasizes the importance of the mechanical reproduction of images.

Before the advent of major urban centres, the average individual was exposed to a relatively limited number of people during their lifetime, perhaps but a few hundred of them. Proliferation of big cities in the nineteenth century intensified visual stimuli and the number of people with whom it was possible to establish some kind of contact in everyday life (Simmel 1976). The advent of mass media and, more recently, digital media has increased these numbers in an even more dramatic way. The faces of actors, talk show hosts, and musicians have become a major presence in people's everyday lives. Ubiquitous in TV shows, movies, and magazines, people follow media personalities' intimate and social lives. For Heinich, the overexposure of faces, mainly of actors and musicians, is both cause and consequence of their celebrity status.

What makes this 'amplified visibility' a type of capital is its imbalance. That is to say that a celebrity is known by the unknown. The greater the imbalance between the number of people that know an individual and the number of people this same individual knows, the greater their capital. This positive differential is what Heinich calls 'visibility capital', which may be transformed into economic capital.

The author recalls Edgar Morin's (1989) work on movie stars, which seeks to analyse the relationship between visibility and profit. Morin argues that the use of movie stars in major film productions results in higher financial returns to the studios. He suggests that the investment the cultural industry makes on the double nature – the divine and the human – of these 'Olympians' guarantees them a mythological position in today's world. On the one hand, movie stars perform parts that turn them into contemporary divinities in the public eye; on the other hand they are humanized by gossip magazines and TV shows that constantly scrutinize the details of their personal lives. According to Morin, this double process, which is responsible at the same time for the projection and identification of the public, is strengthened when the participation in leading movie roles is combined with the increased visibility of the actors' or actresses' personal life (Morin 1997, 107). In other words, the more familiar the public gets with the celebrity's personal life (this is to say, with their 'human side'), the higher the economic feasibility of the productions in which they participate.

According to Heinich, this visibility capital can be measured quantitatively. The French sociologist lists many indicators created by the industry itself to measure the visibility of celebrities: the numbers of paying audience in concerts, media attention to their public appearances, the size and number of fan clubs, number of social media followers, and the number of search results on Google are some of them (Heinich 2012, 47–48).

Forbes magazine adopts similar criteria in its Celebrity 100 list, which ranks the 100 most influential media personalities in the world. *Forbes* editor Dorothy Pomerantz reveals that the magazine combines a range of quantitative drivers such as entertainment-related earnings and exposure in TV, radio, print, and online to compose the list (Forbes 2012).[12] Most of these exposure indicators are objectively collected through counting magazine covers, number of followers in social media profiles, number of appearances on television, and so on. Yet they do not say much about the specifics of the type of visibility produced by these celebrities. That is to say, these indicators do not attest to whether some forms of visibility are more economically rewarding than others.

Although it is not possible to establish a simple cause-and-effect relation here, this chapter suggests that there are indeed certain types of visibility that are more efficient than others when it comes to their transformative material or economic capacity. I specifically propose that the public participation of celebrities in activism is able to generate a symbolic capital that is qualitatively distinct from the one attached to other forms of visibility. *Solidarity capital* is distinguished by its connection to the moral field. It is created through the participation of celebrities in media actions based on very clearly defined principles of idealism, selflessness, and justice. Even when media campaigns trying to raise public awareness point to the imbalance of environmental, social, or humanitarian orders – often with no consensus on possible solutions – they are presented simply and unambiguously

(Curtis and McCarthy 2012; Martín 2010; Polman 2010; Sankore 2005). As a consequence, one is left with the impression that the path to the end of global warming or hunger in developing countries is known and can be easily followed.

Unlike visibility capital, the economic benefits generated by solidarity capital cannot be measured directly, since this form of capital is linked to a moral attribute ascribed to media visibility. It gains materiality when media outlets make reference to socially engaged actions performed by a celebrity, a materiality that varies depending on the social context. For example, a campaign to stop the construction of a hydroelectric dam that threatens indigenous communities in the Amazon region, like the one supported by film director James Cameron in 2010, is not experienced the same way everywhere. While praised by US environmentalist groups, some conservative segments of Brazilian society described Cameron's message as interventionist. Furthermore, despite the polemics it stirred up, news reports around the world that showed Cameron meeting exotic indigenous leaders in the deep Amazon forest drew attention to his blockbuster film *Avatar*, which was being released at that time. In both cases, Cameron's narratives speak of an indigenous culture threatened by greed and Western capitalist values. Such proximity between fiction and reality seemed almost irresistible to newsrooms around the world. The *New York Times*[13] (2010), The *Observer*[14] (2010), CNN[15] (2010), and *Forbes* magazine[16] (2011), among other major media vehicles, ran positive stories about Cameron's campaign, whilst also noting its similarities with the film plot. If, on the one hand, it is impossible to measure the potential financial benefits accrued by Cameron's intervention in the Amazon, on the other, it seems reasonable to argue that the film director gained a kind of legitimacy as a storyteller of such narratives. Did this translate into a significant increase in box office sales for *Avatar*, considering the visibility that his trip to Brazil gave to his film? Probably not. But his well-timed campaign to defend indigenous populations in the Amazon may have boosted his credentials as someone in tune with contemporary environmental challenges, thus fostering new professional opportunities and deals in the film industry.

In some situations, however, this transubstantiation process can be more clearly recognized. The case of Brazilian TV host Luciano Huck is representative in this respect. He commands the TV show *Caldeirão do Huck* (literally, *Huck's Cauldron*), broadcast by the Globo Network, which offers a balanced mix of entertainment and charity, producing local variations of the internationally known *Extreme Makeover: Home Edition* and *Pimp my Ride*. Huck likes to use his social media profiles – he has around 18 million Facebook fans and almost 13 million Twitter followers[17] – to publicize the philanthropist initiatives he supports, segments from his TV program, pictures of private moments with his family, and awards for personal achievements, such as when he was a Man of the Year nominee[18] (IG 2011). He and his wife, Angelica, who is also a TV host, have been referred to by the Brazilian newsweekly *Veja* magazine – the most influential of its sort in the country – as exemplary: 'the perfect celebrity couple for a politically correct world' (*Veja*). He is a celebrity who has both great visibility and considerable solidarity capital. Messages regarding civically engaged actions that are posted through his Twitter and Facebook accounts are often the ones that get the largest number of likes and positive commentaries. Actions promoted include the sale of T-shirts publicizing 'peace culture',[19] whose proceeds go to disaster victims[20] and the exposure of personal transformation stories in his TV shows. The effort to publicize Huck's concern for social and humanitarian issues have, in addition to magazine covers and prize nominations, provided him with contracts with corporations that want to be associated with his 'do-gooder' image. A credit card company, for example, launched a project that was built up around Huck's reputation as social benefactor. During the launching of the campaign, the TV host invited his Facebook and Twitter followers to post descriptions of personal or professional projects in need of some kind of financial aid. Those that Huck and his team chose were awarded half of the financial resources needed to make their dreams come true[21] (Banco Itaú 2013). According to *Alfa* magazine, which also published a cover story about the TV host, Huck receives nearly \$2 million annually to participate in advertising actions for the sponsoring credit card company that created the promotion. In this case, it is easy to see how solidarity capital can be directly translated to a quite advantageous endorsement contract.

Another illustrative example is the 'expedition' that Brazilian top model Gisele Bündchen recently made to Kenya as a Goodwill Ambassador for the United Nations Environment Program. The trip resulted in photo opportunities with the local population and interviews for a variety of media outlets, which praised her commitment to humanitarian and environmental issues. Yet it did not generate any kind of concrete debate about contemporary challenges faced by the environment. At best, the fashion model was able to give some trivial suggestions about her own experience as a consumer: 'Many things need to be changed in the world', declared Bündchen, 'a considerable part of the energy consumed in my house is generated by solar panels. Besides that, I use more efficient and economic light bulbs'[22] (Caras 2012) The fact that she constantly moves about in her own private jet – hardly an environmentally friendly way to travel – was never an issue. Maxwell and Miller (2012, 66) are also mindful of this contradiction when they argue, '[. . .] stars love to add awareness of their shrinking carbon footprints to their enviable personal traits, even as they jet around the world'.

Although it is not possible to make clear assessments of any positive environmental impact to the resulting from Bündchen's engagement in such causes, it is easy to verify the benefits such involvement brings to her image. 'Good example' and 'She is awesome . . . Big fan!' are some of the comments left by the readers of the articles that reported the 'solidarity run-away show' created by the top model.[23]

The humanitarian, social, or environmental campaigns that work with celebrities hardly propose deeper discussions on the issues they raise; nor do they present the structural facts that lie at their root. This is to say, there is no concrete attempt to 'democratize the public sphere', as suggested by some authors that research related phenomena (Cooper 2008; Hartley 1999), nor to include issues that are a part of broader political projects. Instead what prevails is the individualist notion that 'conscientious' consumption or support given to overexposed media actions led by celebrities is the best way to overcome major contemporary humanitarian, social, and environmental imbalances.

As well as the immaterial forms of capital described by Bourdieu and Heinich, solidarity capital is not self-evident as a kind of capital; rather it appears as a set of legitimate skills developed by a given agent. In particular, solidarity capital conveys an individual's ability to make himself or herself visible in the media along with their capacity to publicly demonstrate exemplary moral behaviour regarding the great challenges of our times. The greater the credibility of a celebrity's humanitarian or environmental commitment and the greater exposure they get, the greater the appeal of their solidarity capital. Although such capital is not easily quantifiable – a fact that sets it apart from the visibility capital described by Heinich – the recent popularization of awards, nominations, public lists, products, and socially engaged campaigns promoted by the entertainment industry clearly indicates the value of a new form of media existence: the civically engaged celebrity

Final considerations

Hasty evaluation might suggest that the increasing commitment of celebrities in humanitarian and environmental campaigns indicates the reinforcement of new models of charity, social aid, and political participation. Media spectacles on social engagement and benevolence could be seem as signs of a new public sphere engaged with the resolution of contemporary challenges. Lipovetsky (2005), however, argues that this phenomenon indicates the current inability of society to address its most fundamental issues through austere political projects that demand feelings of obligation and duty. According to the French philosopher, media solidarity demonstrations fuse a generous spirit with marketing, an ideal with personalization. Pain becomes a reason to entertain. More than any other, it is revealing of our current hedonistic culture. The solidarity trend is epidermal and brief and resembles an interactive show. At most, predicts Lipovetsky (2005, 112), we act on the impulse of an 'occasional generosity'. The author sustains that the austere character demanded by obligations of duty, which characterized the West from the eighteenth until the middle of the twentieth centuries – period coined by the author as the 'Moralist Era' – has come to an end. In a 'post-moralistic society', concern with the strengthening of Western ethical values has yielded to concerns for the happiness of the spectator citizen.

Although the thesis of the 'moral decay' supported by Lipovetsky seems a bit simplistic, almost an updated version of similar arguments proposed by other authors throughout the twentieth century (Boorstin 1992 [1961]; Ortega Y Gasset 2007 [1930]), the French philosopher is correct in relating the process of the individualization of society with the entertainment industry expansion and the popularization of 'media benevolence'.

As bearer of the codes that define contemporary models of solidarity, the 'media' (Couldry 2005, 60) is able to legislate on them and simultaneously legitimate them. Our reflections upon the constitution of the solidarity capital and the assumptions that surround it helps to elucidate how it works as a form of capital. The disinterested involvement of celebrities in social, humanitarian, and environmental activism meets the market demands of our current individualistic society based on neoliberal capitalist principles (Boltanski and Chiapello 2007; Chouliaraki 2013). Thus, even though this commitment to solidarity reflects the positive ideals of media stars in relation to great world challenges, it conveniently rewards the visibility of these celebrities. In summary, in order to 'break the spell' that solidarity capital creates, we must show how it functions as a form of capital and go on to propose alternative ways of acting upon the key structural problems faced by contemporary society.

Notes

1 Businesspeople, politicians, scientists, and so forth.
2 Actors, singers, sports figures, and so on.
3 Littler (2015, 3) nonetheless identifies a class and gender bias in Lowenthal's argument. She claims that the anxieties that he expresses reveal a prejudice toward feminized mass culture, in opposition to more 'serious' middle-class culture.
4 In order to simplify my argument, this article does not examine distinctions between social, humanitarian, and environmental campaigns. All these forms of activism are discussed within a broad and generalizing concept that involves what I call 'solidarity' (or 'engaged') campaigns, that is, campaigns that are meant to generate a positive impact on the major world imbalances whether humanitarian, social, or environmental.
5 Samantha Leal, Marie Claire '71 Times Celebrity Did Impressively Selfless Stuff'. www.marieclaire.com/celebrity/news/g2955/celebrities-doing-good-things [accessed: 10 June 2019].
6 The actor was released on bail on the same day.
7 *The Guardian* 'George Clooney Arrested in Planned Protest at Sudanese Embassy'. www.guardian.co.uk/world/2012/mar/16/george-clooney-arrested-sudanese-embassy [accessed: 10 June 2019].
8 Nesrine Malik, *The Guardian*, 'George Clooney Isn't Helping Sudan'. www.guardian.co.uk/commentisfree/2012/mar/19/george-clooney-isnt-helping-sudan [accessed: 10 June 2019].
9 *Sudan Tribune* 'Sudan Change Now Open Letter to George Clooney'. www.sudantribune.com/spip.php?article41950 [accessed: 10 June 2019].
10 Cision *PR Newswire* 'Taylor Swift Honored with RFK Center's Ripple of Hope Award'. https://www.prnewswire.com/news-releases/taylor-swift-honored-with-rfk-centers-ripple-of-hope-award-182081831.html [accessed: 10 June 2019].
11 Translation by the author.
12 Dorothy Pomerantz, *Forbes*, 'Celebrity 100: How We Create the List'. www.forbes.com/sites/dorothypomerantz/2012/05/16/celebrity-100-how-we-create-the-list/#3528172a48f2 [accessed: 10 June 2019].
13 Alexei Barrionuevo, *New York Times*, 'Tribes of Amazon Find an Ally Out of "Avatar"'. www.nytimes.com/2010/04/11/world/americas/11brazil.html [accessed: 10 June 2019].
14 Tom Philips, *The Guardian*, 'Avatar Director James Cameron Joins Amazon Tribe's Fight to Halt Giant Dam'. www.theguardian.com/world/2010/apr/18/avatar-james-cameron-brazil-dam [accessed: 10 June 2019].
15 Alan Duke, *CNN*, 'James Cameron Joins Real-Life "Avatar" Battle'. http://edition.cnn.com/2010/SHOWBIZ/04/20/james.cameron.rain.forest/ [accessed: 10 June 2019].
16 Kenneth Rapoza, *Forbes*, 'Brazil's Vale Joins "Avatar" Battle as Belo Monte Dam Investor'. www.forbes.com/sites/kenrapoza/2011/04/28/brazils-vale-joins-avatar-battle-as-belo-monte-dam-investor/#23e057b04af2 [accessed: 10 June 2019].
17 Figures of June 2019.

18 The election was promoted by *Alfa* magazine. The information can be found at IG 'Luciano Huck faz campanha para ser eleito "Homem do Ano"'. https://gente.ig.com. br/luciano-huck-faz-campanha-para-ser-eleito-homem-do-ano/n1597118952472.html [accessed: 10 June 2019].
19 Message posted on March 27, 2012, and also published by Instituto Sou da Paz, the NGO which developed the partnership with Huck. The message can be read at: https:// twitter.com/isoudapaz/status/184721305873022976 [accessed: 10 June 2019].
20 As an example, see the message Huck posted supporting the victims of the storms in Rio de Janeiro state. https://twitter.com/LucianoHuck/status/26377814122962944 [accessed: 10 June 2019].
21 Banco Itaú 'Itaucard facilita realização de sonhos e racha a conta com até R$ 15 mil'. www.itau.com.br/imprensa/releases/itaucard-facilita-realizacao-de-sonhos-e-racha-a-conta-com-ate-r-15-mil.html [accessed: 10 May 2019].
22 Caras 'Top Gisele Bündchen faz expedição ao Quênia'. https://caras.uol.com.br/ arquivo/top-gisele-bundchen-faz-expedicao-ao-quenia.phtml [accessed: 10 June 2019].
23 Extra, 'Gisele Bündchen desfila sua solidariedade na Africa'. http://extra.globo. com/famosos/gisele-bundchen-desfila-sua-solidariedade-na-africa-3763860.html [accessed: 10 June 2019].

References

Banco Itaú (2013) 'Itaucard facilita realização de sonhos e racha a conta com até R$ 15 mil', 16 April.
Bardia, A.S. (2010) 'Fifty Years of Songs and Large Concerts for Solidarity', paper presented at the Arts and Peace Programme, School for a Culture of Peace, 1–11.
Barrionuevo, A. (2010) 'Tribes of Amazon Find an Ally Out of "Avatar"', *The New York Times*, 10 April [online] Available: www.nytimes.com/2010/04/11/world/americas/11 brazil.html?_r=0 [accessed 10 May 2016].
Baym, N. (2013) 'Fãs ou amigos? Enxergando a Mídia Social Como Fazem os Músicos', *Matrizes*, 7 (8): 13–46.
Bennett, L. (2014) '"If We Stick together We Can Do Anything": Lady Gaga Fandom, Philanthropy and Activism through Social Media', *Celebrity Studies*, 5 (1–2): 138–152.
Boltanski, L. and Chiapello, È. (2007) *The New Spirit of Capitalism*, London: Verso.
Boorstin, D. (1992 [1961]) *The Image: A Guide to Pseudo-Events in America*, New York: Vintage Books.
Bourdieu, P. (1977) *Outline of a Theory in Practice*, Cambridge: Cambridge University Press.
Bourdieu, P. (1986) 'The Forms of Capital', in J.G. Richardson (ed.) *Handbook of Theory and Research for the Sociology of Education*, Westport, CT: Greenwood: 241–258.
Bourdieu, P. (2000) *Distinction: A Social Critique of the Judgement of Taste*, London: Routledge.
Brockington, D. (2014) *Celebrity Advocacy and International Development*, London and New York: Routledge.
Campanella, B. (2012) 'Vendedores de "Consciência": Celebridade, Vida Privada e Consumo em Campanhas Humanitárias e Ecológicas', in V. Franca *et al.* (eds.) *Celebridades no Século XX: Transformações no Estatuto da Fama*, Porto Alegre: Sulina.
Caras (2012) '*Top Gisele Bündchen faz expedição ao Quênia*', 24 January.
Chouliaraki, L. (2013) *The Ironic Spectator: Solidarity in the Age of Post-Humanitarianism*, Malden, MA and Cambridge, UK: Polity Press.
Cooper, A.F. (2008) *Celebrity Diplomacy*, London: Paradigm Publisher.

Couldry, N. (2005) 'Media Rituals: Beyond Functionalism', in E. Rothenbuhler and M. Coman (eds.) *Media Anthropology*, Thousand Oaks, CA: Sage Publications: 59–69.

Couldry, N. and Markham, T. (2007) 'Celebrity Culture and Public Connection: Bridge or Chasm?', *International Journal of Cultural Studies*, 10 (4): 403–421.

Curtis, P. and McCarthy, T. (2012) 'Kony 2012: What's the Real Story?', *The Guardian*, 8 March [online] Available: www.theguardian.com/politics/reality-check-with-polly-curtis/2012/mar/08/kony-2012-what-s-the-story [accessed 17 February 2016].

Devereaux, R. (2012) 'George Clooney Arrested in Planned Protest at Sudanese Embassy', *The Guardian*, 16 March [online] Available: www.theguardian.com/world/2012/mar/16/george-clooney-arrested-sudanese-embassy [accessed 10 May 2016].

Driessens, O. (2013) 'Celebrity Capital: Redefining Celebrity Using Field Theory', *Theory and Society*, 42 (5): 43–560.

Duke, A. (2010) 'James Cameron Joins Real-Life "Avatar" Battle', *CNN*, 21 April [online] Available: http://edition.cnn.com/2010/SHOWBIZ/04/20/james.cameron.rain.forest/ [accessed 10 May 2016].

Dyer, R. (1998) *Stars*, London: British Film Institute.

Extra (2012) 'Gisele Bündchen Desfila sua Solidariedade na África', *Extra*, 26 January [online] Available: http://extra.globo.com/famosos/gisele-bundchen-desfila-sua-solidarie dade-na-africa-3763860.html [accessed 10 June 2019].

Hartley, J. (1999) *The Uses of Television*, London: Routledge.

Heinich, N. (2012) *De la Visibilité: Excellence et Singularité en Régime Médiatique*, Paris: Éditions Gallimard.

IG (2011) 'Luciano Huck faz campanha para ser eleito "Homem do Ano"', IG, 05 August [online] Available: https://gente.ig.com.br/luciano-huck-faz-campanha-para-ser-eleito-homem-do-ano/n1597118952472.html

Kapoor, I. (2013) *Celebrity Humanitarianism: The Ideology of Global Charity*, Oxon: Routledge.

Lawrence, C. (2009) *Celebrity: What Our Fascination with the Stars Reveals about Us*, Guilford, CT: Skirt!.

Leal, S. (2017) '71 Times Celebrity Did Impressively Selfless Stuff', Marie Claire, 13 August [online] Available: www.marieclaire.com/celebrity/news/g2955/celebrities-doing-good-things [accessed 10 June 2019].

Lipovetsky, G. (2005) *A Sociedade Pós-Moralista: O Crepúsculo do Dever e da Ética Indolor dos Novos Tempos Democráticos*, Barueri: Manole.

Littler, J. (2008) '"I Feel Your Pain": Cosmopolitan Charity and the Public Fashioning of the Celebrity Soul', *Social Semiotics*, 18 (2): 237–251.

Littler, J. (2015) 'Celebrity', in T. Miller (ed.) *Routledge Companion to Global Popular Culture*, London: Routledge.

Lowenthal, L. (2006) 'The Triumph of Mass Idols', in P.D. Marshall (ed.) *The Celebrity Culture Reader*, New York: Routledge: 124–152.

Malik, N. (2012) 'George Clooney Isn't Helping Sudan', *The Guardian*, 19 March [online] Available: www.theguardian.com/commentisfree/2012/mar/19/george-clooney-isnt-helping-sudan [accessed 10 June 2019].

Marshall, P.D. (1997) *Celebrity and Power: Fame and Contemporary Culture*, Minneapolis: University of Minnesota University Press.

Marshall, P.D. (ed.) (2006) *The Celebrity Culture Reader*, New York: Routledge.

Martín, R.D. (2010) 'Celebridades y Cooperación al Desarrollo: Manejar con Cuidado', *Análisis del Real Instituto Elcano*, [online] Available: www.realinstitutoelcano.org/wps/portal/rielcano/contenido?WCM_GLOBAL_CONTEXT=/elcano/elcano_es/zonas_es/cooperacion+y+desarrollo/ari142-2010 [accessed 10 May 2016].

Marwick, A. and Boyd, C. (2011) 'To See and Be Seen: Celebrity Practice on Twitter', *Journal of Research into New Media Technologies*, 17 (2): 139–158.

Maxwell, R. and Miller, R. (2012) *Greening the Media*, New York: Oxford University Press.

McRobbie, A. (2005) *The Uses of Cultural Studies*, London: Sage Publications.

Merton, R. (2004 [1946]) *Mass Persuasion*, New York: Howard Fertig.

Morin, E. (1989) *As Estrelas: Mito e Sedução no Cinema*, Rio de Janeiro: José Olympio.

Morin, E. (1997) *Cultura de Massas no Século XX*, Rio de Janeiro: Forense Universitária.

Nash, K. (2008) 'Global Politics as Show Business: The Cultural Politics of Make Poverty History', *Media, Culture and Society*, 30 (2): 167–181.

Ortega Y Gasset, J. (2007 [1930]) *A Rebelião das Massas*, São Paulo: Martins Fontes.

Panis, K. (2012) *Celebrities' Societal Engagement: A Quantitative Analysis of Non-Profit Organisations' Motivations, Public Perception and Media Coverage*. PhD. Thesis, Universiteit Antwerpen.

Phillips, T. (2010) 'Avatar Director James Cameron Joins Amazon Tribe's Fight to Halt Giant Dam', *The Guardian*, 18 April [online] Available: www.theguardian.com/world/2010/apr/18/avatar-james-cameron-brazil-dam [accessed 10 May 2016].

Polman, L. (2010) *War Games: The Story of Aid and War in Modern Times*, London: Penguin.

Pomerantz, D. (2012) 'Celebrity 100: How We Create The List', *Forbes*, 16 May [online] Available: www.forbes.com/sites/dorothypomerantz/2012/05/16/celebrity-100-how-we-create-the-list/#3f2cde9048f2 [accessed 10 May 2016].

Putnam, R. (2000) *Bowing Alone: The Collapse and Revival of American Community*, New York: Simon and Shuster.

Rajagopal, A. (1999) 'Celebrity and the Politics of Charity: Memories of a Missionary Departed', in A. Kear and D. Steinberg (eds.) *Mourning Diana: Nation, Culture and the Performance of Grief*, London and New York: Routledge: 126–141.

Rapoza, K. (2011) 'Brazil's Vale Joins "Avatar" Battle as Belo Monte Dam Investor', *Forbes*, 28 April [online] Available: www.forbes.com/sites/kenrapoza/2011/04/28/brazils-vale-joins-avatar-battle-as-belo-monte-dam-investor/#112a27c54af2 [accessed 10 June 2019].

Richey, L.A. and Ponte, S. (2008) 'Better (Red) Than Dead? Celebrities, Consumption and International Aid', *Third World Quarterly*, 29 (4): 711–729.

Rojek, C. (2013) 'Celanthropy, Music Therapy and "Big-Citizen" Samaritans', *Celebrity Studies*, 4 (2): 129–143.

Said, E. (2003 [1978]) *Orientalism*, London: Penguin Books.

Sankore, R. (2005) 'Behind the Image: Poverty and Development Pornography', *Pambazuka News*, 21 April [online] Available: https://www.pambazuka.org/governance/behind-image-poverty-and-development-pornography [accessed 10 June 2019].

Simmel, G. (1976) 'A Metrópole e a Vida Mental', in. O. Velho (ed.) *O Fenômeno Urbano*, Rio de Janeiro: Zahar Editores.

Sudan Change Now (2012) 'Sudan Change Now Open Letter to George Clooney', *Sudan Tribune*, 19 March [online] Available: www.sudantribune.com/Sudan-Change-Now-Open-Letter-to,41950 [accessed 10 June 2019].

Veja (2011) 'The Perfect Celebrity Couple for a Politically Correct World', *Veja*, 2 February: 1.

Yrjölä, R. (2012) 'From Street into the World: Towards a Politicised Reading of Celebrity Humanitarianism', *The British Journal of Politics and International Relations*, 14 (3): 357–374.

3 Funded by philanthropy, founded for activism

Nobel Peace Prize laureates and their organisations' political endeavours

Lukasz Swiatek

For decades, a select set of celebrity activists has been leaving Norway enriched by the fortune of a long-deceased dynamite magnate. International media organisations' interest in the Nobel Peace Prize and its annual winner(s) rises each year in early October (at the time of the prize announcement) and falls around mid-December (after the awarding ceremonies and other festivities end). As a result, substantial attention is paid to Peace Prize pageantry, but much less scrutiny is given to the winnings and how they are used by the recipients.

The money accompanying each Nobel Prize – currently 8 million Swedish Krona (Nobel Foundation 2016a), equivalent to almost 700,000 British pounds, or nearly a million US dollars – is often donated to charitable causes or, in the case of the Nobel Prizes in the sciences, reinvested into research. The winnings are used in many other ways, though, with the laureates often creating funds and foundations. Indeed many Nobel Peace Prize winners have created organisations to further their humanitarian and political projects.

This chapter investigates these institutions and argues that they wield 'soft power'; that is, they attract other individuals and groups to share and act on the institutions' goals (Nye 2004). Additionally the organisations enhance the laureates' personal soft power. They do this through various humanitarian projects and their communications. However, the organisations established by the peace laureates are problematic, and their activities can cause political friction.

The chapter also examines the other windfall that this prominent group of celebrity activists receives. In addition to being awarded a substantial sum of economic capital, the laureates receive a considerable amount of symbolic capital (Bourdieu 1989). This second, intangible capital strengthens their esteem, increasing their perceived authority. While it aids them in their activist undertakings, it too can be problematic. Together, the economic and symbolic capital in this political economy help the actors wield soft power that is double-edged, generating both benefits and disadvantages that are explained here with reference to several prominent winners and their organisations.

The chapter begins by considering Nobel Peace Prize laureates as celebrity activists and examining their symbolic capital. It then details the uses of their economic capital, particularly in establishing organisations to advance their interests, before discussing the soft power wielded by these institutions, as well as the challenges and tensions that they face. The chapter not only develops our under-standing of Nobel Peace Prize laureates as celebrity activists, it also deepens our knowledge about the under-researched institutions that they establish: institutions that continue to grow around the world and play significant roles in tackling inter-national issues of particular, personal concern to the laureates.

Nobel Peace Prize laureates as celebrity activists

Before delving into the organisations, it is necessary first to canvass the actors behind them: the Nobel Peace Prize laureates. Some were celebrity activists before receiving the prize, while others became celebrities after winning it. For instance, Al Gore, the former US vice president-turned international climate change activ-ist, was already an influential celebrity activist before being awarded the acco-lade (Castells 2013) jointly with the Intergovernmental Panel on Climate Change. Malala Yousafzai too became a 'globe-trotting celebrity activist' following her recovery from the notorious, near-fatal 2012 Taliban assassination attempt (Saeed 2012). By contrast, the 1995 awarding of the Peace Prize to the anti-nuclear physicist Joseph Rotblat (along with the Pugwash Conferences on Science and World Affairs) 'made a celebrity of him' and 'had a major impact on his life', leading to numerous calls for interventions and interviews (Calogero 2007, 67). Shirin Ebadi, the Iranian lawyer and human rights activist, also became a world-wide celebrity after the prize announcement in 2003 (Rashid 2003). Likewise, Mohamed ElBaradei, the former director-general of the International Atomic Energy Agency, became an international celebrity after receiving the prize, jointly with the Agency, in 2005 (Dahl and Westall 2011). El Baradei (2011, 188) even recounts that, after the announcement had been made, an avalanche of Egyptian and international media poured into the home of his mother in Cairo and she became 'an instant celebrity', as well. The announcement of the prize recipient(s) each October then makes international celebrities of the unknown and further raises the statures of already-known. To echo Huijser and Tay's (2011, 113; origi-nal emphasis) observation about such internationally high-profile activists, 'the question is not whether the term "celebrities" is applicable to this group, but *how* it is applicable and enacted in a changing global mediascape'.

For the most part, Nobel Peace Prize-winning activists' celebrity is earned. It can be described as 'achieved' celebrity, rather than 'ascribed' or 'celetoid'-based celebrity, to draw on Rojek's (2015) framework. That is, the peace laureates' celeb-rity derives from recognised accomplishments instead of being familial or relating to heredity (ascribed) or deriving from any short-lived burst of fame generated by popular media (celetoid-based). In this respect, laureates represent celebrities who are not simply 'well-known for their well-knownness' (Boorstin 1992 [1961], 58). However, determining what counts as 'achievement' can be highly problematic; as Drake and Miah (2010, 51) note, achievements can be subjective and 'bound up with relative assumptions of cultural value and politics'. Indeed various laureates' achievements have been called into question over the last century. Critics such as Andrews (2012) and Zinn (2012) have pointed out, for example, that Henry

Kissinger, the former US Secretary of State and National Security Advisor, signed the final agreement ending the war in Vietnam but condoned President Richard Nixon's expansion of the war and the bombing of peasant villages and that President Barack Obama made eloquent speeches about peace but continued military actions of various kinds.

Peace Prize laureate-activists' celebrity also embodies the original definition and usage of the concept. Celebrity, from the Latin *celebrem/celebritas/celeber*, originally referred to a form of ceremony or ritual (Drake and Miah 2010). It denoted pomp and dignity and carried 'history's weight of solemnity and religiosity' in its meaning (Marshall 1997, 6). The Nobel Peace Prize Awarding Ceremonies, held annually on December 10 (the anniversary of Alfred Nobel's death) in the stately Main Hall of Oslo City Hall, reflect such a view of celebrity. The laureates are extolled (celebrated) in a speech given by the chairperson of the Norwegian Nobel Committee, which selects the recipients, and then solemnly conferred their prizes (with all celebrity) during the sombre ceremony, which is attended by international dignitaries and members of the Norwegian royal family. The exclusivity and formal protocol of the awarding ceremonies, whose careful construction changes minimally over time (Swiatek 2015), along with the strict procedures and secretiveness surrounding the selection of the winners, inverts more modern understandings of celebrity and their emphasis on popular and democratic culture. The Peace Prize and its rituals certainly do not reflect 'celebrity [that] embodies the empowerment of the people to shape the public sphere symbolically' (Marshall 1997, 7). The Nobel institution, as a whole, can be seen as an artefact of the era of 'solid modernity', characterised by production, tradition and industry, in the current era of 'liquid modernity', defined by consumption, change, and ephemerality (Bauman 2000).

Nobel laureate-activists then are marked by exclusivity or uniqueness. Their receipt of a singular, rare honour sets them apart from others. As such, they do not engage in the commercially driven form of celebrity activism that attempts to establish 'a greater sense of connection and intimacy between the famous and their admirers'. The laureates' goal, in undertaking their varied efforts for peace, is not to help 'collaps[e] the distance between us and them' (Tsaliki, Frangonikolopoulos and Huliaras 2011, 10) as it is for 'politicised celebrities' (Wheeler 2013), such as entertainment professionals. The laureates are high-level 'transformative' (rather than 'conforming') celebrity activists, to use Wheeler's (2011) distinction. That is, they actively participate in world politics, becoming central figures in issues such as aid, conflict, and human rights, rather than simply being international role models and developing publicity-enhancing relationships with bodies such as the United Nations. Their social and economic capital enable them to take part in global governance as unelected representatives: a group that is growing in numbers around the world and representing a key trend in neoliberalisation (Kapoor 2013). Elite government representative- or diplomat-laureates like Martti Ahtisaari (the former president of Finland), Ellen Johnson Sirleaf (the president of Liberia) and Jimmy Carter (the former president of the United States) illustrate this. The Peace Prize often rewards such high-level leaders who have greater social and intellectual skills and are often from elite socio-economic back-grounds (Swiatek 2015). This strengthens the perception that the Nobel Prizes are 'really knighthoods of a new and unusual kind, perhaps the only true aristocracy in our democratic, levelling age' (Feldman 2012, 1).

Nobel peace laureate-activists' work also differentiates them from other celeb-rity activists. Drawing on McCurdy's (2013) typology, the majority of Nobel peace laureates are 'CA2' activists: individuals who have gained celebrity status as a result of their activism. They differ from 'CA1' activists: prominent figures who have used their celebrity status to undertake activism. CA2 activists, who are already active in particular causes, often beneficially use the honour conferred upon them to differentiate themselves from others also active in those causes. However, this can lead to divisions between and in groups. As Marshall (1997, 246) notes, celebrity, by acting as a marker of distinction, typically valorises indi-viduals and separates them from others, contributing to the wider modern 'spec-tacle of individuals', especially in Western societies. One of the most prominent examples of this type of atomisation involved the International Campaign to Ban Landmines (ICBL) and its founding coordinator, Jody Williams. The conferral of the accolade in 1997 to the ICBL and Williams led to bitter infighting between the organisation's coordinators over who deserved the accolade, how the win was handled, and how the winnings were spent. Williams, singled out by the award-ing committee, became 'the star of a movement that isn't supposed to have stars', and the prize 'split a campaign that set out simply to do good, with the idealistic notion that hundreds of ordinary people in scores of countries . . . can make a difference outside conventional diplomatic forums' (Murphy 1998, F1). Indeed McCurdy (2013) notes that most activists were, and still are, not celebrities by choice; they deliberately seek anonymity in order to focus on their campaigns.

Nobel Peace laureate-activists and their symbolic capital

Nobel laureates' celebrity is enhanced by the symbolic capital that they receive from the prize. This type of capital, originally theorised by Bourdieu (1989), refers to the '[r]esources available to a social actor on the basis of prestige or rec-ognition' (Calhoun 2002, 474). It helps define and strengthen actors' positions by enabling them to be seen as 'authority figures and . . . natural claimants to status or recognition' (Hancock and Garner 2009, 180).

Many Nobel peace laureates have found that this symbolic windfall from the prize has indeed enhanced their stature, in turn aiding their activist undertakings. Thanks to their symbolic capital, they have been able to gain access to elite-level actors, particularly political leaders. For instance, the 1980 laureate, Pérez Esquivel, discovered that, after being honoured with the prize, he was able to meet prominent individuals in the United States, including members of Congress, offi-cials from the State Department, as well as the United Nations secretary-general (Pagnucco 1997). After the Nobel festivities (including the awarding ceremony), Esquivel was also able to visit high-ranking government officials in various Euro-pean countries, including Pope John Paul II. The prestige granted by the prize also helped strengthen and expand activist efforts, and many international non-government organisations (INGOs) and national government officials became more accessible and supportive of the work being undertaken (Pagnucco 1997). Likewise, for the Dalai Lama, the Peace Prize 'opened the White House's door' in April 1991 and 'led the U.S. Congress to recognize Tibet as an occupied country' (Krebs 2009, 599). It also ignited popular interest in the Tibetan cause and rekindled a global movement through 'familiar faces, like Robert Thurman, along with fresh converts drawn from the ranks of celebrities, musicians and students' (Roberts and Roberts 2009, 191).

Other laureates have also benefited from the symbolic capital generated by the prize, particularly in elevating their voices above others in international media. For instance, the 1984 laureate, Desmond Tutu (in Alford 2008, 62), remarked that the 'prestigious prize possessed the remarkable powers of an Open Sesame'. As he found, the '[t]hings you said before you got the Nobel Peace Prize, and not too many people paid attention – you say the same things, and people think it's pearls from Heaven!' (Tutu in Hopkins 2000, 47). Al Gore (2007) similarly found that:

> In the weeks that have passed since the decision on the award was made, I have seen everywhere in the world the enormous respect the Nobel Peace Prize met with both politicians and industry leaders. Whether they basically agree with me in my views on climate change, they say that they should look at the case again.

Shirin Ebadi's increased stature also helped galvanise various Iranian publics, according to Monshipouri (2004). The conferral of the accolade became a morale boost and victory, 'not only for Iranian women and the democratic and peaceful reform movement in Iran but also for Muslim feminists throughout the world'. Upon returning from Norway, Ebadi encountered enthusiasm and hopefulness among Iranian women and received gender-neutral support from many individuals. The conservative establishment was unable to deny 'neither the actual impact of th[e] award nor the importance of legitimacy and the worldwide support that it . . . generated' (Monshipouri 2004, 5).

The high levels of symbolic capital that the Peace Prize is able to grant peace laureate-activists derives from the significant amount of symbolic capital that it, the awarding body, along with the wider 'family' of Nobel Prizes (including the prizes in the sciences), have accrued over time. This symbolic capital has been generated through many factors, including the Peace Prize's emulation by imitators; its immense monetary value and regular awarding; its recognition of different peace categories and international nominees, a steady growth in nominations, and the laureates' often high-profile statuses; its membership in the Nobel 'family' and the dignity of the official events, especially the awarding ceremony; the Norwegian Nobel Committee's autonomy and its (generally) respectable record; and the unrivalled media attention (and controversy) that it attracts, as well as international public's fascination with fame and desire for peace (Van den Dungen

2001). Symbolic capital, like financial capital, also grows if it is invested well. The Nobel Foundation acknowledges that 'The Nobel Laureates, their contributions to mankind [sic.], and the meaning the prize has had in their lives constitute the basis for the Foundation's enormous goodwill-capital' (Ramel 1999). Additionally, due to the fact that the Norwegian Nobel Committee remains detached from international politics, it can strategically mobilise its capital on specific occasions to heighten the resonance of its messages. For instance, in 2009, when Aung San Suu Kyi was transferred from house detention to Burma's Insein prison, the Committee (in Acher 2009) issued a rare statement of protest, 'urg[ing] that she and other political prisoners be immediately and unconditionally released' and 'demand[ing] that she be given the necessary medical assistance without delay'.

However, symbolic capital is problematic and has not brought many peace laureate-activists the benefits that it has brought others. Crucially, symbolic capital depends on perception. As Bourdieu (1989, 17) notes, it must be 'perceived and recognized as legitimate' by others. Many authoritarian states have viewed their laureates' symbolic capital as insignificant, in addition to feeling threatened by it. Concerned that their authority could be undermined, authoritarian leaders have become anxious and brutal after laureates have been announced as prize-recipients. As Krebs (2009, 601) explains, 'regimes desperate to hold on to power are more sensitive to threats to their rule than to the good opinion of the international community'. When the Dalai Lama, for example, was announced as the prizewinner in 1989, a sense of galvanisation among Tibetans compelled the Chinese government to undertake vicious crackdowns and to clamp down on Tibetan nationalism. After Aung San Suu Kyi's win, the Burmese regime became fearful of international encirclement and struck at the pro-democracy movement (Krebs 2009). The prize's own symbolic capital has also been diminished in the eyes of critics after particular choices of laureates. For instance, Tantillo (2009) argued that the Norwegian Nobel Committee inflicted 'significant long-term damage' on the Peace Prize, lowering its prestige, by awarding it to Barack Obama.

The symbolic capital bestowed on Nobel celebrity-activists has also been a double-edged sword: benefiting laureates in some ways while harming them in others. The ICBL and Jody Williams are again a prime example. While the conferral of prize did split the international anti-landmine movement, it also helped it achieve particular goals. For example, the group was 'convinced that it was the prestige and the impact of the Nobel Peace Prize that made many governments rethink their position [on the Mine Ban Treaty]'[1] (Williams 1999). The Japanese government's actions illustrate this type of rethinking, as Williams recounts:

> [The Japanese] Foreign Minister Obuchi said very clearly that, because of the peace prize, he was going to re-think the contradictions in Japanese policy [on landmines], contradictions being that they give a lot for aid for mine victims in clearance. At the same time, they weren't going to sign the treaty. And, he ended up signing. And, they've already ratified. So, it's had a huge impact.

The symbolic capital also helped the activists access high-level leaders. As Williams comments, 'When we travel now, we meet with the foreign minister or the president. Before, we used to meet with second secretary twice removed on my ex-cousin. . . . [N]ow, people want to meet with us'. The symbolic capital conferred by the prize also helped the ICBL to generate funds. Before its win, the Campaign received an average of $64.75 million per year between 1992 and 1995; in 1998, this amount increased to $189 million and $309 million in 2002 (Krebs 2009). Hence, though its decision divided the organisation, the Norwegian Nobel Committee 'might plausibly claim credit for drawing resources to the Campaign' (Krebs, 600).

Nobel Peace laureate-activists' economic capital and their organisations

The economic capital attached to the Nobel Peace Prize gives laureates a significant financial sum on top of the symbolic capital they receive. As the introduction noted, the winnings currently total 8 million Swedish krona, the same amount for each full Nobel Prize. This amount derives from the majority of Alfred Nobel's estate, which amounted to more than 31 million crowns (Nobel Foundation 2016b), today more than £145 million, or $210 million.

The peace laureates have directed their winnings into a variety of different projects over time. For example, Martin Luther King Jr. donated his prize-sum to ten other civil rights organisations (Bryant 2015). Barack Obama replicated this gesture by donating his winnings to ten different charities, with most of the funds going to the military charity Fisher House and the Clinton-Bush Haiti Fund for earthquake relief in Haiti (O'Brien 2010). Such strategic donations have not always been free of complications or controversies. For example, Greg Mortenson, the former head of the Central Asia Institute charity (the recipient of one of Obama's $100,000 donations), admitted in 2014 to mismanaging and personally profiting from the money that the organisation had received (Fleischaker 2014). Albert John Lutuli – the South African teacher, activist, and politician who won the prize in 1960 – used his prize-sum to buy two farms in Swaziland that, he hoped, would provide a safe haven for African National Congress (ANC) refugees escaping from repression in South Africa (Asmal, Hadland and Levy 2011). As Suttner (2011) notes, though, some viewed the action as a contribution to rebuilding the ANC and, problematically, Mkhonto we Sizwe, the military wing of the ANC. The Burmese pro-democracy activist Aung San Suu Kyi announced, after receiving the prize in 1991, that she would use her winnings to establish a health and education trust for the people of Myanmar. However, it remains unclear whether the trust was ever able to be established. Friebe (2008) found that Myanmarese Internet discussion forums suggested that people in the country had never heard of the project, expressing doubts that the state's military rulers would have allowed Suu Kyi to proceed with the endowment. To this day, no clear evidence exists online definitely proving that the trust was created.

A number of peace laureate-activists have used their winnings to establish organisations that are being used to pursue the laureates' objectives and projects. For instance, after receiving the prize in 1992, Rigoberta Menchú Tum established an eponymous foundation that promotes the rights of indigenous peoples worldwide. Its activities are essentially an extension of the indigenous rights and social justice work for which the laureate won with the prize. The foundation, on its website, aligns its particular mission with the general goal of working for peace (also aligning its strategic objectives with the Nobel Peace Prize and its symbolic capital), stating that its 'most fundamental mission is the pursuit of peace. The Nobel Institute provided a launching block with the economic resources for the foundation to answer the call for the respect of human rights and the recognition the rights of indigenous villages' (Rigoberta Menchu Tum Foundation n.d.). Over the last twenty years, the organisation has campaigned for justice for the victims of the Guatemalan Civil War (of 1960 to 1996), exhuming mass graves, fighting for ancestral lands to be returned to Mayan communities, and legally documenting around 36,000 women, among other activities (Bevan 2013).

The Arias Foundation for Peace and Human Progress is another NGO created from Nobel Peace Prize winnings, specifically from the purse given to Óscar Arias Sánchez, the 1987 laureate. It claims to have developed over 400 programs and projects, run numerous fora in Costa Rica and regionally, and published over 220 documents, manuals, and guides (Fundación Arias 2016). The prize-sum has not been a sufficient source of funding for the Foundation, which has also relied on income from other sources, such as the MacArthur Foundation; the Ford Foundation; the United States Agency for International Development; UNESCO; the governments of Finland, Canada, Japan, the Netherlands, Germany, and Switzerland; ASFI; AECID (the Spanish government Agency for International Development Cooperation); the European Union; HIVOS (a Dutch organisation for development); and the United Nations, among others. The funding from these mostly Western institutions helps explain why the organisation states that its official mission is to 'promote fair, peaceful and just societies', but also that it seeks specifically to 'foment more just and peaceful societies in *the Western Hemisphere* and beyond' (Fundación Arias 2016; emphasis added). In some ways, it also reflects neoliberalisation's bent for market logics.

The 1989 Peace Prize winner, the 14th Dalai Lama (Tenzin Gyatso), used part of his winnings to establish the Foundation for Universal Responsibility of His Holiness the Dalai Lama. The other parts of the winnings, he announced in 1989 (in Shiromany 1995, 130), would be donated 'for the many who are facing starvation in various parts of the world', 'for some of the leprosy programs in India', and 'to some existing institutions and programs working on peace'. The Foundation's three missions are to:

> promote universal responsibility in a manner that respects difference and encourages a diversity of beliefs, practices and approaches. To build a global ethic of nonviolence, coexistence, gender equity and peace by facilitating secular processes that cultivate personal and social ethical values. To enrich educational paradigms that tap the transformative potential of the human mind.
>
> (FURHHDL 2012)

The Foundation produces books and films relating to its missions, in addition to organising events such as film screenings, pilgrimages, educational programs, and public fora.

One final prominent organisation established from the prize winnings is the Elie Wiesel Foundation for Humanity. Created in 1987, the Foundation aims to 'combat indifference, intolerance and injustice through international dialogue and youth-focused programs that promote acceptance, understanding and equality' (Elie Wiesel Foundation for Humanity n.d.). The organisation states that its conferences – on the themes of peace, education, health, the environment, and terrorism – have brought together world leaders and Nobel laureates to engage in vital dialogue. For twenty-six years, its Ethics Essay Contest has given American college students the chance to examine today's key ethical issues. It has also operated two Beit Tzipora Centers for Study and Enrichment in Israel for over twenty years, educating the Ethiopian-Jewish community and giving Ethiopian-Israeli students the opportunity to participate fully in Israeli society. It also presents two humanitarian awards (Elie Wiesel Foundation for Humanity n.d.).

The organisations' problematic soft power

In undertaking their various activities, the celebrity peace activists' foundations wield 'soft power'. That is, they aim to 'shape the preferences of others' by getting them to want the same outcomes that the foundations want (Nye 2004, 5). They seek to co-opt or persuade others to embrace their values and support their efforts. This approach contrasts with 'hard power' and its use of force (through approaches such as coercion, threats, and the application of sanctions). For non-state actors – including NGOs, corporations, and private organisations – soft power can be wielded through attractive values and policies, credibility, popularity, cultural elements (including cultural products or artefacts and events), and, for some, universality (Nye 2004).

The Nobel peace laureates' organisations have successfully attracted some to share their values and participate in their ventures. For example, the fellowship that Parris (in Finn 2011) undertook at the Arias Foundation (while a student at Princeton University), working on issues such as demilitarisation and women's rights, was instrumental to shaping her future. As she reflects, 'That year spurred me on to get back to the public service mind-set and also to apply to law school'. Another student, Modi (2012), comments that his internship in the Gurukul Programme – a one-month educational experience aimed at raising awareness of Tibetan Buddhism and the lives of Tibetans in exile organised by the Dalai Lama's Foundation – was a 'life-changing experience'. His reflection clearly illustrates the organisation's success in attracting and co-opting him to its values:

> The whole programme has also instilled in me compassion for the Tibetans and Tibet itself. I am more than motivated to share their stories and the story of Tibet to my own people here at home. The whole programme has had such

a huge impact on me that it has almost changed the way I look at life, for the good. The religious and spiritual teachings made me aware of what the reality should be while the political situation of Tibet and its refugees have showed me how fortunate I am to have a country and family of my own.

The soft power initiatives of the organisations also enhance the personal soft power (Naoyuki 2008) of their founders. They help the Nobel peace activists strengthen their personal relationships and build trust with publics-at-large and government officials, making them and their values more attractive to audiences. The organisations' communications – ranging from their publications (such as books, reports, and websites) to their events – help to do this by presenting the celebrity activists as both authoritative and personable. For instance, the website of the Rigoberta Menchu Tum Foundation (n.d.) features a banner with a photograph of the laureate superimposed against a photograph of a traditional Guatemalan stone carving. Menchu, dressed in native garb – symbolising her closeness to her society and its customs, enhanced by the stone carving behind her – looks directly ahead, establishing a connection with viewers accessing the website. The homepage of the Elie Wiesel Foundation for Humanity website (n.d.) similarly enhances the laureate's personal soft power. Four photographs of Wiesel are salient on the page. Two capture the laureate in the course of his activist work (meeting others), and two are of him alone. In one from this second set, he gazes out from a window (evoking a forward-thinking attitude); in the other, he smiles, looking directly at the camera in a close-up whose tight framing establishes intimacy, at eye-level (suggesting equality with the viewer). In all four, he wears a navy-coloured business suit and blue tie, signifying his authority.

However, the organisations' efforts at inviting publics to share their values and support their activities are problematic. The success of soft power depends on a 'receptive audience' (Nye 2004, 95). If others do not find a particular soft power effort or item attractive – if they feel threatened by it, for example, or find it deceitful – it will fail. This has been the case for some of the Nobel peace laureates' efforts. The Rigoberta Menchu Tum Foundation found itself embroiled in controversy in 2003 after the Nobel laureate became the president of the company Salud para Todos ('Health for All') and planned to open pharmacies across Guatemala selling low-cost generic medicines. The Foundation said that proceeds from the pharmacies would fund its human rights work (AP 2003a). As Raya (in AP 2003b) observed, 'She (Menchu) is playing a double role as an ambassador of human rights and a business woman at the same time. That is questionable'. The criticism shadowed the support she gave earlier that year for a law to reduce patent protection on medicines while sitting on the board of the Guatemalan division of the Mexico-based Farmacias Similares drugstore chain. Menchu denied any conflict of interests in her actions. Responding to the suggestions that she was using her celebrity to lobby for the law, which would enhance Farmacias Similares's business prospects, the Foundation issued a statement calling the criticisms a 'racist campaign, clothed as a scandal or revelation' (in AP 2003b). Some reports (see, for example, AP 2003b) at the time resurrected the 1999 controversy over her autobiography, *I, Rigoberta Menchú*, parts of which were seen to have been fabricated or exaggerated.

Likewise, publics have not always been positively attracted to the Arias Foundation's members and work. One lecture given by Arias himself at York College in 2000 received a decidedly mixed response, with some students calling the laureate's remarks that criticised the U.S. 'appalling' and 'misguided' (Ledington 2000). In 2013, the Public Ministry of Costa Rica opened an investigation into the Foundation to determine if a $200,000 donation received by the organisation in 2008 – days before an open-pit gold development proposed by a Canadian mining company and opposed by citizens was declared of 'national interest' – was connected to the mining company (ICR 2014). The Foundation confirmed that there had been an offer of $250,000, but denied it had accepted any money (Hunka 2013).

The Dalai Lama's Foundation for Universal Responsibility is also problematic. The organisation's financial activities are not fully transparent. Its 'Financial Statements' page provides a thumbnail (rather than a detailed document) of its 2009–2010 Balance Sheet, but the other balance sheets (from 2007–2009), located on a separate site, are not accessible and open to a 'File Not Found' page.[2] No balance sheets are provided from 2010 onwards (FURHHDL 2012). Additionally the work being undertaken by the Women in Security, Conflict Management and Peace (WISCOMP) think-tank in South Asia, established by the Foundation in 1999, diverges from the Dalai Lama's original intention to use the prize-sum to 'implement projects according to Tibetan Buddhist principles' (FURHHDL 2012). WISCOMP's modern action research and 'innovative and experiential pedagogies', which focus on 'UN global compacts such as the SDGs (Sustainable Development Goals), CEDAW (Convention on the Elimination of All Forms of Discrimination Against Women), and other resolutions' (WISCOMP n.d.), are a distinct departure from the initial principles.

The soft power efforts of the Elie Wiesel Foundation have also been contested. The organisation lost $15.2 million (virtually its whole endowment) in the 2008 Bernie Madoff investment (Ponzi scheme) scandal, which also decimated the laureate's life savings (Strom 2009). Critics (Heyman 2015) have noted, though, that Madoff was once honoured by the Foundation. The organisation Charity Navigator (2016) now gives the Foundation an accountability and transparency rating of 85 percent, noting that (at the time of its review) key documents were not provided on the Foundation's website, including a Donor Privacy Policy, Form 990, and Audited Financials. Some (Yeager 2012) have also found the Foundation's suite of awards opaque. The Arts for Humanity Award has only been given twice (to Tom Hanks in 2012 and George Clooney in 2014). The Humanitarian Award has been given seven times to Danielle Mitterrand (1989), George H. W. Bush (1991), King Juan Carlos of Spain (1991), Hillary Clinton (1994), Laura Bush (2002), Oprah Winfrey (2007), and Nicolas Sarkozy (2008). No pattern is discernible in these choices of honourees; the awards are not conferred regularly either. The Foundation's website (n.d.) provides few details about how the awarding system works. This makes it seem fairly arbitrary and consequently represents one of the organisation's tension-filled soft power activities.

Conclusion

Nobel Peace Prize laureates are influential celebrity activists whose activities often have far-reaching and deep social, political, and cultural implications. Some prizewinners achieve fame before they receive the accolade, while others become global celebrities after they are announced as winners. This chapter has investigated the nature of this celebrity and its impact on the work undertaken by the laureate-activists. It has shown that the symbolic capital conferred to the recipients has largely enhanced their stature; at the same time, it has proven to be a mixed blessing, sometimes hindering the laureates' (and their supporters' and colleagues') work. It has also canvassed the ways in which the economic capital from the prize has been used, paying particular attention to several organisations established by the laureates from the winnings. These organisations wield soft power and enhance the laureates' personal soft power. However, the soft power initiatives are often problematic, and publics around the world have not always felt persuaded to share and support the foundations' visions and activities. Hence, this political economy, fuelled by both economic and symbolic capital, ultimately generates mixed outcomes often lacking widespread agreement and adequate transparency.

A number of lessons can be drawn from these findings. Awarders of accolades need to bear in mind the circumstances of the winners they seek to honour and determine whether the symbolic capital of the award or prize is likely, for the most part, to help or hinder the honouree. The organisations established by winnings from accolades would do well to operate with integrity and transparency, invest their resources soundly, and fully disclose their financial dealings.

The chapter also opens a number of avenues for further investigation. Only Nobel Peace Prize winners and their organisations have been examined here. The celebrity and symbolic capital of other accolade recipients could be analysed as well. The organisations established by those recipients could also be studied, with a view to understanding even more clearly how soft power operates in relation to such institutions. Other political economy approaches – relating, for example, to ideology or using different theories of power – could also be used to examine these topics, in addition to frameworks such as audience analysis, to understand how audience members view celebrity laureate-activists' undertakings.

Notes

1 This treaty is formally known as the Convention on the Prohibition of the Use, Stockpiling, Production and Transfer of Anti-Personnel Mines and on their Destruction.
2 http://uttardayee.freewebspace.com [accessed April 25, 2016].

References

Acher, J. (2009) 'Nobel Committee Blasts Suu Kyi Detention', *Reuters*, 15 May [online] Available: www.reuters.com/article/us-suukyi-nobel-sb-idUSTRE54E2VZ20090515 [accessed 15 February 2016].

Alford, R.P. (2008) 'The Nobel Effect: Nobel Peace Prize Laureates as International Norm Entrepreneurs', *Virginia Journal of International Law*, 49 (1): 61–153.

Andrews, J. (2012) *Barack Obama and Leadership: 10 Reasons the 44th President Squandered Unprecedented Goodwill*, Washington, DC: Steward Publishing.

AP (2003a) 'Nobel Prize Winner Launches Discount Pharmacy Business', *Associated Press Newswires* [Factiva: The Associated Press], 12 November.

AP (2003b) 'Nobel Laureate Rigoberta Menchu Calls Criticism of Pharmacy Deal "Racist"', *Associated Press Newswires* [Factiva: The Associated Press], 1 October.

Asmal, K., Hadland, A. and Levy, M. (2011) *Kader Asmal: Politics in My Blood: A Memoir*, Auckland: Jacana Media.

Bauman, Z. (2000) *Liquid Life*, Cambridge: Polity Press.

Bevan, A.C. (2013) 'Central America Snapshot: For Guatemala's Rigoberta Menchú, Votes Aren't Everything', *The Tico Times*, 21 October [online] Available: www.ticotimes. net/2013/10/21/central-america-snapshot-for-guatemala-s-rigoberta-menchu-votes-aren-t-everything [accessed 22 March 2016].

Boorstin, D. (1992 [1961]) *The Image: A Guide to Pseudo-Events in America*, New York: Vintage Books.

Bourdieu, P. (1989) 'Social Space and Symbolic Power', *Sociological Theory*, 7 (1): 14–25.

Bryant, J.H. (2015) 'What You Didn't Know about Dr. King's Father', *John Hope Bryant*, 29 June [online] Available: http://johnhopebryant.com/2015/06/didnt-kings-father.html [accessed 22 March].

Calhoun, C. (2002) 'Symbolic Capital', in *Dictionary of the Social Sciences*, New York: Oxford University Press.

Calogero, F. (2007) 'Rotblat and Pugwash: Some Personal Reminiscences', in R. Braun *et al.* (eds.) *Joseph Rotblat: Visionary for Peace*, Weinheim: Wiley: 57–70.

Castells, M. (2013) *Communication Power* (2nd ed.), Oxford: Oxford University Press.

Charity Navigator (2016) 'Elie Wiesel Foundation for Humanity', *Charity Navigator*, [online] Available: www.charitynavigator.org/index.cfm?bay=search.summary&orgid=11924#. Vx3guY9OJaR [accessed 22 March 2016].

Dahl, F. and Westall, S. (2011) 'U.N. Nuclear Chief Defies Pressure, Takes on Iran', *Morocco World News*, 9 November [online] Available: www.moroccoworldnews.com/ 2011/11/14571/u-n-nuclear-chief-defies-pressure-takes-on-iran/?print=print [accessed 22 March 2016].

Drake, P. and Miah, A. (2010) 'The Cultural Politics of Celebrity', *Cultural Politics*, 6 (1): 49–64.

El Baradei, M. (2011) *The Age of Deception: Nuclear Diplomacy in Treacherous Times*, London: Bloomsbury.

Elie Wiesel Foundation for Humanity (n.d.) *The Elie Wiesel Foundation for Humanity*, [online] Available: www.eliewieselfoundation.org/ [accessed 22 March 2016].

Feldman, B. (2012) *The Nobel Prize: A History of Genius, Controversy, and Prestige*, New York: Arcade.

Finn, R. (2011) 'Looking at the Whole Defendant', *The New York Times*, 23 March [online] Available: www.nytimes.com/2011/03/24/nyregion/24entry.html?_r=0 [accessed 10 May 2016].

Fleischaker, J. (2014) 'Greg Mortenson Goes on Today to Apologize for Three Cups of Tea Scandal', *Melville House*, 22 January [online] Available: www.mhpbooks.com/greg-mortenson-goes-on-today-to-apologize-for-three-cups-of-tea-scandal/ [accessed 10 May 2016].

FURHHDL (2012) 'Mission', *The Foundation for Universal Responsibility of His Holiness the Dalai Lama*, [online] Available: www.furhhdl.org/mission [accessed 10 May 2016].

Friebe, R. (2008) 'How Nobel Winners Spend Their Prize Money', *Time*, 10 October [online] Available: http://content.time.com/time/specials/packages/article/0,28804,1848817_1848816_1848803,00.html [accessed 10 May 2016].

Fundación Arias (2016) 'Quiénes Somos', *Fundación Arias Para la Paz y el Progreso Humano*, [online] Available: http://arias.or.cr/quienes-somos/ [accessed 10 May 2016].

Gore, A. (2007) 'Peace Prize Meets with Respect [Fredsprisen møter respekt]', *Nobels Fredspris*, Interviewer O. Aune, The Norwegian Broadcasting Corporation [Norsk Rikskringkasting AS], 7 December [online] Available: www.nrk.no/nobel/-fredsprisen-moter-respekt-1.4241911 [accessed 15 May 2016].

Hancock, B.H. and Garner, R. (2009) *Changing Theories: New Directions in Sociology*, Toronto: University of Toronto Press.

Heyman, M. (2015) 'Heard and Scene: Lauded for a Hard Look at Tough Topic', *The Wall Street Journal* [Factiva], 31 January.

Hopkins, J. (2000) *The Art of Peace: Nobel Peace Laureates Discuss Human Rights, Conflict and Reconciliation*, Ithaca: Snow Lion Publications.

Huijser, H. and Tay, J. (2011) 'Can Celebrity Save Diplomacy? Appropriating Wisdom through "The Elders"', in L. Tsaliki, C.A. Frangonikolopoulos and A. Huliaras (eds.) *Transnational Celebrity Activism in Global Politics: Changing the World?*, Bristol: Intellect: 105–120.

Hunka, J. (2013) 'Costa Rica Investigating Canadian Mine Approval, Trials Pending', *Global News*, 7 October [online] Available: http://globalnews.ca/news/887810/costa-rica-investigating-canadian-mine-approval-trials-pending/ [accessed 15 May 2016].

ICR (2014) 'Infinito Gold Files for Arbitration: Seeks Millions from Costa Rica', *ICR News*, 11 February [online] Available: http://insidecostarica.com/2014/02/11/infinito-gold-files-arbitration-seeks-millions-costa-rica/ [accessed 12 May 2016].

Kapoor, I. (2013) *Celebrity Humanitarianism: The Ideology of Global Charity*, Oxon: Routledge.

Krebs, R.R. (2009) 'The False Promise of the Nobel Peace Prize', *Political Science Quarterly*, 124 (4): 593–625.

Ledington, S. (2000) 'Nobel Winner Skewers United States for Superpower Role', *York Daily Record*, 19 October.

Marshall, P.D. (1997) *Celebrity and Power: Fame in Contemporary Culture*, Minneapolis: University of Minnesota Press.

McCurdy, P. (2013) 'Conceptualising Celebrity Activists: The Case of Tamsin Omond', *Celebrity Studies*, 4 (3): 311–324.

Modi, Y. (2012) 'An Internship That Was Life-Changing', *SPIC MACAY Gujarat, Society for Promotion of Indian Classical Music and Culture amongst Youth*, [online] Available: http://spicmacayahmedabad.weebly.com/internship-with-the-dalai-lama.html [accessed 15 May 2016].

Monshipouri, M. (2004) 'The Road to Globalization Runs through Women's Struggle: Iran and the Impact of the Nobel Peace Prize', *World Affairs*, 167 (1): 3–14.

Murphy, C. (1998) 'The Nobel Prize Fight; Claims of Jealousy and Betrayal: A Friendship in Ruin: How the World's Most Prestigious Award Turned into a Land Mine', *The Washington Post*, 22 March.

Naoyuki, A. (2008) 'Japan Does Soft Power: Strategy and Effectiveness of Its Public Diplomacy in the United States', in Y. Watanabe and D.L. McConnell (eds.) *Soft Power Superpowers: Cultural and National Assets of Japan and the United States*, New York: M.E Sharpe: 224–244.

Nobel Foundation (2016a) *Prize Amount and Market Value of Invested Capital Converted into 2015 Year's Monetary Value*, [online] Available: www.nobelprize.org/nobel_prizes/about/amounts/prize_amounts_16.pdf [accessed 15 May 2016].

Nobel Foundation (2016b) *The Nobel Prize Amounts*, [online] Available: www.nobelprize.org/nobel_prizes/about/amounts/ [accessed 15 May 2016].

Nye, J. (2004) *Soft Power: The Means to Success in World Politics*, New York: Public Affairs.

O'Brien, M. (2010) 'Obama Doles out $1.4 Million in Nobel Peace Prize Winnings to 10 Charities', *The Hill*, 11 March [online] Available: http://thehill.com/blogs/blog-briefing-room/news/86277-obama-doles-out-14-million-in-nobel-winnings-to-10-charities [accessed 15 May 20116].

Pagnucco, R. (1997) 'The Transnational Strategies of the Service for Peace and Justice in Latin America', in J. Smith, C. Chatfield and R. Pagnucco (eds.) *Transnational Social Movements and Global Politics: Solidarity Beyond the State*, New York: Syracuse University Press: 123–138.

Ramel, S. (1999) 'Celebrating Nobel', *Nobelprize.org*, [trans. B. Savage], 15 December [online] Available: www.nobelprize.org/ceremonies/eyewitness/ramel/ [accessed 15 May 2016].

Rashid, H. (2003) 'First Muslim Woman Nobel Laureate', *The Daily Star*, 16 October [online] Available: http://archive.thedailystar.net/2003/10/16/d310161502101.htm [accessed 15 May 2016].

Rigoberta Menchu Tum Foundation (n.d.) 'What Is The Rigoberta Menchu Tum Foundation?', *Fundación Rigoberta Menchú Tum*, [online] Available: http://frmt.org/en/informaciongeneral.html [accessed 15 May 2016].

Roberts, J.B., II and Roberts, E.A. (2009) *Freeing Tibet: 50 Years of Struggle, Resistance and Hope*, New York: AMACOM.

Rojek, C. (2015) 'Celebrity', in D.T. Cook and J.M. Ryan (eds.) *The Wiley Blackwell Encyclopedia of Consumption and Consumer Studies*, Chichester and New York: Wiley-Blackwell: 71–74.

Saeed, S. (2012) 'Despite Being the Youngest-Ever Nobel Recipient, Malala's Come a Long Way', *The Express Tribune*, 10 October [online] Available: http://tribune.com.pk/story/773348/despite-being-the-youngest-ever-nobel-recipient-malalas-come-a-long-way/ [accessed 15 May 2016].

Shiromany, A.A. (1995) *The Spirit of Tibet: Universal Heritage: Selected Speeches and Writings of HH the Dalai Lama XIV*, New Delhi: Allied Publishers.

Strom, S. (2009) 'Elie Wiesel Levels Scorn at Madoff', *The New York Times*, 26 February [online] Available: www.nytimes.com/2009/02/27/business/27madoff.html [accessed 15 May 2016].

Suttner, R. (2011) 'Luthuli and MK', *Polity.org.za*, 13 December [online] Available: www.polity.org.za/article/luthuli-and-mk-2011-12-08 [accessed 10 May 2016].

Swiatek, L. (2015) 'Constructing the Cosmopolitan Arena Concert', in R. Edgar *et al.* (eds.) *The Arena Concert: Music, Media and Mass Entertainment*, New York: Bloomsbury: 87–97.

Tantillo, J. (2009) 'The Peace Prize Is Damaged Goods', *Fox News*, 13 October [online] Available: www.foxnews.com/opinion/2009/10/13/john-tantillo-nobel-peace-prize-damaged-goods.html [accessed 15 May 2016].

Tsaliki, L., Frangonikolopoulos, C.A. and Huliaras, A. (2011) 'Introduction: The Challenge of Transnational Celebrity Activism: Background, Aim and Scope of the Book', in L. Tsaliki, C. A. Frangonikolopoulos and A. Huliaras (eds.) *Transnational Celebrity Activism in Global Politics: Changing the World?* Bristol: Intellect: 7–24.

Van den Dungen, P. (2001) 'What Makes the Nobel Peace Prize Unique?', *Peace & Change*, 26 (4): 510–524.

Wheeler, M. (2011) 'Celebrity Politics and Cultural Citizenship: UN Goodwill Ambassadors and Messengers of Peace', in L. Tsaliki, C.A. Frangonikolopoulos and A. Huliaras (eds.) *Transnational Celebrity Activism in Global Politics: Changing the World?* Bristol: Intellect: 45–62.

Wheeler, M. (2013) *Celebrity Politics: Image and Identity in Contemporary Political Communications*, Cambridge: Polity Press.

Williams, J. (1999) 'Interview: Jody Williams', *America's Defense Monitor*, interviewer R. Stohl, 4 February [online] Available: www.cdi.org/adm/1226/williams.html [accessed 15 May 2016].

WISCOMP (n.d.) 'Our Mission', *Women in Security, Conflict Management and Peace*, [online] Available: http://wiscomp.org/sample-page/our-mission/ [accessed 15 May 2016].

Yeager, C. (2012) 'Still No Reply from AP or Their Reporter', *Elie Wiesel Cons the World*, 30 November [online] Available: www.eliewieseltattoo.com/tag/elie-wiesel-foundation-for-humanity/ [accessed 15 May 2016].

Zinn, H. (2012) *The Historic Unfulfilled Promise*, San Francisco: City Lights.

4 The value-form of persona

Celebrity scandal, activism, and commodities

Hilary Wheaton and Samita Nandy

This discussion provides insight into the concept of celebrity persona, and indeed the concept of persona more widely, in light of instances of scandal. Persona must be understood for its utilisation in not only enhancing celebrity power but also its paradoxical production by virtue of the power of celebrity. The scandals of Jimmy Savile and Rolf Harris, both previously celebrated as 'national treasures', serve as infamous examples of how an entertainment industry, founded on personality and commodification, may be complicit in the abhorrent abuse of the children and adults it sought to entertain. Both celebrities carefully crafted their personas as a brand, commodifying their activities and cultural productions such as television shows, artwork, music, and activism, while simultaneously commodifying their self as a result. This process of establishing celebrity persona and positive parasocial identification aided in camouflaging sinister, immoral, and criminal personality traits and activities. This chapter must also be read as an exploration of the dialectical nature of both Harris and Savile, and the social, emotional, and political damage they inflicted for various organisations and charitable causes. This dialectic is situated as the question of individual qualities (paedophile, deviant, or other) in contrast to the camouflage of celebrity persona. The dialectical nature of examining these two individuals has prompted society to question our tendency to attribute positive traits to those we admire, rather than see them within the context of their situation as celebrity, and demonstrates the complexity of the individual within the social constructs of media and fame that obscures any attempt to define the truth behind celebrity persona. The result once the scandal broke damaged the various social, emotional, and economic capital they had cultivated and, by extension, the organisations and causes they had engaged in activism for.

Child abuse scandals

Between 2012 and 2014, numerous high-profile celebrities were exposed as a result of Operation Yewtree, the Metropolitan Police Service investigation that occurred in the wake of an ITV programme titled *Exposure – The Other Side of Jimmy Savile*, broadcast on 3 October 2012 (Gardiner 2012; Gray and Watt 2013). Two celebrity figures, Jimmy Savile and Rolf Harris, both of whom had been previously labelled 'national treasures' in the UK, were now relabelled as paedophiles, deviants, perverts, and predatory sex offenders. Both celebrities had used their fame, power, and influence as respectable figures of charity, activism, and television to perpetrate horrible crimes against young and old victims. Disturbingly, in the case of Savile, these assaults occurred in various institutions such as the BBC Television Centre, Broadmoor Hospital, Duncroft School, Leeds General Infirmary, and Stoke Mandeville Hospital (Gray and Watt 2013, 12–13).

Australia and the UK, though separated by over 9,000 miles of land and sea, were subsequently tightly bound in grief and outrage at the abuse revelations attached to their native-born celebrity figures; both of whom heavily influenced the iconography of childhood. Savile died before he could be officially tried, and therefore his guilt or innocence can neither be confirmed nor denied; however, Harris has been judged by his peers and sentenced to five years and nine months in jail (Miller 2014). Harris's conviction included twelve charges of indecent sexual assault on four girls in the UK between 1968 and 1986 (Miller 2014), though his alleged assaults and those yet to surface increase this number and include both adults and children (Miranda 2014; Williams 2014; Miller 2014). With regard to Savile, it is likely that his total victims exceed 450 (Brown 2013), include both males and females, and are aged between 8 and 47 years old (Gray and Watt 2013, 3–6, 12).

As a celebrity, Rolf Harris's career spanned music, television, and art. He was granted numerous awards during his decades of entertainment, including an MBE, OBE, CBE, and Officer of the Order of Australia (Chapman 2014). Harris sang at the Queen's Diamond Jubilee in 2012, also receiving a BAFTA that year and was going to be given the title of Australian of the Year in 2013 before the outcome of his case emerged (Miranda 2014). Harris was, after all, a man commissioned by the BBC to paint the queen's portrait in 2006 (Chapman 2014) as a result of his *Rolf on Art* television show; a pop chart-topping singer of 'Two Little Boys', 'Sun Arise', 'Jake the Peg', and 'Tie Me Kangaroo Down, Sport'; winner of BBC Personality of the Year during the 1960s; host of *The Rolf Harris Show*, and from 1994 *Animal Hospital*, sharing the nation's sympathy for injured and ill pets (Guilliatt and Magnay 2014). While Harris's numerous chart-topping hit songs and television shows cannot be deleted from history, his various paintings in institutions in Australia and the UK, awards, and honours have since been removed, stripped, or rescinded.

Savile's celebrity status was equally, if not more, extraordinary than that of Harris. Savile had been awarded an OBE in 1971; was knighted for his services to charity and entertainment and given a Knight Commander of the Pontifical Equestrian Order of Saint Gregory the Great by the Vatican in 1990; awarded a green beret from the Royal Marines and various honorary degrees; was friendly with such figures as Margaret Thatcher and showed familiarity with the Duke of Edinburgh, the Prince of Wales, and the Queen ('Obituary: Sir Jimmy Savile' 2011; Brown 2013). Savile was best known in the world of youth entertainment, where he initially begun as a DJ playing records live in dance halls and then managed ballrooms; eventually his career led him to radio and then television, where he presented *Top of the Pops* in the 1960s and later *Jim'll Fix It* in the 1970s

(Brown 2013; Gray and Watt 2013, 8). These two shows respectively situated him as a 'cool' youth icon and charitable 'wish-come-true' figure. Even more, his dedication to charity work further endeared him in the hearts of many, as stated in his obituary

> It was once estimated that he had personally raised more than £40 million for various charitable causes, and that up to 90 per cent of his own income was given away, although Savile never disclosed the extent of his charitable donations. He took part in more than 200 marathons and innumerable 'fun runs' for charity, without ever bothering to train.
>
> ('Obituary: Sir Jimmy Savile' 2011)

However, as mentioned in the official Yewtree report, there were rumours connecting him with child abuse in his lifetime; notably these came up in a 1990 interview with journalist Lynn Barber, then again in 2000 with a documentary by Louis Theroux, and in an actual police investigation in 2009 (Gray and Watt 2013).

Both Savile and Harris tended to hide in plain sight, using their celebrity persona as camouflage, revealing at times drastically different attitudes to sex, abuse, and children. In this sense, as we try to piece together who Savile and Harris were or are, we question the risk of fundamental attribution error. Are their criminal actions or their goodwill and charitable work a result of the acceptance and affordance that fame allowed? They often seemed to either claim a complete disinterest and dislike of their young fans or even more astonishingly promote children's protection from such deviants as they turned out to be. These actions and any hints at an ulterior personal disposition undoubtedly results in both those close to Savile and Harris, and the wider public, suffering a degree of cognitive dissonance as an attempt is made to truly identify 'who' these celebrities are.

Harris reportedly took numerous risks by groping women without shame, for which he became notorious amongst the more junior women of the BBC (Guilliatt and Magnay 2014), while rumours regarding Savile were apparently so prevalent that colleagues would have needed to be 'tone deaf' (Brown 2013). Savile even went so far as to publicly defend the convicted paedophile Gary Glitter in 2009 by unashamedly remarking

> He just watched a few dodgy films and was only vilified because he was a celebrity, it was for his own gratification. Whether it was right or wrong is up to him as a person.
>
> (Gray and Watt 2013, 9)

Then, by contrast, Savile made numerous comments in an attempt to deflect any connection between himself and paedophilia, such as stating he disliked children and that this was the key to his success (Gray and Watt 2013, 8). For Harris, this dichotomy was even greater. He became a 'global campaigner against the evils of paedophilia', and he opened the world's largest conference on child abuse in 1986

(Guilliatt and Magnay 2014). This honour followed Harris's own production of an educational film for children instructing them on how to protect themselves from predatory adults, with a particular focus on the 'good feelings' and 'bad feelings' of being touched (Guilliatt and Magnay 2014; Parkinson and Westcott 2014). Were these actions those of a man wracked with guilt and attempting to atone for his actions by participating in activism for those he abused, or a contribution to his celebrity camouflage?

There was another participant, or some might argue conspirator, present in the child abuse scandals of Harris and Savile, and that was the BBC. The perceived failure of the BBC to act has been seen to, at worst, constitute an institutional cover-up and, at best, illustrate complete ignorance to what was occurring (in many instances, within its own buildings) and a denial of responsibility. Greer and McLaughlin, in their academic paper on the Savile scandal, focused on the critical transitions and phases of the scandal process, remarking on how the BBC's institutional cover-up triggered a 'trial by media' (2013). However, even the media was accused of shying away from suggestions of abuse during Savile's lifetime and for a time after his death; similarly, the police had little success in their attempts to follow up on reports that did surface (Brown 2013). What could possibly protect these celebrities for so long?

The answer is a combination of factors. The first, and most obvious, is the threats that victims or reporters were faced with if they attempted to expose the truth. It has been claimed that Savile used a 'variety of techniques' for preventing any allegations against him gaining traction and legitimacy; he would either manipulate or confuse reporters with his words and carefully constructed deflections, or he would simply sue (Brown 2013). Brown goes on to state the following, which reveals in Savile a far more sinister tone:

> On earlier occasions he [Savile] had threatened probing editors that exposure would mean he would give up raising money for charity or he would be able to call on friends in high places to cover up on his behalf or cause trouble. And he did not fear the police.
>
> (2013)

Second, the sheer potency of Harris's and Savile's celebrity personas obscured any temptation to see them as anything other than good with people and trustworthy with children (Conrad 2014) or as men who felt their duty was to brighten everyone's day and uphold the role of cheery national benefactor ('Obituary: Sir Jimmy Savile' 2011). Either an eerie prediction or an insightful observation, Savile's obituary written before the scandal broke remarked that '[h]is public persona was his best camouflage' ('Obituary: Sir Jimmy Savile' 2011). This statement is particularly powerful, as it reveals a judgement as to the 'real' Savile. It can be read to imply that the true nature of this individual was concealed by an aspect of his personality, one that could not be considered a sincere reflection of who he was but rather who he wanted us to see.

The third factor that contributed to why both Harris and Savile succeeded for so long with their abuse can also be linked to this power of persona and what can be considered the institutional aspect of fame (and that of the BBC itself) that allowed any potential red flags associated with eccentricity or suspicious behaviour to be accepted. As remarked by Conrad,

> One of the most perceptive comments about Rolf was made by a conservationist who worked with him on a wildlife program in Scotland. After watching him fraternise with an armada of dolphins, the scientist said, 'If he wasn't well known, he'd be quite mad.' Like Shakespearean fools, celebrities are free to be crazy or zany, and we dispense them from the customary rules about manners and morals.
>
> (2014)

These sentiments of acceptance based on celebrity value reveal something of our fascination with their eccentricity and are similarly evident with regard to Savile. After all, these two individuals were not lone outliers in their abusive dispositions, but as many of the journalists and indeed Operation Yewtree observed, they are simply indicative of many who use fame for nefarious gain (Gray and Watt 2013; Middleton *et al.* 2014; O'Hagan 2012). All that it takes to become a celebrity is 'personality' and for O' Hagen

> At the BBC these people became like gods. Even the weird ones. Even the ones whom everybody could tell were deranged . . . .We never asked whether a certain derangement was a crucial part of their talent.
>
> Bosses and colleagues who knew what he was doing say he was just being Jimmy. And he was just Jimmy to the public as well. It is the kind of concession a sentimental society makes to its worst deviants.
>
> (2012)

Indeed it seems that guilt should rest upon the shoulders of those within the BBC who turned a blind eye to the deviance of their avuncular celebrities, but as an audience and perhaps likewise accessory in the success and fame of both Savile and Harris, we cannot ignore our own acceptance of their eccentricities and dubious nature. Perhaps we turned a blind eye to any niggling doubt of their good intent because we were afraid of our moral difficulty with reconciling their good deeds? After all, the famed psychiatrist Anthony Clare had remarked that 'Jimmy Savile appeared to be a man without feelings' (*The Telegraph*, 2007), a fact that seems particularly odd of someone so engrossed in charity work, activism, and selfless acts. It is on this note that we can turn to consider biography as a tool for analysing the nature of the celebrity persona and their indexical substitutes in the wake of scandal.

Celebrity biography

Biography is a loosely used term that indicates life writing in which an artist turns into a metaphor of a personality brand, whereby the brand is a 'differentiating mark' and 'value indicator'. This metaphor offers multiple possibilities for exploring individual experience as an artist, as persona, and as value indicators, whereby their brand is a differentiating mark (Rentschler 2005, 2). Both Savile and Harris were eccentric bodily performers, and each was heavily biographed/ autobiographed whereby their eccentric nature and bizarre past were clearly recorded. While Harris's paintings, music, and eccentric physical acts like Jake the Peg, wobbleboards, and British Paint can-tapping expressed his personality, his written letter to the father of an alleged victim combined with his autograph caricatures in retrospect revealed his dark side (Conrad 2014). Meanwhile, Saville's hallmarks were his peroxide-blond hair, outlandish fashion (in the frequent form of tracksuits), jewellery, and cigars, coupled with his famous catchphrases or 'Savilisms' (Greer and McLaughlin 2013, 248). But just as in Harris's letter, Savile's biographical representation in the Louis Theroux episode *When Louis Met . . . Jimmy* (Theroux 2000) could apparently be considered an obvious indicator of his paedophilic activity (according to the YouTube comments that have since been disabled). For Savile and Harris, their biographies and mediated versions of biographical accounts represent revelations and confessions that are central to understanding their artistic and performative celebrity personas. They also offer an alternative viewpoint that potentially reveals the distinction between commodified persona and the more authentic individual behind the celebrity (whether good or bad).

The sensational responses surrounding these celebrities in media, and the confessions of emotional expression in biographical accounts, show that the heroic persona is not singular but rather dichotomous. The media (and perhaps other institutions pivotal to the persona's fame, such as the BBC) shaped this dichotomy and overlooked the contextual elements presented in their biographical accounts. Savile and Harris' representations in media and biographies are not just contingent on merit-based talent but measured against the nation's moral consciousness. Both media and biographical accounts had portrayed Savile and Harris as heroic figures in arts and activism, but with the changing tide of allegations that tarnished their reputable branding, it instead became representations of their infamy filling media spaces to sell their reconstructed inauthentic personas as newsworthy content. The dichotomy of their personas has become more and more, a singular reflection of the previously unobserved 'truth' that was camouflaged. Is this an accurate process with the potential to establish a sense of certainty as to the true and stable identity-form of Harris and Savile as deviant paedophiles?

As Greer and McLaughlin have remarked, 'scandal is a prime time news genre that galvanises and empowers news organisations' (2013, 244), allowing media to raise social issues and encourage public opinion, while simultaneously sensationalising and privileging celebrated personas over similar violent acts that often go unreported or fail to receive attention. But in the instance of Savile and Harris, the destruction of these celebrated personas actually facilitated a wider public awareness of acts of abuse, specifically when sanctioned and potentially enabled by wider 'trusted' organisations and those in power. It prompted society, as an audience and complicit participant in the success of Savile and Harris's personas, to reflect on our acceptance of the inferential structure created by media and the entertainment industry that promotes a dominant framework within which celebrities are kind and charismatic, holding social and emotional capital rather than simply weird, perverted, or creepy. This inferential structure also problematises our understanding of persona and its relation as camouflage to the authentic self because we are unable to identify any attribution error we may be participating in and simultaneously unable to reconcile the cognitive dissonance inherent in an individual who is charitable for the benefit of good and yet criminally evil.

While journalists can 'remain silent regarding criminals who also happen to be celebrities' (Nandy 2015, 224), the public and various other stakeholders invested in the study of celebrity have learned to be wary of the 'default inferential structure' (Greer and McLaughlin 2013, 251), which frames celebrities according to commercial demand rather than moral accuracy or accountability. As society moves on, we do not forget such instances of scandal and have become weary of both major celebrities, such as Bill Cosby, and those of minor celebrity, such as Jared Fogle, who influence our social and emotional lives while camouflaging their own destruction of others.

When Savile's and Harris's infamy is measured against the moral consciousness of the nation, the media reconstructs their personas in a way that contradicts the former national fame and unfolds their duplicity, consequently highlighting the dichotomy of activists who simultaneously abused the causes for which they advocated. Their personas, both famous and infamous, become reconstructed in ways that are ultimately meaningful to the nation as ideology while simultaneously meaningless to the individual. The sensation shifts attention away from the original contexts of social activism, charity, and cultural production to alternative contexts that also promote activism but of a different form – the interrogation and calls for justice from complicit institutions and corrupt officials, the seeking out of further paedophiles and protection of the future innocent. In the process of media production, distribution, and consumption of scandals, the scandal itself can generate new forms of persona power and associated celebrity activism. Savile's and Harris' deviant personas and criminal behaviours then act as alternative conditions of fame, offering grounds for future research on how their beneficial works might be managed within the loss and transformation of personas. Indeed academics who research celebrity must become more discriminating in their understanding of persona, interrogating the potential flaws and inauthentic biographical moments or acts that hint towards the divide between celebrity persona and the individual. This is particularly pertinent with activism; is it the individual who is the activist or the celebrity and their invested endorsers, and what motivates their involvement?

Value of celebrity persona

In the wake of such scandals as Harris and Savile, the lasting impact to the celebrity persona and their associated indexical substitutes or traces such as television shows, music, artwork, honours, branded places or organisations, charities, and monetary donations, is that of a loss in value or complete elimination of the indexical connection. To clarify,

> An indexical sign always points to an object or is a sample of that object. Smoke, for an example, is an indexical sign of fire.
>
> (Hillis 2015, 79)

Thus, in the instance of either Harris's or Savile's indexical substitutes, such as art, we are always physically or mentally pointed towards the celebrity persona. This can also be extended to their activism, in the form of recorded events, associated organisations, and monetary donations. Indexical substitutes, or signs, can be traced directly back to their origin due to their being a causal relation between the sign (art, television show, song, and so on) and object (Harris as artist, Savile as host, and so forth). The persona with its ability to brand products or places and thus increase their commercial value takes on a very special power in the form of understanding the relation between celebrity, their affective labour or emotional work, and the value of their commodities. Greer and McLaughlin note that 'Scandal news generates profit through a surge in scandalised consumers' but that hard news scandals, such as those of Harris and Savile, which involve acts of immorality or criminality, receive an intense negative social reaction with lasting reputational consequences (Greer and McLaughlin 2013, 244–245). Consequently, while reporting on the damaged persona or generating commercial interest around it might produce profit, the persona itself and any indexical substitute is devalued by reputational consequence.

This section seeks to understand the relationship that exists between the celebrity persona and any indexical substitutes it creates and how those substitutes can still exist in an identical physical or commercial state and yet be devalued within the market as commodities. After all, Harris's painting is still the same painting incorporating identical labour time and materials in production, and yet post-scandal its value decreases;[1] in reference to Marxist labour theory of value, this decrease in value makes no sense. Similarly Savile's charity funds, in the form of existing donations and current charity houses with funding still to give, have not altered in monetary value. This is perhaps the most perplexing because the indexical trace between Savile and money, which is itself a highly abstracted value-form, has still experienced a similar devaluing within the commercial market. How can we account for this, and is it simply a result of the linkage to persona or something more?

To understand the relationship between celebrity persona and its indexical substitutes, it is useful to refer to Marxist theory regarding labour and commodities, of which King (2010, 10–11) provides an excellent summary, and the theory of 'value-effect' put forth by Negri (1999), later examined by Arvidsson and Colleoni (2012). King provides the best starting point by advising that celebrity has reached a point where the 'commodification of personality and the formation of exchange value out of what appear to be the natural values of the person' has emerged (2010, 10). He further remarks

In this manner the contemporary star encourages (or is compelled to encourage) the development of a persona as a universal equivalent or, in more accessible parlance, a brand – a generic name for a bundle of affects that incorporates a suite of commodity goods and services.

(King 2010, 14)

Thus celebrities take on a value-form abstracted from their use-value as an actor or producer of labour and can even be considered to become a money-form circulated among film, television, and media; celebrity guarantees a specific box office income, a boost in news or magazine circulation, an endorsement that boosts sales of products, or a proportionate chunk of audience-share.

Marxist labour theory of value, however, seems insufficient for the purpose of understanding celebrity persona because labour-time is not a suitable measure for the value of persona. Arvidsson and Colleoni (2012) investigate value in informational capitalism on the Internet and offer at the same time a means by which to understand the nature of celebrity value. Rejecting the labour theory of value in online prosumer practice, they instead suggest an alternative framework based on affective relations.

Instead, value is ever more related to the ability to create and reaffirm affective bonds, like the ties that bind consumers into a community of interest or 'tribe,' or the link structure that underpins the network centrality of valuable 'influencers'.

(Arvidsson and Colleoni 2012, 136)

Both Harris and Savile existed in a network of prominent influencers and within an institution that labelled them as influencers with regard to children, charity, and social justice work. These affective bonds are produced by using so-called 'intangible' resources (Arvidsson and Colleoni 2012, 140); for the celebrity, these intangible resources are used in the production of their persona, which is itself an intangible resource (brand), none of which are measurable by time. After all, it is not time that a celebrity invests in generating their persona, but rather the intangible resources successfully cultivated and utilised as a result of personality and its affects.

Furthermore, the creation of value in this way mostly employs resources, such as communicative and social skills, the 'skills' of 'the social individual', the value-creating potential of which are poorly related to the quanta of time in which they are employed.

. . . the value of intangible resources is less susceptible to measurement in terms of productivity of time, and depends more on the ability to attract affective investments such as reputation, goodwill or employee motivation.

(Arvidsson and Colleoni 2012, 140)

For the indexical substitutes and traces of celebrities, such as artwork or monetary donations, not only should Marx's labour theory of value be applied, but in addition the affective relation between those commodities produced by virtue of the persona used.

Of course the celebrity persona does not maintain a static form of value; it can vary from context to context, but also from moment to moment. As King remarks,

> Public-self presentation, however, involves to a variable degree, the presentation of aspects of the use value of the self as exchange value. In other words, the use value of personality, the psychological and affective content of a person, varies with the context of the exchange of services. . . .
>
> (2010, 11–12)

In addition to context, the affective investment of both celebrity and public is important for determining use-value and consequent exchange-value. The use-value of the self, as exchange-value or money-form, can vary due to the public affective investment in the persona. The public must see the correct performance embodied in the celebrity, that of Savile or Harris, as avuncular or charitable figures; otherwise they cease to function as suitable exchange-values for that context. If the celebrity's affect is incorrect, as was the result in the instance of scandal, the use-value and consequent exchange-value of their indexed commodities will decrease as they are not abstract representations of charity, goodwill, activism, and avuncular compassion.

Prior to scandalous revelations, both Harris and Savile were perceived to undertake the correct emotional labour for their celebrity roles; they were adored and in demand. Nunn and Biressi discuss how audiences wish to see public figures reference a meaning that is evocative, authentic, and connective (2010, 50). Savile had achieved this so successfully in *Jim'll Fix It*, making dreams come true and prompting tears of joy and happiness while similarly embodying the image of tireless charity worker; Harris endeared himself as the lovable and fun children's artist in his two cartoon-focused TV shows and later a more matured comrade who embodied our emotional responses to loss and suffering on *Animal Hospital*. In these instances, audiences

> . . . witness what sociologist Arlie Hochschild described as 'emotion work': work requiring one to perform the 'right' feeling and ultimately even 'feel' the right feeling according to the rules of the setting and often in the service of commerce.
>
> (Nunn and Biressi 2010, 50)

In these instances, the use-value of the persona is reinforced by the value-effect, but of course in the wake of scandal, this is illegitimatised as insincere. Savile used his role purely for selfish and abusive gain, targeting those who were the weakest and most in need of help. Meanwhile, Harris revealed his narcissism, as opposed to compassion, in a letter to the father of one of his victims during the trial in which he referred to his time spent on *Animal Hospital* (Conrad 2014).

Having proved, in the wake of scandal, that the value-effect of both Savile and Harris was not only insincere but camouflage for immoral and criminal self-interest, the problem becomes that the indexical substitutes embody this same immoral and criminal value. A celebrity's activism, such as their work with a social cause or charity (and associated funding), is dependent on the exchange-value of the celebrity. For example, the charity work of Harris, especially that related to children and safeguarding them from abuse, highlights the potential political and economic costs to an activist organisation that works with a celebrity if they are involved in a scandal. This point can be highlighted again by referring to King, who states

> The various indexical substitutes, traces, and surrogates of stardom – the autograph, the pin-up, the magazine article, and the interview – are a kind of 'paper' money resting on the 'gold' standard of the star's persona. Such exchangeable promissory notes of presence rely for their *currency* on the persona of the star being reaffirmed as a force at the box office.
>
> (2010, 14: italics in original)

This makes perfect sense from a Marxist perspective if we also consider the value-effect of persona rather than the labour-value; consequently the indexical traces, no matter what they entail, are literally exchangeable only to the affective-value ascribed to the persona of the celebrity. Thus, after scandal, all work by an associated activist organisation or charity will be brought into question alongside the inevitable 'guilt' by association and concerns that it may have enabled the activity it was seeking to fight against or injured those it sought to protect due to the indexical trace back to the celebrity. However, should it be that such indexical substitutes, especially when they are commodities or value-forms such as art of money that exist in their own right, can experience a loss of affective-value?

Rosewarne muses on why the works of scandalised artists might lose their value and why they should not by drawing reference to Roman Polanski and Woody Allen (2014); but of course these artists, while involved to a certain extent in similar sexual scandals, had not committed the same affective dishonesty by performing false emotional work as a part of their persona. What is so hard to forgive, from the perspective of the audience, is that both Harris and Savile portrayed the emotion work of a persona reliant upon avuncular charity, activism, and goodwill while in reality perpetrating acts of child abuse. As Rosewarne concludes that

> while in practice fans may completely understand that the work itself is unchanged, fans look at art and listen to music with the baggage of our humanity. It's insufficient therefore, that the work hasn't changed, we have changed by virtue of our new insights into the producer.
>
> (2014)

Therefore, to take the Marxist analysis to its full course, the problem of devaluation exists because these indexical substitutes have become fetishised. They are fetishistic commodities or abstracted value-forms (in the instance of money) that do not obscure labour-value but affective-value. Our own affective guilt as an audience and that of the celebrity is fetishised by these artworks, charity organisations and money, songs, and television shows and reflected back at us as our failure to recognise the insincerity of the persona whom we idolised. The indexical substitutes of Harris and Savile are the resolution of their dialectic, the synthesis of individual and persona into emblems of our cognitive dissonance, and our attribution error and thus prompt the further dialectic between traditional labour-value and affective value.

Persona and activism in the wake of celebrity scandal

In the wake of celebrity scandal, we start to see the difficulty inherent in the value of persona; its fragility rests on the fact that both the owner and consumer of persona must truly express an authentic and required emotional response for it to function and produce value. If the affective response of persona is negatively impacted, then the indexical value associated with it will be lost. Persona and indexical value is contextual, temporary, and at risk of being manipulated for both positive and negative social, emotional, and political gain. With this usage, persona consequently risks those commodities it becomes affiliated with, whether through direct or indirect indexical relations, and taints any positive activist work that the individual may have been involved in.

We must ask whether the damage done by scandal and persona should remain indexically attached to commodities that have the potential to do good, both now or in the past. For some, Saville's charity work and show *Jim'll Fix It* will have either saved their life or provided untold joy by fulfilling a wish. For Harris, his work on raising awareness of child sex abuse may have prevented many from being abused or given children the knowledge of how to express abuse that may have occurred. The question is: how do we reconcile and rightfully acknowledge the immense damage done by these individuals when simultaneously through their activism they achieved positive and influential acts? Is it possible to separate this activism and the various commodities (including money) from the persona that was integral in generating it? If not, why not? And what does this say about persona? More importantly, how can those impacted by either the abuser or beneficiary reconcile this experience? We are therefore left with difficult questions regarding how we approach persona and its use and whether celebrity involvement in activism is to be valued or treated with caution.

The first step is in what approach we might use to further understand persona and in also situating the relationship between celebrity and persona. By taking a sociological perspective, we may be able to identify how persona can influence our attitudes towards individuals and obscure elements of their personality. Our own culture shapes the success or failure of persona by taking into account the historical influences and biographical elements of the individual; we can see how persona emerges in response to both the celebrity who utilises it and the society to which it appeals. Persona is not simply the product of the individual who uses it, but of those around it. And the need to understand our own role in the construction and success of celebrity persona may go some way in being able to repair the damage of scandal. If we consider celebrity persona, such as that of Savile and Harris, in light of the three approaches to conceptualising stardom – as commodity, text, or object of desire – (Nelmes 2012) then a sociological perspective is the only method by which we can truly analyse the celebrity. Harris and Savile are inevitably celebrity texts operating within the intertextual layers of commodification, activism, art, entertainment, and BBC institutional ideology. It is at this crossroads, between intertextual layers that generate the celebrity persona and maintain its validation and circulation within society and the alternate reality of the individual where perversion or ill-intent may be present, where analysis can truly occur.

In the wake of scandals such as Harris and Savile, effort must be made in terms of both academic and public responsibility to understand the dangers of celebrity and the persuasive power of its persona. Further research by academics that may seek to draw back the curtain on the reality of celebrity, separating the individual from the intertextual persona that grants them power and influence, is key. This is especially important if activists continue to invite or welcome celebrity engagement in social causes to increase awareness and raise money for aid and assistance. Distinguishing between the individual and the persona and the motivations and reasoning behind celebrity affiliation and involvement is necessary – along with increased transparency. Breaking down the institutional ideology that establishes celebrities as other and untouchable and replacing it with one that is ethically and morally accountable to all stakeholders, of which the BBC may already been seen to have acknowledged this transition with its sacking of Jeremy Clarkson.

Conclusion

The scandals of Savile and Harris have been discussed and analysed in this brief exploration of the use and function of persona for achieving celebrity influence and eventual disgrace. Persona is a powerful concept, used by many celebrities to create an emotional connection and sense of authenticity with their audience, and persona also lends power to social activism when celebrities endorse or champion a cause. However, persona can also be utilised to understand how moral, ethical, and legal crimes may be committed by high-profile and often admired individuals within society. Persona is a central aspect of what it means to become and maintain celebrity in our society, and in the wake of scandal and the revelation of an inauthentic persona, we see how its indexical substitutes in the form of commodities and other cultural productions may fluctuate in value. These indexical substitutes are more than just emblematic of the dialectical nature of celebrity and any attempt to understand their true identity; they are affective emblems of our cognitive dissonance between labour-value, associated guilt, and the inferential structure of celebrity as kind and good.

This article has taken the first steps in exploring this relationship and suggesting some future directions for how we might recover the indexical loss caused by celebrity persona and prevent persona from functioning to aid in the concealment of crimes. As academics, we must seek to improve the methods by which we access celebrities and understand their use of persona for both professional and personal gain and whether the distinction between public and private life is also a distinction between admired persona or less-than-admirable individual.

Note

1 Though it should be mentioned that in some instances the macabre association could increase the value of such substitutes for certain buyers or collectors.

References

Arvidsson, A. and Colleoni, E. (2012) 'Value in Informational Capitalism and on the Internet', *The Information Society*, 28: 135–150.

Brown, J. (2013) 'Jimmy Savile: A Report That Reveals 54 Years of Abuse by the Man Who Groomed the Nation', *The Independent*, [online] Available: www.independent.co.uk/news/uk/crime/jimmy-savile-a-report-that-reveals-54-years-of-abuse-by-the-man-who-groomed-the-nation-8447146.html [accessed 26 February 2016].

Chapman, J. (2014) 'Rolf Harris Faces Being Stripped of Honours Awarded by the Queen in Britain and Australia after Indecent Assault Verdicts', *Daily Mail Australia*, [online] Available: http://dailym.ai/1sSQX50 [accessed 26 February 2016].

Conrad, P. (2014) 'Inside the Strange World of Rolf Harris: Behind the Wobbleboard', *The Monthly*, July [online] Available: www.themonthly.com.au/issue/2014/july/1404178677/peter-conrad/inside-strange-world-rolf-harris [accessed 20 May 2016].

Gardiner, L. (2012) 'The Other Side of Jimmy Savile', in *Exposure, 50 Minutes*, London, UK: ITV Studios.

Gray, D. and Watt, P. (2013) *Giving Victims a Voice: Joint Report into Sexual Allegations Made against Jimmy Savile*, London: Metropolitan Police Service & NSPCC.

Greer, C. and McLaughlin, E. (2013) 'The Sir Jimmy Savile Scandal: Child Sexual Abuse and Institutional Denial at the BBC', *Crime Media Culture*, 9 (3): 243–263.

Guilliatt, R. and Magnay, J. (2014) 'The Dark Double Life of Rolf Harris', *The Weekend Australian Magazine*, [online] Available: www.theaustralian.com.au/news/features/the-dark-double-life-of-rolf-harris/story-e6frg8h6-1226981773650 [accessed 26 February 2016].

Hillis, K. (2015) 'The Avatar and Online Affect', in K. Hillis, S. Paasonen and M. Petit (eds.) *Networked Affect*, Cambridge, MA: MIT Press: 75–88.

King, B. (2010) 'Stardom, Celebrity, and the Money Form', *The Velvet Light Trap*, 65: 7–19.

Middleton, W. *et al.* (2014) 'Institutional Abuse and Societal Silence: An Emerging Global Problem', *Australian & New Zealand Journal of Psychiatry*, 48 (1): 22–25.

Miller, B. (2014) 'Rolf Harris Sentenced to More than Five Years' Jail for Indecent Assault at London's Southwark Crown Court', *ABC News*, [online] Available: www.abc.net.au/news/2014-07-04/rolf-harris-sentenced-to-more-than-five-years-jail/5572768 [accessed 26 February 2016].

Miranda, C. (2014) 'Rolf: A Life Well Lived . . . Until the End', *The Daily Telegraph*, [online] Available: www.dailytelegraph.com.au/news/nsw/rolf-a-life-well-lived-until-the-end/story-fni0cx12-1226976734754 [accessed 26 February 2016].

Nandy, S. (2015) *Fame in Hollywood North: A Theoretical Guide to Celebrity Cultures in Canada*, Kingston: WaterHill Publishing.

Negri, A. (1999) 'Value and Affect', *Boundary*, 26 (2): 77–88.

Nelmes, J. (2012) *Introduction to Film Studies* (5th ed.), London: Routledge.

Nunn, H. and Biressi, A. (2010) '"A Trust Betrayed": Celebrity and the Work of Emotion', *Celebrity Studies*, 1 (1): 49–64.

O'Hagan, A. (2012, Winter) 'Light Entertainment, Child Abuse and the British public', *British Society of Criminology Newsletter*.

Parkinson, J. and Westcott, K. (2014) 'The Story Behind Rolf Harris's Child Safety Film', *BBC News Magazine*, [online] Available: www.bbc.com/news/magazine-28112605 [accessed 26 February 2016].

Rentschler, R. (2005) 'An Early Painter's Persona as Metaphor', Paper presented at the Marketing: Building Business, Shaping Society the 2005 Academy of Marketing, Dublin Institute of Technology Faculty of Business, Dublin, Ireland.

Rosewarne, L. (2014) 'Rolf Harris: Guilty Man, Guilty Art?', *ABC: The Drum*, [online] Available: www.abc.net.au/news/2014-07-01/rosewarne-rolf-harris-guilty-man-guilty-art/5561640 [accessed 26 February 2016].

The Telegraph (2007) 'Obituary: Professor Anthony Clare', [online] Available: www.telegraph.co.uk/news/obituaries/1567778/Professor-Anthony-Clare.html [accessed 26 February 2016].

The Telegraph (2011) 'Obituary: Sir Jimmy Savile', [online] Available: www.telegraph.co.uk/news/obituaries/8857428/Sir-Jimmy-Savile.html [accessed 26 February 2016].

Theroux, L. (2000) 'When Louis Met Jimmy', [online] Available: https://vimeo.com/76002148 [accessed 26 February 2016].

Williams, P. (2014) 'Rolf Harris Investigators Say 10 New Alleged Victims Have Come Forward: British Media Reports', *ABC News*, [online] Available: www.abc.net.au/news/2014-10-12/rolf-harris-10-new-alleged-victims-come-forward-say-reports/5808050 [accessed 26 February 2016].

5 'Bring back our girls'

Social celebrity, digital activism, and new femininity

Susan Hopkins and Eric Louw

In April 2014, 276 female students, aged sixteen to eighteen years, were kidnapped from an all-girls secondary school in Chibok in northeastern Nigeria by Boko Haram Islamist militants. Boko Haram targeted schools for supposedly teaching 'sinful' Western values and diverting students from traditional Islamic life and teachings. Girls in particular were targeted because, according to Boko Haram Islamic militants, girls and women should be married and not educated. The kidnapped girls were, according to the group's spokesperson, sold into sexual slavery or forced 'marriages' with Boko Haram soldiers (BBC News 2014).

Although Chibok was not the first or last Nigerian school to be attacked, burnt, and raided, the scale of the kidnapping of girls there was unprecedented and attracted international attention (see BBC News 2014; Chandler 2015; Cleven and Curtis 2015; ABC News 2016). Protests demanding government action were held in Nigeria and later around the world, including in Western cities such as London and Los Angeles. At this point, the hashtag #BringBackOurGirls had begun to trend worldwide on the social media platform Twitter. Through the digital campaign, activists demanded the Nigerian government do more to recover the kidnapped girls and ensure access to education and freedom from violence for women and girls in Nigeria. While the first tweet using the #BringBackOurGirls (BBOG) hashtag was posted by Ibrahim Abdullahi, a Nigerian lawyer based in Abuja, it took Twitter and Instagram postings by key Western public figures, such as US First Lady Michelle Obama and supermodels and actors, such as Cara Delevinge, Emma Watson, Julia Roberts, and Keira Knightley, to raise global awareness of the kidnappings and influence national governments (Britain, the US, France and China) to send advisers, including hostage negotiators, and logistical support to Nigeria to assist in the recovery of the missing girls.

The initial rapid rise of the BBOG digital campaign can be explained in part by contemporary political and cultural preoccupations with terrorism around the world and particularly in the United States. The terms 'Islamic terrorism' or 'jihadist militants' appeared in almost all media accounts of the Chibok kidnappings – a process which, as Newman (2005, 100) explains, 'immediately brings into play a whole discursive apparatus and a series of moral assumptions which have concrete political effects'. As Said (1981) observed some time ago, in the Western mediated consensus, Islam has come to represent barbarism, medieval theocracy, and threats to the Western way of life. While the Chibok events do of course deserve widespread condemnation, another means of accounting for the rise of the BBOG digital campaign was its familiar juxtaposition of American heroism and Islamic barbarism, with the former being embodied by Western female celebrities. Indeed the female pop culture celebrity is frequently celebrated as the ultimate (Western) hero, a symbol of modern, empowered, individual strength and progress who stands in distinction from oppressed, weaker, or unenlightened others (see Hopkins 2002; see McRobbie 2009).

The BBOG digital campaign was celebrated at the time in women's magazines, such as *Marie Clare*, for demonstrating 'how powerful and positive social media can be' (Webster 2014, 8). 'Led mainly by high-profile women the world over', #BringBackOurGirls was supposedly 'a global hashtag activism movement', which 'created an international push for action that had never been seen before' (Frank 2014, 10). The digital BBOG campaign appeared to be an example of the 'clicktivism' of hashtag activism movements or social movements that use social media to generate publicity for social justice causes. Unfortunately, however, a number of years later, it appears the BBOG digital campaign has had little impact on the position of girls and women in Nigeria. As Cleven and Curtis (2015) have observed, the efforts of the #BringBackOurGirls social media campaigners 'went mostly for naught', and the kidnapped Nigerian schoolgirls have 'slowly slipped from the radar of major American media outlets'. Tragically, at the time of writing, most of the kidnapped Chibok girls (219) are either missing or still held captive by Boko Haram (ABC News 2016; Motlagh 2016). Despite a change of government and the current president Muhammadu Buhari promising to crush Boko Haram, the Nigerian leadership has thus far been unable to find or recover the Chibok girls, prompting activists to maintain that Nigeria is still not doing enough (ABC News 2016; Motlagh 2016).

Since the BBOG campaign, thousands more girls and women have been kidnapped, treated as sexual objects, and sold into sexual slavery in Nigeria. In its more recent and less optimistic updates on the BBOG digital campaign, *Marie Clare* has reported that at least 2,000 girls have been abducted since 2014 and millions more displaced as Boko Haram's 'campaign of terror continues' (Motlagh 2016, 98). As Chandler (2015) observes in *The Atlantic* magazine, BBOG was ultimately unable to meet its primary objectives, joining Kony 2012 and other hashtag campaigns 'in the junkyard of digital activism'. The rise and fall of the BBOG digital campaign on the Western media landscape seemed to illustrate the limitations of ultimately ephemeral and superficial contemporary social media campaigns and their individualistic, micro-political approaches to activism. On another level, the campaign also unearths complex and unanswered questions about who has the right to represent and speak on behalf of the Subaltern 'other' in the distant Global South (see Spivak 1993).

Through critical analysis of the recent appropriation of the BBOG digital campaign by white Western female celebrities, this chapter explores some of the contradictions in postfeminist celebrity activism, which advocates for global gender equality through a celebrity performativity intimately linked to Westernised consumerism, economic inequality, and sexualised patriarchal culture. The chapter draws on feminist analysis of popular culture, which questions the contemporary 'postfeminist phenomena' of linking discourses of celebrity with sexualisation and empowerment (see Gill 2009; McRobbie 2000, 2004). Particularly important is feminist intersectional analysis, which draws attention to the role of race, class, and age in sexualisation processes in popular culture texts featuring and targeting women (see Crenshaw 1995; see Gill 2009). This critical and intersectional reading of the BBOG digital campaign also follows Repo and Yrjölä (2011, 44) in questioning the class-specific, 'privileged, neo-colonial position' from which Western celebrities speak, often on behalf of less privileged others. The chapter interrogates the connections between neoliberal narratives of successful 'new femininity' and female celebrity performances of transnational activism and global humanitarianism (see McRobbie 2000; see Gill and Arthurs 2006; see Repo and Yrjölä 2011) that are evident in the BBOG campaign. It explores the multilayered objectification at the heart of celebrity focused gender equality campaigns, as female celebrities, who profit from their own sexual objectification, reinvent themselves as empowered 'white saviours' (see Cole 2012) by speaking on the behalf of less powerful women in the Global South. As the attractive face of neoliberal globalisation, female celebrity activists frequently represent and call for female agency and power, without adequately acknowledging their own investment in the practice architectures of global exploitation and inequality. The celebritisation of feminist politics, with feminine beauty and sexiness at its heart, transforms political issues into (pseudo)political personalities, through staged performances that reduces social complexity to simplistic morality tales (see Louw 2005). Increasingly, it is the female celebrity who purports to teach girls and women how to be a 'good', successful, and valuable global citizen. Moreover, the performance of global justice activism becomes part of the online construction and circulation of branded celebrity on Twitter, Instagram, and other social media platforms. This is often the case for female celebrities in particular, who are typically rewarded for fitting in with contemporary gender norms of being a strong and successful but caring and compassionate woman. This chapter argues that, in the name of self-actualisation through postfeminist digital activism, female celebrities frequently privatise politics by absorbing the complex stories of distant others into their own mediated identity narratives of self-growth and 'making a difference'. In campaigns, such as BBOG, it is frequently the celebrity herself and all she represents that takes centre-stage.

The female celebrity and her mirror

As Marshall (1997), Turner (2004), and Redmond (2006) have pointed out, contemporary culture is often defined and determined by celebrity power. This is exemplified, among other things, by the frequent intertwining of celebrity and politics, as celebrities increasingly take an interest in global causes (Street 2004; Louw 2005; Drake and Higgins 2006; Repo and Yrjölä 2011; Farrell 2012). In addition, 'ordinary people' often interpret their experiences of everyday life through the lens of multi-mediated fame (Hopkins 2002; Redmond 2006; Evans and Riley 2013), particularly as significant media attention is paid to the private and personal lives of celebrities. Typically it is female celebrities, more often than men, to whom this type of media attention is paid and who are more likely to be defined through their personal lives (see Geraghty 2000). As such, the influence of celebrity in the construction of meanings and identities is particularly evident in the editorials and advertisements found in women's magazines. In these spaces, female celebrities are often celebrated as exemplars of successful, cosmopolitan, and enlightened femininity (Hopkins 2002; Evans and Riley 2013; LaWare and Moutsatsos 2013).

Social media has also accelerated and reproduced celebrity culture and the image-making potential of female celebrities, particularly as celebrities and celebrity marketers increasingly use social media to (re)position the personal brand of celebrities, to connect with fans, and to maximise potential sales (Tsaliki, Frangonikolopoulos and Huliaras 2011; Johns and English 2016). As Marshall (2010) points out, celebrity discourses of the self are not only a key element of new media, they are also a tool in which ordinary people use to express and mediate themselves online. Building on Marshall's (2010) insights, it appears female celebrity discourses on Twitter and Instagram not only visualise what is considered important and significant to the modern woman, they also teach girls and women how to produce the modern gendered self. The female celebrity social media feed may be a tangle of both feminist and postfeminist discourses that offer implicit and explicit moral lessons to her followers. Social media provides a new platform to both perform 'private' lives and to privatise politics. Thanks to these new digital networks, the celebrity and her followers may enjoy more immediate and 'personal' relationships, in an imagined global village of connectivity, which is supposedly outside more traditional institutions and structures of power. In recent years, female film actors and female fashion supermodels (or 'social supers') have extended their media exposure, found their 'voice', and built their global celebrity brands via personal posts on social networking sites. Although they also exuded the power and sexuality of ideal or hegemonic femininity, the original supermodels of the 1980s and 1990s were mostly seen, but not heard, on the pages of women's magazines. Today, as the female celebrity is strategically staged through multiple layers of digital mediation, 'personality is arguably the trump card for a model right now' (Rippon 2016, 136). As Rippon (2016, 136) points out, thanks to Snapchat, Twitter, and Instagram, fans can now follow the 'social supers' of celebrity femininity 24/7, or 'the full 360 degrees'. This type of ubiquitous presence on social media, which is more intimate, constant, and content-hungry than traditional broadcast media, rewards celebrities for staging multiple sides to their intertwined public/private 'personality'.

In 2014, using the hashtag #BringBackOurGirls, several female film actors, fashion supermodels, and other celebrities shared photographs of themselves on social media holding up handwritten signs reading 'Bring Back our Girls', referring to the 276 kidnapped female students. Celebrities such as Cara Delevingne, Emma Watson, Julia Roberts, and Keira Knightley were joining a social media campaign that aimed to raise awareness of the tragedy, put pressure on the Nigerian government, and encourage Western intervention to recover the kidnapped girls. As these images were shared or retweeted across social media websites like Twitter and Instagram, they also received significant attention in the traditional broadcast media, television news, and women's magazines. Along the way, as the BBOG digital campaign became increasingly celebritised, these images picked up and produced meanings and messages about new politics and new femininities. As Gill and Arthurs (2006, 443) have explained, 'new femininities' refers to 'the ways in which representations and lived experiences of femininity are changing in a cultural context marked by extraordinary rapid technological change, unprecedented globalisation and the increasing hegemony of a neoliberal form of governance'. In terms of political economy, this neoliberal age is marked by a global Western hegemony, a resexualisation of women's bodies, intense focus on women's appearance, economic inequality, and empowerment through attractive femininity as a kind of moral obligation (Gill and Arthurs 2006). All these convergent trends are evident to some extent in the celebrity appropriation or celebritisation of the BBOG digital campaign.

Contemporary Western female celebrities are uniquely well positioned to profit from the postmodern cultural trend of presenting young women as the ultimate metaphors of progress, hope, and social change (see McRobbie 2000, 198; McRobbie 2004, 2009). Moreover, as McRobbie (2000, 198) has pointed out, the increasing presence of young women in our visual culture is defined and delimited by a 'slim blondeness', which perpetuates 'violent exclusions' of the nonwhite. In postfeminist times, girls and women are celebrated for their business savvy and career success, so long as they do not challenge hegemonic masculinities and the dominant, Westernised ideal of sexy femininity promoted by women's magazines and the fashion, beauty, and cosmetics industries (McRobbie 2009; Evans and Riley 2013). Like any hierarchical system in a competitive neoliberal economy, the system of celebrity sexiness richly rewards those who meet the ideal, while disciplining and penalizing those who fail to measure up (see Evans and Riley 2013). In a postfeminist age, glamourous celebrities appear to have obtained the strong, powerful, and perfect but likeable selves that women and girls are encouraged to pursue (LaWare and Moutsatsos 2013). Contemporary female celebrities now learn to speak the language of 'empowerment', 'equality', 'compassion', and 'solidarity', while simultaneously profiting immensely from the reality of persistent inequality in both local and global contexts. Moreover, new ways of being a successful young woman in neoliberal times (see McRobbie 2000; see Gill and Arthurs 2006), which prioritise wealth, fame, and individualism, are influencing the terrain of digital activism in the name of global gender justice.

Feminist celebrity politics, in the postfeminist, mobile, and global media age, embodies a number of contemporary cultural contradictions. On the one hand, it appears fame has never been more democratic and celebrities have never been more open, accessible, and cosmopolitan. On the other hand, celebrity culture exemplifies the gendered, individualistic, competitive, hierarchical, and exploitative processes of late global capitalism. Most women and girls, even in the wealthy

West, will never have access to the elite brand of empowered self-actualisation glamourous models, pop stars, and actresses promote on social media. The female pop icon becomes wealthy in the first place by embodying what her mostly female followers desire but cannot reach. Such issues of admiration and envy, power, and inequality pose difficult moral and political questions for both the female celebrities themselves and for the social justice campaigns that enlist them to attract attention. Ironically the new style digital or social celebrity activist promises social connection and deploys social capital through social media platforms while simultaneously embodying and profiting from the hyper-individualisation of neoliberal modernity. Without deep knowledge and some experience of the different forms of oppression suffered by different groups of women, celebrity digital activism may appear patronising, staged, and hollow, if not actually harmful. As social media campaigns, like Bring Back Our Girls, absorb various forms of feminism, the line between 'authentic' activism and artful self-promotion is increasingly blurred. In such self-referential 'selfie' activism, both feminist and postfeminist meanings may mix and merge. Through narcissistic 'selfie' images and strategic sound bites, distant, exotic others are enlisted as mirrors to reflect back the fame, power, and moral righteousness of the modern celebrity activist.

The model citizen: politics as fashion

One of the world's richest and most famous fashion models, Cara Delevingne, is an interesting and contemporary case in point of celebrity activism and new femininity (see *Cleo* 2015a; *Elle* 2015; Rippon 2016). Part of the growing pack of fashion supermodels who also have enormous social media followings, Delevingne was one of the first celebrities to present with the Bring Back Our Girls sign on her Instagram account in 2014. The image caught all the visual characteristics for which the fashion model celebrity is most well-known and celebrated (the long blonde hair, the supermodel stare, the heavy eye makeup, and the hand tattoo) above the caption: 'Everyone help and raise awareness #regram #repost or make your own! Let's @bringbackourgirls #bringbackourgirls'. Of all the BBOG celebrity portraits subsequently reposted or circulated in women's magazines, girl culture websites, and blogs, the picture of striking 'it girl' Cara Delevingne received much of the screen time.

With over 21 million Instagram followers, online feeds filled with celebrity feminist friends (her 'girl squad') and multiple collaborations with luxury designer brand labels, Cara Delevingne is the type of individual that girls' and women's magazines now celebrate as a 'successful' and 'empowered' woman (see, for example, *Cleo* 2015a, 25; *Elle* 2015, 80). *Cleo* (2015a, 25) declares that 'queen Cara' has 'Instagirl power', representing 'a new wave of celebrity who take control of their own public image through social media, and reeling in the dollars' (*Cleo* 2015a, 25).

In the same year, Delevingne also led the simulated 'feminist street protest' (carrying signs such as 'history is her story') orchestrated by designer Karl Lagerfeld as part of Paris Fashion Week. When wealthy supermodels literally and figuratively carry the signs of feminism, as part of a publicity pseudo-event designed to sell luxury clothes, it is another indication of 'how far a version of feminism can be pulled in the direction of the political right' (see McRobbie 2000, 211). Moreover, it is exemplary of the new wave of celebrity postfeminist activists and their army of minders, marketers, and managers, mastering the art of 'pseudo-politics' (see Louw 2005). Delevingne, or perhaps her publicist, has built a media presence that extends beyond the role of fashion model to make political statements and to construct a public/private personality (or personal 'brand') as an anti-establishment rebel. As the 'face' of multiple beauty/fashion/cosmetics companies, she loans this star power and its associations to other elite brands, particularly those that wish to be seen as 'edgy' as well as exclusive. In both sexy advertisements and reverential editorials, women's magazines, such as *Vogue*, *Cleo*, and *Elle*, have also celebrated Delevingne's style, attitude, body art, and sexual relationships for 'breaking the rules' – except of course the unspoken rule that decrees that powerful young women must also be sexually desirable objects.

The 'hot' activist and the beauty myth

Of course, not all fashion model celebrities succeed in their performances of 'good girl' global citizen and 'correct' or authentic, feminist-inspired digital activism. Some staged performances fail in the sense that they generate more negative than positive interpretations of the aspiring celebrity gender justice activist. One telling incident during the Bring Back Our Girls digital campaign demonstrates what happens when the celebrity sexiness of the 'hot activist' is apparently pushed too far. Irina Shayk, *Sports Illustrated Swimsuit* model, 'brand ambassador' for elite designers, and actor in music videos, contributed to the cause by posting pictures of herself pouting and topless with only the Bring Back our Girls sign covering her semi-naked body. Shayk's own Twitter followers were offended by this, criticising the supermodel for being 'tasteless' and 'disrespectful' while reminding her that BBOG was meant to be about global activism, not just another magazine photoshoot (Marcus 2014). As a model and idealized sex object, Shayk was simply doing what she was famous for, but apparently without realising the marketing of intense sexuality was unsavoury in a campaign against sexual violence. This celebrity 'fail' reveals the hypocrisy and shallowness of those celebrity activists, who make moral claims for female equality and freedom, while at the same time profiting as a symbol of material success and ideal femininity within an inherently unequal and exploitative system. It is also a perverse manifestation of the underlying postfeminist pressures on the modern, empowered woman to prove that she is 'hot' enough to be heard and to be valued in visual culture, even when she is performing traditional women's work of caring for others (see Levy cited in Gill 2009).

The minor media scandal that Irina Shayk created alongside the Bring Back Our Girls campaign suggested this particular female celebrity was not subtle or 'classy' enough in her performance of the sexualised or 'hot' new femininity (see McRobbie 2009; Evans and Riley 2013). It is worth noting, however, that almost every film/fashion celebrity who posted for Bring Back Our Girls is also complicit in promoting sexualised hyper-femininity through her role as spokesperson for potentially exploitative and oppressive beauty and fashion industries. Moreover, celebrities may call for global equality while also representing and celebrating the luxury, wealth, elitism, and exclusivity of global designer brands. Julia Roberts, for example, represents Lancôme. Keira Knightly appears for Chanel, and Emma Watson has represented Burberry and Lancôme. Currently, and significantly, model Cara Delevingne has replaced female sports stars as the face of Tag Heuer. Delevingne also appeared in sexualised poses alongside veteran supermodel provocateur, Kate Moss, in her modelling work for Burberry fragrance around the same time frame as the BBOG campaign. In that staged and mediated performance, however, Delevingne was apparently playing the role of the 'hot lesbian' (see Gill 2009) rather than the 'hot activist'. In a visual and postfeminist culture, the commercial representations of the 'hot' sex object merge with celebrity discourses of global humanitarianism. Of course, in contemporary postfeminist times, the modern empowered woman may be expected to perpetually self-monitor and carefully manage multiple, contradictory roles. Model Irina Shayk embarrassed the digital Bring Back Our Girls campaign not because she is a professional sex object *per se*, but because she presented herself as a sex object and a gender justice activist *in the same picture*, thereby revealing contradictions in celebrity-focused feminist activism. The resexualisation of women's bodies in contemporary popular culture and advertising, like the expansion of celebrity activism, is part of, not opposed to, the processes of neoliberalism, globalisation, and inequality. Despite her calls to female solidarity, the 'hot activist' is bound up with 'new femininities' that remain profoundly divided along lines of class, race, age, and appearance.

Essentially, female celebrity activists may mean well, but they operate within the confines of what bell hooks (cited in LaWare and Moutsatsos 2013, 191) has termed a 'white supremacist, capitalist patriarchy', which may be ultimately painful and damaging for many girls and women. Picking up on the signs of the times, where neoliberal or 'corporate' postfeminism meets neo-imperial humanitarianism, model Irina Shayk apparently sought to present herself on #BringBackOurGirls as a successful sex object and a celebrity saviour *at the same time*. These tensions in constructions of gender and power in the mediated, visual performances of female celebrity activism deserve further critical investigation. Although the social media postings of the Bring Back our Girls celebrities have since moved on (and some have been deleted), it is important to, as Gill (2009, 155) suggests, 'freeze the frame' to consider the social currency of the hot activist and what she communicates about the intersection of new femininity and new media activism. Selfie activism and supermodel humanitarianism lives on (in the Pink Hope Pinky Promise health campaign, for example) because 'nothing exists unless it's on social media' and 'your next selfie could help save your (and your bestie's) life' (Elle 2016). At the time of writing, the supermodels and celebrated 'hot girls' Rosie Huntington-Whiteley and Lily Aldridge were being celebrated as women's health ambassadors for their 'looks, bodies, personalities, social-media sense, hearts and #girlsquad to match' (Elle 2016). As Wolf (1991) pointed out some time ago, the health of women and girls may actually be undermined by such dominant, narrow ideals or models of white, slender, youthful beauty. The kind of power, agency, and 'women's rights' embodied by female celebrity activism is most often realised, not as a global 'sisterhood', but as an individual's right to pursue material self-interest and self-promotion at the expense of (and even in the name of) less 'empowered' women.

Emma Watson and the business of being a feminist activist in neoliberal times

Similar to the fashion model Cara Delevingne, the young model and film actor Emma Watson, with over 20 million Twitter followers, was one of the most visible and retweeted (or reposted) faces of the BBOG digital campaign. Like Delevingne, Watson has also appeared on the cover of *Cleo* and *Vogue* magazines and served as the 'face' of elite, luxury designer label campaigns directed at female consumers. Although best known for her roles in films, such as the *Harry Potter* franchise and *The Bling Ring*, Watson has recently expanded her multimedia profile to include social media humanitarian, celebrity diplomat, and United Nations Women Goodwill Ambassador. Watson has been applauded in women's magazines and websites for speaking on behalf of girls and other women in her 2014 *HeforShe* campaign and speech (which went viral) and in the Bring Back Our Girls campaign in the same year (*Cleo* 2015b). *Cleo* [original emphasis] (2015b, 24) young women's magazine, for example, applauds Emma Watson for being both a 'passionate feminist and stylish babe': 'This talented A-lister and activist has found a dual purpose – starring in critically acclaimed films and *being the voice of a generation*'. Due in part to her effective promotion and presentation of herself in new media spaces as a celebrity activist, Emma Watson has emerged as a kind of global gender equality spokesmodel for the digital age (see *Cleo* 2015b, 26). As Roxane Gay (2014) pointed out, 'The feminist movement found a new brand, even though Emma Watson wasn't saying anything feminists haven't already said for more than 40 years'. The recent reinvention of model/actress Emma Watson as global activist raises questions about what, aside from celebrity power, qualifies a twentysomething, white, Western celebrity, reportedly worth over $32 million (Lee 2010), to speak on behalf of poor women and girls in rural northeast Nigeria.

The image of Emma Watson posted on Twitter holding her handwritten sign in support of Bring Back Our Girls speaks also to the image of a new kind of feminine ideal that aims to strike the right balance between attractiveness and intelligence. As Jackson and Lyons (2013) have pointed out, postfeminist culture presents a moral lesson to girls and women that they must be sexy enough to be successful, visible, and modern, but not so sexualised as to appear 'skanky', 'cheap', or aggressive. The BBOG Twitter image of Watson as a headshot, with sombre expression and understated makeup in front of a bookcase, presented a celebrity 'selfie', which, unlike the photo Irina Shayk took of herself, seemed to hit the 'right' note of sobriety and sincerity. As a successful feminist celebrity spokesperson, Watson is able to bring attention to global issues while accumulating further value and public admiration of her celebrity brand. In digital and broadcast media, Watson is frequently held up as an example to all women for her ethics of hard work, gender equality, and heroic individualism. The self-mediation and commercial construction of Watson as celebrity humanitarian and goodwill ambassador works because it fits within the 'empowered' ideal of middle class, educated, youthful, and intelligent but attractive femininity. Successful model femininity is expected to make a claim to agency and power, without being seen as too strident, too old, too angry, or 'wild' (Jackson and Lyons 2013). While claiming to advocate for gender equality, Watson simultaneously plays to the attractive, well-groomed 'good girl' role that reasserts hegemonic meanings about gender, class, and power. As a self-identified feminist, celebrity activist, and film star, she produces meanings that are both progressive and oppressive for other women and girls.

It is important to note that social media followers will not always read celebrity messages in the preferred way, even in the case of legitimated 'good girl' activist Emma Watson. Hence under the Bring Back Our Girls 'selfie' on Emma Watson's Twitter feed, comments appear such as 'Oh please. We don't need fake media and fake people getting on a cause' and the satirical 'how can Boko Haram keep these girls now Emma Watson is involved'. Such is the nature of postmodern popular culture that the contemporary cliché of celebrity humanitarianism will of course also be satirised and reflected back upon itself in intertextual art forms. The satirical 'White Saviour Barbie' Instagram site, for example, pokes fun at narcissistic Western activists in Africa posting selfies, with the catch-phrase, 'It's not about me . . . but it kind of is' (*The Huffington Post* 2016). At the time of writing, Emma Watson had gone back to tweeting about her latest film, *Beauty and the Beast*, promoting both her primary product and cultural fairy tales that reassert ideal, 'attractive' femininity.

As the reigning 'it girl' of celebrity humanitarianism, Emma Watson seems to have mastered the arts of new media and new femininity. If Watson wishes to be the flag-bearer of global gender equality, however, her own privileged positioning within the Western celebrity 'hero' narrative is relevant. Her empowered white 'goddess' status (and its claim to moral high ground) comes in part from positioning herself in opposition to less fortunate 'backward' others, ultimately sustaining simplistic neo-imperial narratives that are circulated, not just in girl culture, but in mainstream news as well. While presumably well intended, Western celebrity activists speaking on behalf of girls in the Global South frequently fall back on the duality of empowered and oppressed, coloniser and colonised, subject and object. What they are really speaking to is their own power. These commercial representations of model/actress celebrities, such as Delevingne and Watson, are indicative of what McRobbie (2000) identified some time ago as the new dominant ways of being young and female in postmodern, postfeminist times. The contemporary political and cultural push toward privatisation and individualisation means the pursuit of individual wealth and fame becomes the new measure of success in girl culture (see McRobbie 2000; Hopkins 2002). Moreover, in this context, even activism, charity, and humanitarianism comes to be seen in individualised, privatised terms as part of the new strategic practice of feminine 'celebrityhood'.

'Insta-girl power': the celebrity sex object does global diplomacy

From Angelina Jolie and Madonna to Cara Delevingne and Emma Watson, celebrity approaches to activism in the Global South, while variable in approach, commonly provide a new layer of meaning to the celebrity personality or brand (see Huliaras and Tzifakis 2011; Finlay 2011). In postfeminist times, when the ideal woman is required to be simultaneously many things to many people (mother, sex object, career woman, role model, activist), ambitious female celebrities cannot afford to be dismissed as superficial or self-serving. Celebrity appropriation of feminist discourses delivers them some claim to a commodity that is increasingly rare and valuable: authenticity (see LaWare and Moutsatsos 2013).

As more model/actress celebrities take a turn with the role of United Nations Women Goodwill Ambassador, global gender issues are increasingly framed through the intersection of celebrity culture, corporate culture, and postfeminism. In turn, this means even complex issues of gender violence come to be explained through the 'compassion' of 'caring' celebrity elites, filtered through the pages of women's magazines and websites alongside the seamless promotion of fashion, beauty, and glamour industries (see *Marie Clare* 2016; see *Daily Mail Australia* 2014). In sycophantic interviews and profiles, female celebrities are now praised as much for being a 'voice of compassion' and 'global advocate' as for their beauty and business success (see *Marie Clare* 2016; see *Daily Mail Australia* 2014). Hence, even events designed to 'raise awareness of global gender inequality' may be reported in terms of the 'right' celebrity femininity narrative – 'formal yet stunning . . . locks swept into a center-parting. . . . make-up understated and natural . . . conservative black pumps' (see *Daily Mail Australia* 2014). Celebrity culture, beauty industries, and glossy women's magazines are intricately linked in their promotion of virtually unattainable standards of perpetual youth, beauty, and wealth, which may in the long term be damaging to women and girls as a group (see Wolf 1991; LaWare and Moutsatsos 2013). Moreover, the female celebrity's 'calculated quasi-godlike' persona (Evans and Riley 2013) is now lent a moral dimension through the performance of 'compassionate' activism for 'good' causes wherein 'it's easy to forget they're goddesses and you're a mere mortal . . . until you get a selfie with them' (*Elle* 2016, 96).

Celebrity humanitarianism, however, does not necessarily challenge the structures of the global economic system. As Huliaras and Tzifakis (2011, 38) observe, '[c]elebrity campaigners' real message to policy-makers is a call for "more attention" to Africa, rather than a demand for radically changed policies'. This, they suggest, explains why Western celebrities often sign up for humanitarian causes in war-torn Africa rather than to more controversial issues closer to home because it is less risky to their brand image, marketability, and long-term career strategy.

Such an approach relegates campaigns such as BBOG to the domain of what Huliaras and Tzifakis (2011, 39) term 'soft' news, which covers international events through the lens of celebrity involvement rather than through highlighting the root causes of particular social problems. As such, while these platforms do often succeed in improving public awareness of global issues, they do not necessarily improve public knowledge or understanding of the events. While Western celebrities acting as transnational activists have effectively publicised some global gender atrocities and made Western governments more attentive (especially where Islamic militants are to blame), 'they cannot equally claim that they have persuaded rich states to do more for the poor countries of the world' (Huliaras and Tzifakis 2011, 39).

Indeed the very moral and social authority female celebrity activists rely upon to bring attention to gender justice issues derives from their privileged 'goddess' position over and above other 'ordinary' women. Most Western female celebrities became wealthy 'stars' in the first place by trading in the currency of female objectification, in industries that demand youth, beauty, and sexual desirability above all else. Female celebrity activism certainly does not operate outside the machinery of sexist and ageist mainstream media representation. Although the fashion industry likes to flirt with the possibility of being rebellious and transgressive, it rarely challenges the rules of the game of patriarchal capitalism and neoliberal globalisation.

Aside from enabling the individual celebrity to 'evolve' or 'actualise', the performance of (pseudo) politics also inevitably generates more press and allows fans, journalists, and media scholars alike to drape new meanings on the angular shoulders of the femininity model. On multiple levels, the feminist celebrity activist presents politics as a kind of fashion, where women can shop for new empowered identities, covet celebrity lifestyles, and 'make a difference', all while staying perpetually modern and mobile. Celebrity fans and followers are encouraged to express gender solidarity via consumerism, for example, by purchasing an 'exclusive' purple scarf for international women's day (see *Marie Clare* 2016). The process recalls the kind of political consumerism campaigns fronted by celebrities, which Farrell (2012, 2015) has critically investigated in the context of philanthrocapitalism (or the assumption that market methods can address social and environmental problems). While white celebrity feminists have also had some success in raising awareness and funding for global gender issues, they do so in a manner that reproduces the ideological underpinnings of global neoliberal capitalism.

Simplistic calls to global gender equality fronted by race and class privileged elites ignore differences in gender discrimination experienced by different groups of women around the world. As a result, Western celebrity feminists run the risk of ultimately reproducing and legitimating the systems of gender inequality they intend to remedy. Where postfeminist celebrity activism mirrors the experiences of extremely wealthy white women, it is limited, even on its own narrow terms of gender solidarity (see Crenshaw 1995). The problem is particularly acute in the context of violence against women because the violence that many women experience is so often shaped by dimensions of race and class as well as gender (see Crenshaw 1995), a fact that is often overlooked in celebrity-focused digital campaigns. Feminist intersectional analysis (see Crenshaw 1995; see Gill 2009) calls for recognition of the differences between women's experiences. Certainly it is difficult to imagine a more radical contradiction between the lived experiences of poor Nigerian girls growing up in rural African villages and the experiences of the obscenely wealthy Western supermodels and Hollywood stars who claim to speak for them on Instagram and Twitter.

Unlike activists in the West (see Scott 2016), poor communities in rural Africa, with no Internet connection, are typically not in position to 'call out' or 'speak back' to Western celebrities who claim to speak on their behalf. As Spivak (1993, 91) suggests, in assuming the right to narrate the story of 'the historically muted subject of the subaltern woman', Western elites and experts leave 'no space from which the sexed subaltern subject can speak' (Spivak 1993, 103). As Engle (2012) observed in her critical examination of the 2007 UN Action Against Sexual Violence campaign, 'while the campaign imagines new global citizens who can take action simply by promoting their own images (assuming they speak English and have access to the Internet, a camera, and equipment for uploading photographs), it denies even that thin form of citizenship to those whom it aims to save'.

White celebrity saviours

Female pop culture celebrities frequently replace other female public figures as the arbiter of all that is desirable, good, and even 'heroic' in contemporary post-feminist culture (see Hopkins 2002). Indeed it is a short step from increasingly pervasive 'hero worship' of celebrities to the emergence of white celebrity 'saviours' in global gender equality campaigns. The BBOG campaign made visible the cultural trend of privileged and powerful female Western celebrities intervening in African problems (see Repo and Yrjölä 2011). Emma Watson, for example, is emblematic of a new kind of post-racial, transnational ideal global citizen who uses celebrity power to pressure states and hold them to account at a distance. The Nigerian-American writer Teju Cole (2012) suggests the misguided 'fresh faced young Americans using the power of YouTube' may actually legitimate a 'White Saviour Industrial Complex', which draws attention away from the root causes of poverty and conflict in Africa. While presumably well-intended, the egotism and exhibitionism of white celebrity 'saviors' has also been interpreted as patronising and offensive to some African commentators and to those they purport to 'save' (see Cole 2012; Mwenda 2013; Ogunlesi 2014). The increasingly ubiquitous figure of the white celebrity 'saviour' nonetheless requires her backward 'other' in need of modernisation and empowerment. As Cole (2012) suggests, 'Africa serves as a backdrop for white fantasies of conquest and heroism' and 'a space onto which white egos can conveniently be projected'. These narcissistic fantasises, reasserted in new ways in digital culture, position celebrity activists, like Emma Watson, as magical or heroic individuals capable of doing what nation states cannot. Yet as Finlay (2011, 206) points out, celebrity activism with its focus on 'personality' and 'charismatic leadership' may actually be fundamentally incompatible with democratic processes, and it leaves them democratically accountable to no one when interventions fail to bring about real change. The BBOG campaign, for example, seems to have been more successful thus far in constructing female celebrities as ideal global citizens than in bringing about lasting change for women and girls in Nigeria.

In contrast to Western celebrities, who loom ubiquitous on multiple media platforms, 'our girls' remained mostly nameless and faceless in the BBOG campaign. While the parents and activists on the ground in Nigeria were mostly ignored, images of Western celebrities holding up handwritten BBOG signs were shared and retweeted thousands of times around the world. Understandably, the fact that the most visible women in the BBOG campaign were actually privileged, white, Western celebrities touched a nerve with some postcolonial critics. By appropriating the Bring Back Our Girls movement, the white celebrity activists were, in effect, preventing other local and/or more credible voices from being heard on the same issues. Nigerian journalist and author Tolu Ogunlesi (2014), for example, criticised the BBOG campaign for (mis)representing the Chibok tragedy as a Twitter hot topic or 'global flavour of the moment', hijacked in the interests of 'celebrity-feel-gooding' and appropriated by Western elites in a new virtual or neo-imperial 'scramble for Africa', recalling the history, traditions, and prejudices of European colonialism.

Ogunlesi (2014) also pointed out the fact that the Chibok kidnappings featured 'a group of young women seeking an education arrayed against a band of turbaned, bearded, women-oppressing extremists' meant the tragedy had 'all the right elements to capture the world's imagination'. As HaidehMoghissi (1999, 20) suggests, the struggle between modernism and Islamic fundamentalism is often perceived as essentially a struggle over the rights and bodies of women. Yet in both the Global South *and in the West*, women and girls are subjected to harmful cultural practices that exert painful control over their bodies (see Bartky 1990). The control, use, and exploitation of female bodies is constant across the East/West, North/South divide (see Eisenstein 2004), and female celebrities, no matter how well-meaning, well-groomed, or well-spoken, are by no means innocent or outside this process. By adding 'global humanitarian' to 'model/actress' on her celebrity CV, the celebrity activist reflects and reasserts postfeminist and neoliberal ideologies that draw attention away from the structural and historical causes of inequality.

Meanwhile, back in Africa: #BringBackOurGirls and bringing back imperialism

Due in part to the time/space compression afforded by new networked communication technologies (Harvey 1990), a tweet from a Nigerian lawyer on the Chibok abductions in 2014 was picked up by celebrities in the West and quickly became one of Twitter's most posted hashtags. Despite the solidarity and inclusion implied by the message of bringing back 'our' girls, the experiences of celebrity activists in the Global North were still a world away from the lived realities of girls and women in the Global South. Even when powered by new media activism, distance is still a significant issue on a number of different levels in global gender equality campaigns fronted by celebrities. As Radley (2016) discovered in his investigation of 'conflict minerals' campaigns, such as 'Stand with Congo', advocacy movements headquartered in Western cities may have only a tenuous relationship and little real engagement with the most disadvantaged groups most directly affected by these campaigns. Radley (2016) suggests Western advocates should 'reorient their efforts to working with, not just for, the non-elites they use to promote their public image and in whose name they justify their external interventions'. Radley (2016) criticises Western campaigns that position Western consumers as the solution to African problems, also acknowledging that it is difficult to mobilise funding and celebrities around multifaceted and long-term goals.

Certainly, in the case of Bring Back Our Girls, the quick and frequent flashes of celebrity photos and short text messages (less than 140 characters) on social media websites did not necessarily encourage deep understandings of global issues. Although it did briefly raise awareness of the Chibok kidnappings, celebrity intervention in the campaign has not necessarily been sustained. Part of the reason celebrity digital campaigns like Bring Back Our Girls frequently fade from view is because, as Nigerian-American writer Teju Cole (2012) puts it, 'there is no single villain to topple' and hence no simple solution to state failure in Africa. The Nigerian government is associated with corruption and a track record of poor governance (Fagbadebo 2007; Khakee 2010; Agbiboa 2012; Cole 2012). Despite huge oil reserves, Nigeria is unable to maintain functioning statist structures and democratic institutions, resulting in an inability to end warlordism, violence, or crime, and has a poor track record in listening to its *own* citizens (Herbst 1997; Khakee 2010; Fagbadebo 2007; Agbiboa 2012).

The BBOG activists were also sending messages to Western governments suggesting that the West should intervene. What is troubling about this message, however, is that it recalls imperialist narratives about Africa as the problem continent that needs the West to 'fix' or 'save' it. This neo-imperial conceptualisation of African nations as lands of barbarism and despair and the West as the only solution to Africa's numerous political and economic difficulties has been described as 'Afropessisim' by de B'beri and Louw (2011). Presumably, few of the liberal BBOG activists realised that, by proposing Western intervention, they were inadvertently and ironically aligning themselves with the Afropessimists, who believe the recolonisation of Africa may be the only way to re-establish effective governance on the continent (see de B'beri and Louw 2011). Nonetheless, the campaign makes visible the (neo)imperial discourses and assumptions of cultural superiority, which sustain much white Western celebrity activism (see Cole 2012; Mwenda 2013; Ogunlesi 2014; Zakaria 2014). While increased publicity is the oxygen that sustains celebrity, it is rarely a magical solution to complex challenges in the Global South. In the case of BBOG, the campaign was effectively pulled away from its African political context as Western hashtag activists came to dominate the flows of communication. In the process, the campaign became a lesson in the limitations of celebrity digital activism, which often provides a simplistic, individualistic, and decontextualized view to complex economic, political, and historical problems.

As Farrell (2012, 405) points out, to appreciate the complexities of such issues, it is necessary to 'navigate a path between celebratory populism and laments regarding a cultural decline'. Where celebrity activism meets corporate postfeminism, extremes of gendered violence are rightly opposed, but the norms of sexual objectification that underpin Western culture and celebrity culture, in particular, remain unchallenged. Female celebrities are right to express moral outrage at gender atrocities in the Global South. However, they are also morally obliged to acknowledge their own class- and race-specific, privileged, speaking position; their lack of in-depth expertise on the African crisis; and their own investment, closer to home, in the commercial sexual objectification of girls and women. Female celebrity activists are not just loaning their names, faces, and popularity to global causes. They are also redefining interconnections between celebrity power, global humanitarianism, new media, and new femininity. As powerful symbols of limitless mobility, wealthy female celebrities have the luxury of 'moving on' in their multi-mediated lives – and it appears most have done so. But what of the outcome of the Bring Back Our Girls digital campaign for the most powerless women and girls involved? Despite raised global awareness; a change of government in Nigeria, the assistance of Western advisers, hostage negotiators, and logistical support; and the #BringBackOurGirls social media campaign, many of the Chibok victims are still missing or captive. Tragically, 'our' girls are still lost.

References

ABC News (2016) 'Boko Haram "Proof of Life" Video of Kidnapped Chibok Schoolgirls Puts Pressure on Nigerian Government', 15 April [online] Available: www.abc.net.au/news/2016-04-15/video-of-chibok-girls-puts-pressure-on-nigeria-government/7328378 [accessed 16 April 2016].

Agbiboa, D.E. (2012) 'Between Corruption and Development: The Political Economy of State Robbery in Nigeria', *Journal of Business Ethics*, 108 (3): 325–345.

Bartky, S. (1990) *Femininity and Domination: Studies in the Phenomenology of Oppression*, New York: Routledge.

BBC News (2014) 'Boko Haram to Sell Nigerian Girls Abducted from Chibok', 6 May [online] Available: www.bbc.com/news/world-africa-27283383 [accessed 10 February 2016].

Chandler, A. (2015) 'Nigeria's Violent Year Since "Bring Back our Girls"', *The Atlantic*, [online] Available: www.theatlantic.com/international/archive/2015/04/nigerias-violent-year-since-bring-back-our-girls/390510/ [accessed 10 February 2016].

Cleo (2015a) 'All Hail Queen Cara', *Cleo* [Australia], July: 24–25.

Cleo (2015b) 'Raising Her Voice', *Cleo* [Australia], November: 24–26.

Cleven, E. and Curtis, S. (2015) 'Hope for the Kidnapped Girls in Nigeria Dimming Even as Boko Haram Loses Steam', *The Conversation*, 17 April [online] Available: https://theconversation.com/hope-for-the-kidnapped-girls-in-nigeria-dimming-even-as-boko-haram-loses-steam-40278 [accessed 16 April 2016].

Cole, T. (2012) 'The White-Saviour Industrial Complex', *The Atlantic*, 21 March [online] Available: www.theatlantic.com/international/archive/2012/03/the-white-savior-industrial-complex/254843/ [accessed 10 April 2016].

Crenshaw, K.W. (1995) 'Mapping the Margins: Intersectionality, Identity Politics and Violence against Women of Colour', in K. Crenshaw *et al.* (eds.) *Critical Race Theory: The Key Writings That Formed the Movement*, New York: The New Press: 357–384.

Daily Mail Australia (2014) 'She Means Business: Emma Watson Is Smart and Sophisticated in Belted White Coat Dress at UN Event in Role of Goodwill Ambassador for Women', *Daily Mail*, 21 September [online] Available: www.dailymail.co.uk/tvshowbiz/article-2763873/Emma-Watson-smart-sophiticated-belted-white-coat-dress-UN-event-role-Goodwill-Ambassador-For-Women.html [accessed 14 April 2016].

deB'beri, B.E. and Louw, E. (2011) 'Afropessismism: A Genealogy of Discourse', *Critical Arts*, 25 (3): 335–346.

Drake, P. and Higgins, M. (2006) 'I'm a Celebrity, Get Me into Politics', in S. Holmes and S. Redmond (eds.) *Framing Celebrity: New Directions in Celebrity Culture*, London: Routledge: 87–100.

Eisenstein, Z. (2004) *Against Empire: Feminisms, Racism and the West*, London: Zed Books.

Elle (2015) 'First Look', *Elle* [Australia], December, 27: 80.

Elle (2016) 'What Hot Girls Know: Hey Sista, Go Sista (Make a Pinky Promise)', *Elle* [Australia], June, 33: 90–99.

Engle, K. (2012) 'Celebrity Diplomacy and Global Citizenship', *Celebrity Studies*, 3 (1): 116–118.

Evans, A. and Riley, S. (2013) 'Immaculate Consumption: Negotiating the Sex Symbol in Postfeminist Celebrity Culture', *Journal of Gender Studies*, 22 (3): 268–281.

Fagbadebo, O. (2007) 'Corruption, Governance and Political Instability in Nigeria', *African Journal of Political Science and International Relations*, 1 (2): 28–37.

Farrell, N. (2012) 'Celebrity Politics: Bono, Product (RED) and the Legitimising of Philanthrocapitalism', *British Journal of Politics and International Relations*, 14 (3): 392–406.

Farrell, N. (2015) 'Conscience Capitalism and the Neoliberalisation of the Non-Profit Sector', *New Political Economy*, 20 (2): 254–272.

Finlay, G. (2011) 'Madonna's Adoptions: Celebrity Activism, Justice and Civil Society in the Global South', in L. Tsaliki, C. Frangonikolopoulos and A. Huliaras (eds.) *Transnational Celebrity: Activism in Global Politics: Changing the World?* Bristol: Intellect: 195–210.

Frank, J. (2014) 'From the Editor', *Marie Claire*, August: 228.

Gay, R. (2014) 'Emma Watson? Jennifer Lawrence? These Aren't the Feminists You're Looking for', *The Guardian*, 11 October [online] Available: www.theguardian.com/commentisfree/2014/oct/10/-sp-jennifer-lawrence-emma-watson-feminists-celebrity [accessed 9 February 2016].

Geraghty, C. (2000) 'Re-Examining Stardom: Questions of Texts, Bodies and Performance', in C. Gledhill and L. Williams (eds.) *Re-Inventing Film Studies*, London: Oxford University Press: 183–202.

Gill, R. (2009) 'Beyond the "Sexualisation of Culture" Thesis: An Intersectional Analysis of "Sixpacks", "Midriffs" and "Hot Lesbians" in Advertising', *Sexualities*, 12 (2): 137–160.

Gill, R. and Arthurs, J. (2006) 'Editors' Introduction: New Femininities', *Feminist Media Studies*, 6 (4): 443-451.

Harvey, D. (1990) *The Condition of Postmodernity: An Enquiry into the Origins of Cultural Change*, Oxford: Blackwell.

Herbst, J. (1997) 'Responding to State Failure in Africa', *International Security*, 21 (3): 120–144.

Hopkins, S. (2002) *Girl Heroes: The New Force in Popular Culture*, Sydney: Pluto Press.

Huffington Post (2016) '"White Saviour Barbie" Hilariously Parodies Volunteer Selfies in Africa', *Huffington Post*, 18 April [online] Available: www.huffingtonpost.com.au/entry/white-savior-barbie-hilariously-parodies-volunteer-selfies-in-africa_us_570fd4b5e4b03d8b7b9fc464?section=australia [accessed 23 April 2016].

Huliaras, A. and Tzifakis, N. (2011) 'Bringing the Individuals Back In? Celebrities as Transnational Activists', in L. Tsaliki, C. Frangonikolopoulos and A. Huliaras (eds.) *Transnational Celebrity: Activism in Global Politics: Changing the World?*, Bristol: Intellect: 27–45.

Jackson, S. and Lyons, A. (2013) 'Girls' New Femininity Refusals and "Good Girl" Recuperations in Soap Talk', *Feminist Media Studies*, 13 (2): 228–244.

Johns, R. and English, R. (2016) 'Transition of Self: Repositioning the Celebrity Brand through Social Media: The Case of Elizabeth Gilbert', *Journal of Business Research*, 69 (1): 65–72.

Khakee, A. (2010) 'Nigeria: Conflict, Energy and Bad Governance', in R. Youngs (ed.) *The European Union and Democracy Promotion*, Baltimore: John Hopkins University Press.

LaWare, M.R. and Moutsatsos, C. (2013) '"For Skin That's Us, Authentically Us": Celebrity, Empowerment and the Allure of Antiaging Advertisements', *Women's Studies in Communication*, 36: 189–208.

Lee, J. (2010) 'Emma Watson: I Felt Sick over My Own Net Worth', *CBS News*, 3 November [online] Available: www.cbsnews.com/news/emma-watson-i-felt-sick-over-my-own-net-worth/ [accessed 23 April].

Louw, E. (2005) *The Media and Political Process*, London: Sage Publications.

Marcus, S. (2014) 'Irina Shayk Slammed for Posing Topless for #BringBackOurGirls Campaign', *Huffington Post*, 16 May [online] Available: www.huffingtonpost.com.au/entry/irina-shayk-topless-bring-back-our-girls_n_5332844.html?section=australia [accessed 23 April 2016].

Marshall, P.D. (1997) *Celebrity and Power: Fame in Contemporary Culture*, Minneapolis: University of Minnesota Press.

Marshall, P.D. (2010) 'The Promotion and Presentation of the Self: Celebrity as a Marker of Presentational Media', *Celebrity Studies*, 1 (1): 35–48.

McRobbie, A. (2000) *Feminism and Youth Culture* (2nd ed.), Houndmills: Macmillan Press.

McRobbie, A. (2004) 'Postfeminism and Popular Culture', *Feminist Media Studies*, 4: 255–264.

McRobbie, A. (2009) *The Aftermath of Feminism: Gender, Culture and Social Change*, London: Sage Publications.

Moghissi, H. (1999) *Feminism and Islamic Fundamentalism: The Limits of Postmodern Analysis*, London: Zed books.

Motlagh, J. (2016) 'Escape from Boko Haram', *Marie Clare (Australia)*, April, 248: 96–99.

Mwenda, A.M. (2013) 'Madonna and Africa's Celebrity Saviours', *CNN*, [online] Available: http://edition.cnn.com/2013/04/16/opinion/madonna-charity-africa-mwenda/ [accessed 14 April].

Newman, S. (2005) *Power and Politics in Poststructuralist Thought: New Theories of the Political*, Oxon: Routledge.

Ogunlesi, T. (2014) 'Hijacking Nigeria's #Bring Back Our Girls Campaign', *Al Jazeera*, [online] Available: www.aljazeera.com/indepth/opinion/2014/10/hijacking-nigeria-bringbackour-2014102213549148465.html [accessed 10 February 2016].

Radley, B. (2016) 'The Problem with Western Activists Trying to Do Good in Africa', *The Conversation*, 19 April [online] Available: https://theconversation.com/the-problem-with-western-activists-trying-to-do-good-in-africa-57917 [accessed 23 April 2016].

Redmond, S. (2006) 'Intimate Fame Everywhere', in S. Holmes and S. Redmond (eds.) *Framing Celebrity: New Directions in Celebrity Culture*, London: Routledge: 27–43.

Repo, J. and Yrjölä, R. (2011) 'The Gender Politics of Celebrity Humanitarianism in Africa', *International Feminist Journal of Politics*, 13 (1): 44–62.

Rippon, R. (2016) 'New Muse', *Vogue* [Australia], April: 136.

Said, E. (1981) *Covering Islam: How the Media and the Experts Determine How We See the Rest of the World*, London: Routledge and Kegan Paul.

Scott, E. (2016) 'Black Lives Matter Protestors Confront Clinton at a Fundraiser', *CNN*, 25 February [online] Available: http://edition.cnn.com/2016/02/25/politics/hillary-clinton-black-lives-matter-whichhillary/ [accessed 15 April 2016].

Spivak, G. (1993) 'Can the Subaltern Speak?', in P. Williams and L. Chrisman (eds.) *Colonial Discourse and Post-Colonial Theory: A Reader*, Hertfordshire: Harvester Wheatsheaf: 66–112.

Street, J. (2004) 'Celebrity Politicians: Popular Culture and Political Representation', *British Journal of Politics and International Relations*, 6 (4): 435–452.

Tsaliki, L., Frangonikolopoulos, C. and Huliaras, A. (2011) 'The Challenge of Transnational Celebrity Activism: Background, Aim and Scope of the Book', in L. Tsaliki, C. Frangonikolopoulos and A. Huliaras (eds.) *Transnational Celebrity: Activism in Global Politics: Changing the World?*, Bristol: Intellect: 9–24.

Turner, G. (2004) *Understanding Celebrity*, London: Sage Publications.

Webster, D. (2014) 'Editorial', *Marie Claire*, No 228, August.

Wolf, N. (1991) *The Beauty Myth: How Images of Beauty Are Used against Women*, London: Vintage.

Zakaria, R. (2014) '#BringBackOurGirls and the Pitfalls of Schoolgirl Feminism', *Al Jazeera*, 19 May [online] Available: http://america.aljazeera.com/opinions/2014/5/-bringbackourgirlsandthepitfallsofschoolgirlfeminism.html [accessed 26 March 2016].

6 Promoting peace and coffee pods

George Clooney, Nespresso activist

Joshua Gulam

Since his rise to prominence in the late 1990s, George Clooney has been one of the most consistently sought-after Hollywood actors for product endorsements, working with major brands including Fiat, Omega, Martini, and Belstaff. The most lucrative of these endorsement deals has been his partnership with Nespresso. An operating unit of the Nestlé Group, Nespresso sells single-serve coffee machines and the gourmet coffee capsules ('pods') that are used in these machines. Nespresso announced Clooney as its 'Global Ambassador' in 2006, with the actor agreeing to appear in a series of television and print media advertisements produced exclusively for European markets.[1] Estimates suggest that the actor earned over $40 million for his work to promote the company in the years from 2006 to 2013 (Said 2013). Significantly, Clooney's ambassadorship coincided with a marked increase in the commercial fortunes of the brand in this period. Although Nespresso products have been on sale since 1989, it was only after his recruitment that the company emerged as a major player in the coffee industry: Nespresso recorded an annual turnover of $4 billion in 2014 (Reuters 2014), as compared to $810 million in 2006, with its sales accounting for approximately 4 percent of Nestlé's total revenue (Gretler 2015).

In the years since he became a Nespresso ambassador, Clooney has also established himself as one of Hollywood's most socially conscious stars (Horn 2011; Harris 2012), advocating for causes including Save Darfur and Cinema for Peace, as well as directing and starring in a series of films that address social issues, such as *Syriana* (2005) and *Good Night and Good Luck* (2005). These activities have earned the actor high praise from aid workers and journalists, in addition to various accolades. For example, the United Nations named Clooney as a Messenger of Peace in January 2008, a role he occupied until April 2014; and *LooktotheStars. org* – a website that chronicles the philanthropic activities of stars – lists him among 'the most charitable hearts' in the entertainment industry (Look to the Stars n.d.).

Clooney's reputation as a celebrated filmmaker-come-humanitarian appears to be at odds with the crudely commercial nature of his Nespresso work. Yet the actor has often sought to link his product endorsements to his charitable and political campaigning. In interviews with the media, Clooney regularly explains how he channels a proportion of his Nespresso salary into his activist endeavours, using this money to support a number of charitable foundations (e.g., Siegle 2013; Woodruff 2012). At the same time, the actor has been cited as a key figure in Nespresso's recent pledges to invest in sustainable farming methods. Clooney currently sits on the Nespresso Sustainability Advisory Board (NSAB), a board of 'experts' that helps to oversee The Positive Cup strategy. Announced in August 2014, The Positive Cup commits Nespresso to sourcing 100 percent of its Grand Cru coffee range sustainably by 2020 (Nestlé-Nespresso 2017).

This chapter asks what is at stake in the pairing of Nespresso with a celebrity activist like Clooney. Through close analysis of Clooney's Nespresso promotions, in addition to a range of film and publicity texts, it considers the complex exchange of meanings between the multibillion-dollar coffee brand and the Hollywood actor. In what ways do Clooney's Nespresso advertisements complicate and/or consolidate the meanings associated with his humanitarian image? And how has the star's involvement helped to legitimise the practices of Nespresso and its parent company? Overall, then, this chapter contributes to a growing body of scholarship that examines the political economic tensions of celebrity activism (Collins 2007; Kapoor 2013; Mukherjee and Banet-Weiser 2012; Brockington 2014). Specifically, it explores the tensions that exist between the celebrity as branded commodity, on the one hand, and their charitable and political activities, on the other. At each stage of the analysis, the chapter is concerned with how such tensions are resolved, and to what extent this works to reproduce hegemonic capitalist inequality.

The chapter begins by examining what the involvement of Clooney communicates about the Nespresso brand. This section looks in detail at Nespresso's branding as an 'ethical' company and the role that Clooney plays in furthering these promotional claims. A second section explores the complex ways in which Clooney's Nespresso ambassadorship intersects with his appearances in a series of anti-corporate films, including *Up in the Air* (2009) and *Michael Clayton* (2007). Here, I consider how the star has sought to frame his endorsements in ways that are consistent with both his on-screen roles and his off-screen campaigning.

Making Nespresso compassionate

From a marketing perspective, the value of celebrities extends beyond the public and media attention that they can bring to a product or brand. Celebrities are also valuable because of what they represent. As various scholars have observed, celebrities communicate certain meanings about the products they endorse (McCracken 1989; McDonald 2013). Grant McCracken (1989) labels this process 'meaning transfer'. According to McCracken, particular meanings and values 'reside in the celebrity'. When a celebrity endorses a product, these meanings and values are transferred from the celebrity to the product and from the product to the consumer. These meanings and values can relate to a general image of stardom – some broader sense of the glamour and romance of the acting profession, for instance – or to a specific set of associations that are 'unique' to the celebrity (McCracken 1989, 310–313).

Paul McDonald (2013) has applied this meaning transfer model to Clooney's endorsement of Nespresso. In his book *Hollywood Stardom*, McDonald explains how partnering with Clooney helps to position Nespresso as a quality brand – a large part of Nespresso's marketing strategy is that its machines allow customers to brew 'barista-quality' coffee in their own homes (Nestle-Nespresso 2017). Central to McDonald's analysis is the sense of style and sophistication that the actor has cultivated through his appearances in the *Ocean's* trilogy: *Ocean's Eleven* (2001), *Ocean's Twelve* (2004), and *Ocean's Thirteen* (2007). Grossing over $1.1 billion at the box office (Box Office Mojo n.d.), these three films cast Clooney in the role of Daniel Ocean, the debonair and handsome leader of an elite group of con artists.[2] For McDonald, Clooney's Nespresso advertisements operate by establishing a correlation between his *Ocean's* persona and the coffee brand. He notes how the suave associations of this character work to frame Nespresso in ways that distinguish it from Nestlé's cheaper products, such as the Nescafé range of instant coffees (McDonald 2013, 60–64).

McDonald's analysis makes an important contribution to our understanding of not just the Clooney-Nespresso partnership, but how celebrity endorsements operate more generally: the way in which these endorsements draw on a broad range of meanings associated with the star, including those surrounding their on-screen roles. McDonald fails to mention Clooney's reputation for charitable and political campaigning, however. By doing so, he neglects a vital part of the meanings that the actor communicates about the Nespresso brand. In addition to a sense of sexiness and sophistication, Clooney bestows upon Nespresso some of 'integrity' and 'compassion' that he has cultivated through his activism.

For over a decade, Clooney has combined his film career with high-profile work on behalf of various causes and charities. Clooney's charitable and political commitments date back to September 21, 2001, when he was one of the organizers of the *America: A Tribute to Heroes* telecast (2001) that raised over $120 million for the victims of the 9/11 terror attacks (Huliaras and Tzifakis 2012). In the intervening years, he has campaigned for organisations as diverse as the UN, Hope for Haiti, and the American Foundation for AIDS Research, receiving both the Nobel Summit Peace Award (2007) and the Bob Hope Humanitarian Award (2010) in the process. Yet the actor is best known for his efforts to raise awareness of the Darfur conflict, which began in 2003. Since 2005, when a series of newspaper articles alerted him to the scale of the violence in the region (Woodruff 2012), Clooney has made a number of visits to Darfur and surrounding areas; documented his experiences in various public appearances and interviews; co-founded a not-for-profit organization that aims to prevent mass atrocities around the globe, Not On Our Watch (NOOW); and lobbied politicians, including US President Barack Obama. Clooney met with then-President Obama in February 2009, for example, to discuss the possibility of the United States appointing a full-time envoy to Darfur (see Gulam 2014a).[3]

On April 30, 2009, *TIME* magazine included Clooney on its annual list of 'the 100 most influential people', as recognition for his campaigning in Darfur. In his profile of the actor for the '*TIME* 100' issue, U2 singer Bono suggested that it was

Clooney's 'commitment' and 'nuance' that set him apart from other Hollywood 'do-gooder[s]' (Bono 2009). This assessment is representative of the high regard in which Clooney's charitable and political activities are held, with many commentators citing the actor as an example of what star power can achieve when it is put to good use (Harris 2012; Look to the Stars n.d.). Writing in 2011, for example, *The Los Angeles Times*'s John Horn observed, 'For better and often for worse, actors have dabbled in politics and causes, but few have shown the kind of sustained and informed [. . .] commitment that Clooney has' (Horn 2011).

Clooney's compassionate and thoughtful image stands in stark contrast to that of Nespresso's parent company. In July 1977, the Nestlé Group became the target of a large-scale consumer boycott over its aggressive marketing of infant formula in the Third World. Proponents of the boycott criticised Nestlé for misleading customers about the benefits of its powdered milk formula. They argued that by persuading mothers to switch to formula instead of breastfeeding, the company had contributed to health problems and deaths among infants in developing countries (Smith 2012; Boyd 2012; Muller 2013). Although this boycott officially ended in 1984, when Nestlé agreed to follow a code of conduct developed by the World Health Organisation, large numbers of consumers continue to boycott the company because of its involvement in the infant formula scandal, as well as a number of other controversies (Muller 2013; Siegle 2013). Nestlé once again became the focus of widespread disapproval in late 2002, for instance, when it emerged that the company was seeking a $6 million payment from the Ethiopian government as compensation for a factory that was nationalised in 1975 (Denny 2002). More recently, the food and beverage multinational has been accused of conspiring to fix the price of chocolate in Canada (BBC 2013), while it was also forced to admit to incidences of forced labour in its supply chain, when allegations of child slavery were brought before the US Supreme Court (Worley 2016).

Since emerging as a major force in the global coffee market, Nespresso has sought to distance itself from Nestlé's tarnished reputation. Alongside a focus on producing barista-quality coffee, therefore, promotional materials for the company emphasise its commitment to sustainability and improving the lives of farmers around the globe. Clooney has played a prominent role in articulating this sense of commitment. In 2013, the actor appeared in a series of videos intended to raise awareness of the AAA Sustainable Quality™ Program. A joint venture between Nespresso and the conservation group the Rainforest Alliance, AAA was launched in 2003 with the aim of managing the ecological and social impacts of the coffee manufacturer's operations – a ten-year goal of the programme was to reduce the carbon footprint required to make a Nespresso coffee by 20 percent (Nestlé-Nespresso n.d.). In one of the videos, gentle guitar music overlays footage of Clooney speaking to Costa Rican farmers employed by the AAA programme. This footage is intercut with a sequence of title cards detailing Nespresso's core values of 'fairness', 'partnership', and 'expertise' (Ecomtrading 2013).[4] Overall, this promotional campaign champions the positive impact AAA has had on local farming communities, documenting the extra training and financial support that the company gives to its employees in the developing world – Nespresso contends that the AAA programme has helped to enhance the lives of more than 70,000 'famer partners' since its formation (Nestlé-Nespresso 2017). Part of the way in which the campaign does this is by creating a slippage between the ethical practices of Nespresso and those of Clooney himself, as per McCracken's account of meaning transfer (McCracken 1989).

The Nespresso videos featuring Clooney draw heavily on his long track record of humanitarianism. At the simplest level, footage of the actor trekking across Costa Rican coffee fields recalls his on-the-ground campaigning in Darfur and other exotic locations. For example, Clooney dons the same cargo vest jacket in the videos that he has worn on many of his field trips for the UN. What is being invoked here is not just the extent of Clooney's humanitarianism. On a more complex level, this promotional campaign also invokes the high regard in which his charitable and political activities are held. 'Fairness' and 'expertise' are both qualities that have been attributed to Clooney, while press reports about the actor regularly praise his ability to forge 'partnerships' across ideological divides: Clooney is said to be one of the few 'liberals' in contemporary Hollywood whose politics reach beyond Democrats (for example, Lowe 2005; Mottram 2007).[5] Despite his long-standing involvement with the coffee company, several of the Nespresso videos also list Clooney as an 'Independent Witness' (Ecomtrading 2013). This designation provides a further reminder of the actor's humanitarian credentials, summoning up the authority that he wields as an ambassador for a variety of NGOs. Each of these associations is invoked for the purpose of legitimising the promotional campaign, so that the effect of Clooney's presence is to lend weight to the ethical credentials of Nespresso itself – the inference being that the *Ocean's* star would only endorse an organisation that shares his own sense of integrity and compassion.

Clooney's appearances in these Nespresso videos are indicative of the way in which celebrity activism and forms of 'ethical consumption' currently intersect (Goodman 2010). Indeed, Clooney is one of a number of contemporary stars who combine their campaigning with the endorsement of 'ethical' products: Hollywood actor and humanitarian Ben Affleck has partnered with the 'ethical' shoe company TOMS, for example; and Bono is the co-founder of Product (RED), an initiative that raises funds to help eliminate HIV/AIDS in Africa via the sale of popular consumer products (e.g., RED iPhone cases and RED iPods).[6] Scholar Patricia Daley (2013) argues that rather than helping to promote social justice, this type of campaigning actually reproduces the worst inequalities of neoliberal capitalism. Pointing to Product (RED) and other examples, she notes how the linking of celebrity activists with ethical consumption has opened up new business opportunities for commercial superpowers like Apple, while also representing the practices of these companies as 'socially responsible' (Daley 2013, 380). For Daley, then, the caring and thoughtful personas of stars such as Bono and Clooney function at the level of ideology: they work to distract from the structural violence that exists within neoliberal capitalism (cf. Kapoor 2013; Littler 2008).

Daley's ideological critique provides a valuable framework for examining the Clooney-Nespresso partnership. Specifically, it offers a useful starting point for discussions about how Clooney's ambassadorship helps to mask a series of eco-logical issues relating to the Nespresso brand. In contrast to conventional coffee machines, Nespresso machines brew coffee using individually portioned alumin-ium pods. Promotional materials for Nespresso claim that these pods are '100 percent recyclable'. For example, customers in the UK can return their used pods directly to Nespresso boutiques, dispose of them at a number of 'dedicated collec-tion points', or arrange a collection via the company's website (Nestlé-Nespresso n.d.). Although these options mark a significant improvement on the early years of the brand (originally Nespresso provided no options for recycling pods outside of Switzerland), a comprehensive rollout of effective sustainability measures has been slow to materialize, with access to recycling facilities remaining limited in many countries. As of May 2018, the option to dispose of pods in household recycling bins is only available in six countries, while free home collection is restricted to fifteen of the seventy-six markets in which the company operates (Nestlé-Nespresso 2018; BBC 2016).[7]

At the same time, concerns arise from the 1.15 grams of aluminium that is used to produce each Nespresso pod. Aluminium packaging is a key feature of Nespresso's brand identity, allowing the company to differentiate its capsules from cheaper, plastic alternatives. The company website trumpets aluminium as the best way to 'preserve aroma' and 'freshness', for example (Nestlé-Nespresso n.d.). Yet these manufacturing choices have significant ecological costs. The extraction and refining of aluminium is an energy-intensive process, which results in high levels of carbon emissions and hazardous waste. Moreover, critics of Nespresso point to the basic problem of getting small quantities of aluminium waste to recycling facilities, as these types of miniature packaging are generally thrown in the bin by consumers – in the UK alone, it is estimated that more than 340 million coffee capsules/pods end up in landfill sites each year (Hamann et al. 2014; Ellson 2016).

All of these ecological issues are compounded by a lack of transparency. At present, Nespresso focuses on 'recycling capacity' as a measure of its sustain-ability efforts. In 2017, Nespresso reported that its 'global collection capacity' had exceeded 86 percent, while The Perfect Cup initiative commits the company to achieving 100 percent capacity by 2020 (Nestlé-Nespresso 2017). Although these figures seem impressive and contribute to Nespresso's overall branding as 'The Sustainable Quality Coffee Company', they fail to give a clear indication of the levels of waste generated by its single-serve aluminium pods. Recycling capacity refers to the percentage of Nespresso pods sold to 'consumers who have accessible collection options' as opposed to *actual* recycling rates, which – at just 24.6 percent – are substantially lower than the company's green branding might suggest (Nestlé-Nespresso 2018). Lisa Hamann et al., in their analysis of sustain-ability in the coffee industry, argue that these records of recycling capacity are 'not really meaningful', and show how they effectively obscure the ecological impacts of the Nespresso brand (Hamann et al. 2014, 34; cf. Gunther 2015). The involvement of a lauded activist like Clooney can be read in similar terms. His recruitment lends Nespresso a degree of moral authority, which helps to distract attention from both the wastefulness of aluminium pods and the misleading data about its sustainability programmes.

Any analysis of Clooney's activism must also take into account his roles in films ranging from the *Ocean's* trilogy to lower-budget productions like *Michael Clayton*. As I have explored elsewhere (Gulam 2014a, 2014b, 2016), films are central to the meanings that Hollywood stars communicate as activists, advocates, and humanitarians: these texts help to shape not just the media and institutional traction of star campaigners, but also the wider instrumentalities that their campaigning performs. Indeed, in the same way that Clooney's Nespresso work draws upon the moral authority that he has accrued through his campaigning, it also invokes the decency and heroism of his on-screen characters. Since winning admirers for his performance of Dr. Doug Ross, a troubled but committed paediatrician on the hit television series *ER* (1994–2009), Clooney has been consistently cast as the hero or saviour. Each of his characters in *Batman and Robin* (1997), *Gravity* (2013), and *The Monuments Men* (2014) risk their lives to save others, for example, while the conman that he plays in *Out of Sight* (1998) sacrifices his share of the loot in order to prevent a violent assault. These cinematic narratives circulate in and around his Nespresso ambassadorship, contributing to the sense of integrity and compassion that he transfers onto the brand. The next section looks in close detail at the complex relationship between Clooney's activism, his on-screen career, and his product endorsements.

From anti-corporate crusader to corporate ambassador

In the same period that he developed a reputation for his off-screen campaigning, Clooney also appeared in a series of films that addressed social and political issues: the geopolitical thriller *Syriana* (2005); *Good Night, and Good Luck* (2005), a War on Terror allegory that he co-wrote and directed; the corporate corruption film *Michael Clayton* (2007); and *Up in the Air* (2009), a picture that touches on issues of consumerism and unemployment. Although these films failed to match the commercial success of the *Ocean's* franchise, they each received widespread critical acclaim, with reviewers praising the filmmakers for producing the kind of 'thought-provoking' stories that Hollywood typically avoids (Lowe 2005; Levy 2008; Ansen 2009). Clooney's work on these issues pictures exists in a feedback loop with his activism, whereby the two aspects of his star image draw off and feed into one another. Footage of his on-the-ground campaigning animates the portrayal of real-world political issues in films like *Syriana*, for example, while the apparent heft of these movies lends credence to the idea that Clooney is one of Hollywood's most accomplished campaigners (Gulam 2014a). In terms of his Nespresso endorsement, however, what is most significant about this body of films is how they each contain a critique of big businesses and corporate capitalism.

This anti-corporate strain is most evident in *Michael Clayton* and *Up in the Air*. Written and directed by Tony Gilroy and co-produced by Clooney's Section Eight Productions, *Michael Clayton* is a tense legal thriller, portraying the greed and corruption that exists within the corporate sector.[8] Clooney plays the role of Michael Clayton, an attorney for a prestigious corporate law firm based in New York, Kenner, Bach and Ledeen (KBL). Clayton acts as the firm's self-declared 'fixer', the person KBL calls upon to deal with incidents that require discretion and expediency. A series of early scenes show Clayton doing the dirty work that keeps the rotten corporate system intact, leveraging his contacts in federal government and the local authorities to achieve the best results for KBL and its shareholders.

The central storyline in *Michael Clayton* focuses on a $3 billion class-action suit involving one of KBL's biggest clients, U/North, a multinational agrochemical company that manufactures pesticides. U/North is being sued over the harmful effects of one of its products, which is accused of poisoning farmland and water supplies, as well as causing the premature deaths of thousands of people. Clayton becomes involved in the case when the litigator representing U/North, Arthur Edens (Tom Wilkinson), dies from an apparent overdose. In his investigation into Edens's death, Clayton uncovers a confidential U/North memo confirming that the company knew about the deadly properties of its pesticide. He also discovers the true details of Edens's 'overdose', when it emerges that a senior U/North executive hired assassins to drug and murder the litigator as a way to cover the company's tracks. Grief-stricken by the death of his colleague and fearing for his own safety, Clayton delivers the memo to the police. In doing so, he not only helps to bring U/North to justice, but also turns his back on the corporate world. A climactic scene sees Clayton claim the symbolic role of corporate avenger when he tells two soon-to-be arrested U/North executives, 'I am Shiva, the god of death'.

Directed by Jason Reitman and starring Clooney, *Up in the Air* also explores the injustices of corporate America, but does so through the genre of the romantic comedy-drama. Clooney plays Ryan Bingham, a professional corporate downsizer employed by companies to implement large-scale layoffs. Bingham is one of the leading consultants at the Career Transitions Corporation (CTC). Specialists in 'outplacement counselling', CTC claim to help former employees begin the 'next chapter' of their working lives. In reality, the company acts as little more than hired hatchet men: the full extent of CTC's counselling is a generic pep talk and a thin envelope of materials, which former employees are invited to peruse at their own leisure. Like Clooney's character in *Michael Clayton*, then, Bingham harbours no illusions about the ruthless nature of his work, recognising that his job is to get workers out the door as quickly and quietly as possible. An early montage shows Bingham dismissing workers with disconcerting ease. In one scene, Clooney's character reassures a recently fired worker that he will be 'in touch', but his voiceover narration confirms that they will never speak again.

Despite these extended montages showing the plight of ordinary workers, *Up in the Air* is principally concerned with the toll that a dehumanising corporate culture has taken on its central character. Large sections of the film are dedicated to showing the aimlessness and vacuity of Bingham's personal life. Travelling back and forth across America to wield the proverbial axe, Clooney's protagonist possesses no meaningful or long-lasting relationships. The person he spends most of his time with is his new colleague, Natalie Keener (Anna Kendrick), while he is also estranged from his two sisters. Echoing the cut-throat philosophy of the companies for whom he works, the only things that appear to motivate Bingham are the desire for efficiency and personal gain. For example, a recurring motif in *Up in the Air* is his quest to reach 10 million frequent flyer miles, a goal that will earn Bingham access to a club that contains just six other members. Clooney's downsizer eventually reaches his goal on a flight back from Chicago and is personally congratulated by the chief pilot (Sam Elliott). When the pilot asks where he is from, Bingham responds, 'Here'. The sense of deflation in his response contributes to the film's central message about the moral bankruptcy of corporate America and the human costs of the drive for ever-expanding profit.

Even more than his charitable and political activities, therefore, Clooney's on-screen roles appear to be at odds with his Nespresso endorsement. Indeed, in a press event to promote *Michael Clayton* at the 2007 Venice Film Festival, the actor was asked how he could reconcile the film's critique of corporate capitalism with his endorsement of a multinational like Nestlé. In his response, Clooney rejected the idea that any conflict existed between these two aspects of his career. Seeking to shift the focus back onto his cinematic endeavours, the actor ultimately refused to apologise for 'trying to make a living every once in a while' (Mottram 2007).

The Venice incident was noteworthy not only for how it crystallised a tension between Clooney's roles as a corporate ambassador and activist, but also for the way in which the star attempted to resolve this tension. Like a number of contemporary film stars who pursue careers behind the camera, Clooney has fostered a reputation as an astute filmmaker – someone working within the commercial structures of Hollywood to make films that are both more 'complex' than the conventional blockbuster and deeply 'personal' (Hornaday 2007; Levy 2008). Journalistic profiles of the actor-director report that he operates according to a one-for-one process, for instance, whereby each commercial hit he delivers for the studios gives him the freedom to make a 'serious' picture like *Michael Clayton* (Levy 2008). By refusing to apologise for 'trying to make a living every once in a while', Clooney sought to rationalise his Nespresso ambassadorship in terms of the same give-and-take that is said to characterise his relationship with commercial Hollywood.

A similar logic was articulated by the star in a July 2013 interview with *The Guardian*. Commenting on his work for the coffee manufacturer, Clooney detailed the way in which he uses a large percentage of his Nespresso salary to fund the Satellite Sentinel Project (Siegle 2013). Co-founded by Clooney in 2010, the Satellite Sentinel Project (SSP) is an organisation that employs satellite imagery to monitor for signs of human rights abuses in several countries, including Sudan, South Sudan, and the Democratic Republic of Congo.[9] In these instances, Clooney seeks to distance himself from accusations of corporate acquiescence and/or 'selling out'. Instead, he claims the identity of the shrewd operator: an individual who sees all the angles, and knows how best to use his stardom for the good of the African citizens he claims to help.

This image of the star overlaps with elements of his representation in the *Ocean's* franchise. Daniel Ocean is the consummate hustler. Although the central focus of the trilogy is the camaraderie that exists among the group of conmen, it is Clooney's character who ultimately assumes the role of 'top dog', marshalling all of the resources at his disposal to pull off a string of elaborate heists (Gulam 2014a). Significantly, there is also an anti-corporate dimension to this character. In each of the films in the trilogy, Clooney's protagonist is pitted against an unscrupulous businessman. Willy Bank (Al Pacino), the 'mark' in *Ocean's Thirteen*, is a predatory casino magnate, and Ocean targets Bank when he cheats one of his crew out of their share of a lucrative hotel-casino. In the David vs. Goliath narratives of the *Ocean's* franchise, therefore, Clooney's character is not just a conman seeking great riches and personal glory. He is also a populist hero, striking a blow against elite interests.

Several of Clooney's films seek to problematize the corporate world, therefore, by depicting the venality of those individuals at the top of the corporate pyramid. At the same time, these films also document the progressive potential that exists within such structures. Clooney's protagonist in *Michael Clayton* outwits U/North using the craftiness that he learned as a corporate fixer, for example, while *Up in the Air* shows how the worst cruelties of corporate capitalism can be ameliorated by small acts of human kindness. By the same token, *Ocean's Thirteen* contains a subplot in which one of Ocean's crew – Casey Affleck's Virgil Malloy – poses as a low-paid worker in a Mexican dice-making factory. Although Malloy is operating under self-interested motives – he is there to tamper with the dice that will eventually end up in Bank's casino – he becomes involved in a protest against poor working conditions, helping to stage a strike with the other employees. This strike is only resolved once Clooney's conman intervenes. Recognising the threat that the strike poses to his intricately planned heist, Ocean agrees to fund a wage increase for the factory employees out of his share of the loot, thereby allowing them to return to work.

Each of these cinematic narratives speaks to important aspects of Clooney's humanitarian image and the broader ideological function that his Nespresso ambassadorship performs. Like the characters in his films, Clooney is represented as a force for 'good', someone who has been able to realise positive results by working within the structures of neoliberal capitalism. The press stories about how he redirects his endorsement money back into 'progressive' projects evoke the shrewdness and moral decency of Daniel Ocean, for instance (Gulam 2014a). Moving beyond a narrow focus on individual agents such as Nestlé, one of the ideological effects of the Clooney-Nespresso partnership is to promote the idea that the answers to global inequality lie within the very structures that produce it. Recalling the star's relationship with commercial Hollywood, media coverage of his Nespresso activism serves to validate a form of give-and-take resistance in which benevolent corporate hustlers like Clooney work to tackle the worst symptoms of global inequality, while the system of neoliberal capitalism that drives this inequality is left unopposed.

In his influential work on stardom, Richard Dyer (2004) suggests that part of the appeal of stars is in the way their images can resolve ideological contradictions for the audience. Central to his analysis is how disparate notions of human identity are brought together in a star's image. For example, he notes how Marilyn Monroe's combination of sexiness and innocence helped to resolve certain contradictory notions of femininity circulating in 1950s America. For Dyer, this process is ideologically significant because of the way in which it obfuscates wider social structures: as these meanings are attached to the figure of the star, what is social appears as if it were 'natural' (Dyer 2004, 17–36). Clooney's star image functions according to the same ideological process described by Dyer, combining his corporate ambassadorship with the populist heroics of his on-screen characters. The combination of these disparate elements naturalises the concept that the worst injustices of neoliberal capitalism can be overcome by individuals working within this system.

Conclusion

In November 2013, Nespresso launched a new series of advertisements featuring Clooney. Building on previous campaigns, these advertisements sought to use Clooney to promote Nespresso's core values of sophistication, rich flavours, and responsible corporate practice. In the first of three interconnected vignettes, Clooney is shown in a Nespresso boutique, sitting beside an attractive woman. When Clooney goes to fetch a drink for the woman, she announces his presence to the other customers, causing a group of fans to swarm the actor. Alone at last, the woman sits back and enjoys Clooney's own cup of Nespresso. The second advertisement sees a bedraggled Clooney in the same boutique, joined by Hollywood actor Matt Damon. When Damon tells his *Ocean's* co-star that he is there to recycle, revealing a bag of empty Nespresso pods, this prompts Clooney to respond, 'Me too'. A final advertisement completes the narrative as Clooney exits the boutique, having pulled the same trick on Damon that he was subjected to in the opening vignette (Gianatasio 2013).[10]

Jointly entitled 'In the Name of Pleasure', Nespresso circulated these three advertisements via its YouTube channel, with staggered release dates for different markets. At the same time, the company linked the advertisements to a series of more in-depth videos about its sustainability efforts. These videos ranged from short trailers featuring Clooney in his role as an NASB member to round-table discussions about the AAA programme. Within six months of premiering the first advertisement, the campaign had received over 50 million views, including 10 million views for the linked content (Google 2014).

The 'In the Name of Pleasure' saga captures the complex interplay between on- and off-screen images of Clooney that has been a key feature of his partnership with Nespresso. In the three advertisements, Clooney does not simply play a version of himself – the glamorous and socially responsible film star-turned-humanitarian. He also plays a version of his *Ocean's* character (McDonald 2013, 63–64). For example, the arrival of Damon in the second advertisement substantiates the connections between the coffee company and the populist heroics of Daniel Ocean, with Clooney's endorsement of Nespresso constructed as just another good-natured escapade.

This chapter has examined the triangulation of Clooney's roles as a film star, activist, and Nespresso ambassador, outlining how the sense of compassion that he has accrued in his on- and off-screen campaigning is transferred onto the coffee brand. Overall, the chapter has argued that the partnership between Clooney and Nespresso is significant not only in terms of the commercial opportunities that it realises for the two parties. It is also significant from an ideological perspective. I have shown how the pairing of a multibillion-dollar multinational with a lauded celebrity activist works to legitimise the concept of a benevolent capitalism – one in which the solutions to social problems rest in the hands of 'ethical' multinationals like Nespresso and the Hollywood stars who endorse them.

Notes

1 The initial contract between Clooney and Nespresso prohibited the use of his image in the United States. Since 2015, however, Clooney's Nespresso advertisements have aired in both European and US markets (Gretler 2015).
2 Significantly this is a role originally played by Frank Sinatra in the 1960s Rat Pack film upon which *Ocean's Eleven* is based, *Ocean's 11* (1960). For further discussion of the *Ocean's* films and how they impact on the meanings associated with Clooney's activism, see Gulam (2014a).
3 Clooney has also participated in the production of two documentary feature movies about the conflict: *Sand and Sorrow* (2007) and *Darfur Now* (2007).The 2007 Nobel Summit Peace Award was awarded jointly to Clooney and fellow Hollywood actor Don Cheadle. Clooney and Cheadle co-founded NOOW, together with their *Ocean's* co-stars Brad Pitt and Matt Damon.
4 Entitled 'George Clooney & Nespresso in Costa Rica', this video is available online at www.youtube.com/watch?v=bHNSg9LxjpY (Ecomtrading 2013).
5 For detailed discussion of Clooney's particular brand of Hollywood liberalism, see Gulam (2014a).
6 In his role as chairman of the Eastern Congo Initiative (ECI), a non-profit organisation that he co-founded in 2010, Affleck collaborated with TOMS to produce a line of limited-edition trainers using 'Congolese-inspired textiles'. TOMS operates according to a 'one-for-one' business model, meaning that for each pair of shoes sold, it donates a similar pair to someone in the developing world. In the case of the TOMS-ECI partnership, shoes were donated to Congolese schoolchildren, while $5 from each sale was directed back into ECI's 'youth and families' projects (Cappadona 2013).
7 In May 2017, Nespresso sought to offset longstanding criticisms of its environmental record by launching a six-month pilot project in the London borough of Kensington and Chelsea, which allowed Nespresso Club members to recycle their used pods through their council household recycling service (Smithers 2017).
8 Clooney and the *Ocean's* director Steven Soderbergh co-founded Section Eight in 2000, with the company operating from 2000–2006.
9 In collaboration with The Enough Project and DigitalGlobe, SSP claims to offer access to 'near-real time' information about events in conflict zones, making this information available via regular reports on its website. In May 2011, for instance, SSP visually confirmed the looting of a World Food Programme facility in the disputed Abyei region of Sudan (Raymond *et al*. 2013, 189–190).
10 Damon reportedly received $3 million for his appearance in this advertisement (Gianatasio 2013). The three advertisements are available online at www.adweek.com/adfreak/matt-damon-joins-george-clooney-nespresso-campaign-its-no-oscar-winner-153810 (Gianatasio 2013).

References

America: A Tribute to Heroes (2001) [TV programme] Fox, ABC, NBC, and CBS. USA: Broadcast on multiple channels, 21 September.

Ansen, D. (2009) 'Jason Reitman: The Grown-Up's Director', *Newsweek*, 25 October [online] Available: http://europe.newsweek.com/jason-reitman-grown-ups-director-76793?rm= eu [accessed 14 April 2016].

Batman and Robin (1997) [Film] Directed by Joel Schumacher. USA: Warner Bros.

BBC (2013) 'Chocolate Firms Nestle and Mars Accused of Price-Fixing', *BBC*, [online] Available: www.bbc.co.uk/news/business-22807887 [accessed 14 April 2016].

BBC (2016) 'Is There a Serious Problem with Coffee Capsules?', *BBC*, 19 February [online] Available: https://www.bbc.co.uk/news/magazine-35605927 [accessed 14 April 2016].

Bono (2009) 'Heroes & Icons: George Clooney', *Time*, 30 April [online] Available: http://content.time.com/time/specials/packages/article/0,28804,1894410_1894289_1894280,00.html [accessed 14 April 2016].

Box Office Mojo (n.d.) *George Clooney*, [online] Available: www.boxofficemojo.com/people/chart/?id=georgeclooney.htm [accessed 11 April 2016].

Boyd, C. (2012) 'The Nestlé Infant Formula Controversy and a Strange Web of Subsequent Business Scandals', *Journal of Business Ethics*, 106 (3): 283–293.

Brockington, D. (2014) 'The Production and Construction of Celebrity Advocacy in International Development', *Third World Quarterly*, 35 (1): 88–108.

Cappadona, B. (2013) 'Ben Affleck Collaborates with TOMS on Charitable Shoe Line', *Boston Magazine*, 15 May [online] Available: www.bostonmagazine.com/arts-entertainment/blog/2013/05/15/ben-affleck-toms-shoe-line-eastern-congo-initiative/ [accessed 2 April 2016].

Collins, S. (2007) 'Traversing Authenticities: The West Wing President and the Activist Sheen', in: K. Riegert (ed.) *Politicotainment: Television's Take on the Real*, New York: Peter Lang: 181–211.

Daley, P. (2013) 'Rescuing African Bodies: Celebrities, Consumerism and Neoliberal Humanitarianism', *Review of African Political Economy*, 40 (137): 375–393.

Darfur Now (2007) [Film] Directed by Ted Braun. USA: Warner Independent Pictures.

Denny, C. (2002) 'Retreat by Nestle on Ethiopia's $6m Debt', *The Guardian*, 20 December [online] Available: www.theguardian.com/world/2002/dec/20/marketingandpr.debtrelief [accessed 14 April 2016].

Dyer, R. (2004) *Heavenly Bodies: Film Stars and Society*, London: Routledge.

Ecomtrading (2013) *George Clooney & Nespresso in Costa Rica*, [online] Available: www.youtube.com/watch?v=bHNSg9LxjpY [accessed 14 April 2016].

Ellson, A. (2016) 'Recycling Row Brews as Coffee Pod Sales Overtake Instant', *The Times*, 6 September [online] Available: https://www.thetimes.co.uk/article/recycling-row-brews-as-coffee-pod-sales-overtake-instant-h730jk2tx [accessed 2 April 2019].

ER (1994–2009) [TV series] Directed by various. USA: NBC.

Gianatasio, D. (2013) 'Matt Damon Joins George Clooney in Nespresso Campaign, But It's No Oscar Winner', *AdWeek*, 13 November [online] Available: www.adweek.com/adfreak/matt-damon-joins-george-clooney-nespresso-campaign-its-no-oscar-winner-153810 [accessed 14 April 2016].

Goodman, M.K. (2010) 'The Mirror of Consumption: Celebritization, Developmental Consumption and the Shifting Cultural Politics of Fair Trade', *Geoforum*, 41 (1): 104–116.

Good Night and Good Luck (2005) [Film] Directed by George Clooney. USA: Warner Independent Pictures.

Google (2014) 'George Clooney Brings in Over 50M Views for Nespresso on YouTube!', [online] Available: www.thinkwithgoogle.com/intl/en-gb/case-study/nespresso-youtube [accessed 14 April 2016].

Gravity (2013) [Film] Directed by Alfonso Cuarón. USA: Warner Bros.

Gretler, C. (2015) 'Nespresso to Bring George Clooney Coffee Ads to U.S. Market', *Bloomberg*, [online] Available: www.bloomberg.com/news/articles/2015-10-29/nespresso-to-bring-george-clooney-coffee-ads-to-u-s-market [accessed 14 April 2016].

Gulam, J. (2014a) '"The Issues Guy": George Clooney's Journey from Film Star to Philanthropist', in A. Barlow (ed.) *Star Power: The Impact of Branded Celebrity*, Los Angeles, CA: ABC-CLIO: 223–248.

Gulam, J. (2014b) 'Film Stardom, Gender, and Philanthropy: Sharon Stone at the World Summit of Nobel Peace Laureates', *Celebrity Studies*, 5 (3): 360–363.

Gulam, J. (2016) 'From Action Babe to Mature Actress: The Place of Humanitarianism in Angelina Jolie's Lasting Screen Career', in L. Bolton and J. Wright (eds.) *Lasting Screen Stars: Images that Fade and Personas that Endure*, London: Palgrave Macmillan: 277–290.

Gunther, M. (2015) 'The Good, the Bad and the Ugly: Sustainability at Nespresso', *The Guardian*, 27 May [online] Available: www.theguardian.com/sustainable-business/2015/may/27/nespresso-sustainability-transparency-recycling-coffee-pods-values-aluminum [accessed 18 August 2014].

Hamann, L. et al. (2014) 'CSR in the Coffee Industry: Sustainability Issues at Nestlé-Nespresso and Starbucks', *Journal of European Management & Public Affairs Studies*, 2 (1): 31–35.

Harris, P. (2012) 'George Clooney's Satellite Spies Reveal Secrets of Sudan's Bloody Army', *The Guardian*, 24 March [online] Available: www.theguardian.com/world/2012/mar/24/george-clooney-spies-secrets-sudan [accessed 11 December 2012].

Horn, J. (2011) 'I Spy', *The Los Angeles Times Magazine*, December [online] Available: www.latimesmagazine.com/2011/12/i-spy.html [accessed 11 December 2012].

Hornaday, A. (2007) '"Michael Clayton": Clooney's Dark Knight of the Soul'. *The Washington Post*, 5 October [online] Available: http://www.washingtonpost.com/wp-dyn/content/article/2007/10/04/AR2007100402309.html [accessed 11 December 2018].

Huliaras, A. and Tzifakis, N. (2012) 'The Fallacy of the Autonomous Celebrity Activist in International Politics: George Clooney and Mia Farrow in Darfur', *Cambridge Review of International Affairs*, 25 (3): 417–431.

Kapoor, I. (2013) *Celebrity Humanitarianism: The Ideology of Global Charity*, London: Routledge.

Levy, E. (2008) 'I Was Unfamous for an Awful Long Time', *The Financial Times*, 28 March [online] Available: www.ft.com/cms/s/2/4bfb2b12-fc5a-11dc-9229-000077b07658.html#axzz34RLLqa5p [accessed 11 December 2012].

Littler, J. (2008) '"I Feel Your Pain": Cosmopolitan Charity and the Public Fashioning of the Celebrity Soul', *Social Semiotics*, 18 (2): 237–251.

Look to the Stars (n.d.) 'George Clooney: Charity Work & Causes', *Look to the Stars*, [online] Available: www.looktothestars.org/celebrity/george-clooney [accessed 10 March 2015].

Lowe, F. (2005) 'How a Heart-Throb Became the Voice of Liberal America', *The Guardian*, 27 November [online] Available: www.theguardian.com/film/2005/nov/27/awardsandprizes.usa [accessed 11 December 2012].

McCracken, G. (1989) 'Who Is the Celebrity Endorser? Cultural Foundations of the Endorsement Process', *Journal of Consumer Research*, 16 (3): 310–321.

McDonald, P. (2013) *Hollywood Stardom*, London: John Wiley & Sons.

Michael Clayton (2007) [Film] Directed by Tony Gilroy. USA: Warner Bros.

The Monuments Men (2014) [Film] Directed by George Clooney. USA: Sony Pictures.

Mottram, J. (2007) 'George Clooney: Hollywood's Conscience', *The Independent*, 13 September [online] Available: www.independent.co.uk/arts-entertainment/films/features/george-clooney-hollywoodsconscience-464212.html [accessed 10 March 2015].

Mukherjee, R. and Banet-Weiser, S. (eds.) (2012) *Commodity Activism: Cultural Resistance in Neoliberal Times*, New York: New York University Press.

Muller, M. (2013) 'Nestlé Baby Milk Scandal Has Grown Up But Not Gone Away', *The Guardian*, 13 February [online] Available: www.theguardian.com/sustainable-business/nestle-baby-milk-scandal-food-industry-standards [accessed 15 April 2016].

Nestlé (2015) *Nespresso's The Positive Cup*, 17 August [online] Available: www.nestle.com/csv/case-studies/AllCaseStudies/Nespresso-Positive-Cup [accessed 1 April 2016].

Nestlé-Nespresso (n.d.) *Sustainability,* [online] Available: https://www.nestle-nespresso.com/sustainability [accessed 24 April 2016].

Nestlé-Nespresso (2017) *The Positive Cup: Creating Shared Value Report*, [online] Available: https://www.nestle-nespresso.com/asset-library/documents/nespresso-positive-cup-csv-report-interactive.pdf [accessed 10 June 2019].

Nestlé-Nespresso (2018) *The Positive Cup: 2017 Status and Outlook*, [online] Available: https://www.nestle-nespresso.com/asset-library/documents/2017%20status%20and%202020%20outlook%20report.pdf [accessed 10 June 2019].

Ocean's 11 (1960) [Film] Directed by Lewis Milestone. USA: Warner Bros.

Ocean's Eleven (2001) [Film] Directed by Steven Soderbergh. USA: Warner Bros.

Ocean's Thirteen (2007) [Film] Directed by Steven Soderbergh. USA: Warner Bros.

Ocean's Twelve (2004) [Film] Directed by Steven Soderbergh. USA: Warner Bros.

Out of Sight (1998) [Film] Directed by Steven Soderbergh. USA: Universal Pictures.

Raymond, N.A. et al. (2013) 'While We Watched: Assessing the Impact of the Satellite Sentinel Project', *Georgetown Journal of International Affairs*, 14 (2): 185–191.

Reuters (2014) *Nespresso Eyes Sales Increase This Year: CEO in Handelsblatt*, [online] Available: www.reuters.com/article/nestle-nespresso-idUSL5N0QW4KR20140826 [accessed 14 April 2016].

Said, S. (2013) *George Clooney Earns $40 Million from Nespresso Deal*, [online] Available: www.therichest.com/expensive-lifestyle/entertainment/george-clooney-earns-40-million-from-nespresso-deal/ [accessed 14 April 2016].

Sand and Sorrow (2007) [Film] Directed by Paul Freedman. USA: Home Box Office.

Siegle, L. (2013) 'George Clooney Tastes Sustainability in Nespresso Coffee', *The Guardian*, 17 July [online] Available: www.theguardian.com/environment/blog/2013/jul/17/george-clooney-nespresso-coffee-ad [accessed 23 July 2015].

Smith, E. (2012) 'Corporate Image and Public Health: An Analysis of the Philip Morris, Kraft, and Nestle Websites', *Journal of Health Communication*, 17 (5): 582–600.

Smithers, R. (2017) 'Nespresso Bid to Recycle Coffee Pods', *The Guardian*, 2 May [online] Available: https://www.theguardian.com/environment/2017/apr/29/recycle-nespresso-coffee-pods-london [accessed 18 August 2018].

Syriana (2005) [Film] Directed by Steven Gaghan. USA: Warner Bros.

Up in the Air (2009) [Film] Directed by Jason Reitman. USA: Paramount Pictures.

Woodruff, J. (2012) 'Interview with George Clooney', *PBS NewsHour* [TV programme] PBS, 14 March. Available: https://www.pbs.org/video/pbs-newshour-george-clooney-puts-spotlight-on-bloodshed-crisis-in-sudan/ [accessed 10 June 2019].

Worley, W. (2016) 'Nestle Battles Slavery Issues on Two Continents', *The Independent*, 1 February [online] Available: www.independent.co.uk/news/world/americas/nestle-battles-slavery-issues-on-two-continents-a6847366.html [accessed 10 March 2015].

7 All under the Same Sky? Celebrity philanthropy and the transnational market for women's empowerment

Annika Bergman Rosamond and Catia Gregoratti

This chapter is an attempt to enable a productive conversation between the budding, interdisciplinary research field of celebrity studies, humanitarianism, and activism and feminist international political economy (IPE) scholarship. Critical development scholarship, political science, and media studies have come to seriously consider the constitutive role of celebrity humanitarianism and activism in the transformation of both domestic and international society in a peaceful and equitable fashion (Brockington 2009, 2014; Kapoor 2013; Chouliaraki 2013; Richey and Ponte 2011; Yrjölä 2012). These scholarly endeavours commonly rest on the assumption that the humanitarian efforts of individuals are worth studying rather than confining such analysis to state actors and international institutions (Bergman Rosamond 2015; Cooper 2008). As much as we might assume that states and other actors are candidates for (moral) agency in global politics (Bergman Rosamond 2013, 2015, 2016), we might be equally willing to accept that individuals may carry transformative powers.

Our second point of departure lies within a strand of literature interested in how women's empowerment is becoming increasingly facilitated by nebulous, transnational constellations of public and private transnational actors. In a powerful feminist historical materialist intervention, Adrienne Roberts (2012, 2015) has termed these 'Transnational Business Feminism'. Situating these assemblages within feminist debates on neoliberalism, Elisabeth Prügl has recently introduced the term 'neoliberalising feminism' to denote the incorporation of feminist claims and aspirations into economic projects and the neoliberal ideology, as well as attending changes in governance mechanisms and rationalities that strive to cultivate 'dependable subjects who hold themselves accountable to norms of market-embedded gender equality' (Prügl 2015, 620). Along with Elizabeth Prügl, we suggest that the kind of neoliberalising feminism operating through various development assemblages converges around the expansion of markets in the name of feminist goals and the constitution of the self-responsibilised and enterprising woman.

Our intention in this chapter is to contribute to such feminist literature by contextually scrutinising how these assemblages work and what kind of empowerment they engender. In particular, we do so by problematising the role of celebrity philanthropy in the everyday production, marketing, and consumption of what we term 'empowering commodities'. Empowering commodities come in different forms – they can be clothes, accessories, household items, or even foodstuff – but what makes them distinct is that they come with a more or less visible promise of women's empowerment. More specifically, such commodities claim to transform women's (and men's) lives in a dual way, empowering the distant predominantly women who produce them while, at the same time, offering moral cleanliness through the enactment of a benevolent deed and emotional fulfilment (Mitchell 2016) to those who consume them.

Merging the aforementioned strands of research through the concept of empowering commodity enables us to foreground the role that celebrities and celebrity philanthropy play in feminist IPE interventions on transnational business feminism and neoliberalising feminism – aspects that arguably have not yet received a large amount of attention – but also to point to the transactional, emotionally loaded and aesthetically pleasing character that empowerment is assuming in contemporary development interventions mediated through uneven processes of production, marketing and consumption. Our interest in these debates arises from a shared feeling of uneasiness about the incorporation and instrumentalisation of feminist critiques (Fraser 2009) to serve the expansion of markets through a commodified empowerment agenda and resorting to celebrity-endorsed shopping for this purpose. Existing feminist research (Pearson 2007; Prügl and True 2014; Prügl 2015; Gregoratti, Roberts and Tornhill 2018) makes us aware of the contingency, inequalities, and differences reinforced through market-based interventions operating under the banner of gender equality and empowerment. Moreover, such research explicitly calls for deeper and more extensive studies on how neoliberalising feminism is articulated, enacted, and sustained in networks of neoliberal solidarity and care towards the distant other.

In this paper, we zoom in on the Same Sky shopping initiative – a New York-based ethical trade and shopping initiative supported by a philanthropic foundation with the same name. The main objective of this chapter is to unravel the women empowerment agenda promoted by its founder Francine LeFrak, an American former producer and recognised woman philanthropist, whose project has been endorsed by over eighty 'celebrity politicians' (Street 2012), including elected politician Hillary Clinton and stars such as Ben Affleck and Meryl Streep. While recent research has broken down celebrity humanitarianism, philanthrocapitalism, and spectacular NGOs (Kapoor 2013) into rather neat categories, the Same Sky initiative exceeds these analytical boundaries by merging women-led philanthropy, partnerships with fashion retailers, celebrity activism, and ethical shopping, all of which have an assumed link to women's empowerment and transnational solidarity. Celebrity-driven initiatives and movements such as Ben Affleck's Eastern Congo Initiative (Richey and Budabin 2016) and Madonna's Raising Malawi Academy for Girls (Mubanda Rasmussen 2015) have clear links to women's and girls' empowerment. Empowering commodities that are entering Northern markets and online retail spaces are situated within similar discourses of empowerment.[1] What, however, drew our attention to Same Sky is the invocation and circulation of notions of transnational solidarity involving 'a whole movement of women supporting other women . . . giving them the tools and means to become entrepreneurs and economically independent' (Blair 2011).

We thus employ the case of Same Sky as a springboard to develop a feminist critique of the type of empowerment promoted by LeFrak and Same Sky. First we argue that alongside the endorsement offered to Same Sky by over eighty celebrities, the construction of the celebrity philanthropist LeFrak – which occurs through biographical self-representations, emotional language, and ways of framing gendered livelihoods – is central in the quotidian legitimation of individualised, gendered, racialised market-based empowerment projects. Thereafter, delving more deeply into how empowering commodities are produced, marketed, and consumed, we suggest that attempts to harness the market for empowerment reinforce class, gender, and racial inequalities in production, social reproduction, and consumption, directing attention away from the structures and institutions that produce these. While the rationality of women's empowerment draws heavily on notions of individual freedom and responsibility, the means to its achievement do little more than give women access to resources such as work training and a piece-rate wage. For the few affluent consumers that can purchase commodities that empower of the distant other, consumption becomes a means to attain gratification and enact solidarity.

Francine LeFrak as Same Sky

Same Sky might not be widely known outside the United States or indeed New York even if the jewellery produced within the initiative is being worn by celebrities such as Goldie Hawn, Halle Berry, Meryl Streep, and Ben Affleck. It is through such celebrity endorsement and support that the business venture has become known to wider audiences and legitimised. The fashion magazine *InStyle* (2014) recently encouraged its readers to wear Same Sky jewellery because it would make them 'Look Good' and 'Do Good', just like 'Halle Berry, Jessica Alba' who '(h)eart Same Sky Jewelry'. The company has been widely endorsed by a range of celebrity politicians such as Hillary Clinton and Jeannette Kagame and political celebrities (Street 2004, 2012). Such high-power endorsements are significant in legitimising LeFrak's business venture and humanitarian project.

The founding of Same Sky is deeply entwined with the life history of Francine LeFrak. The daughter of the real estate magnate Samuel J. LeFrak,[2] she did not join the family company, which was passed down to her elder brother, but embarked on a career as a theatrical, television and film producer, social entrepreneur, and philanthropist (particularly for the Christopher and Dana Reed Foundation). More recently, LeFrak has become an occasional columnist for the *Huffington Post*, where she writes on ethical trade, ethical consumption, women's philanthropy, and women's rights and empowerment. In 2013, alongside celebrity philanthropist such as Bono and Bill Gates, she was also a speaker at 2013 Forbes 400 Philanthropy Summit held at the United Nations. We might think of her as an *achieved* rather than *ascribed* or *attributed* celebrity, having initially become known to the American public through her producing skills (Rojek 2001, 17–18), like so many other celebrity philanthropists who seek to change the world through their ethical interventions, whether in discourse or practice (Hansen 2006) or both.[3] LeFrak is well connected, has considerable personal wealth, and has 'access to places, events and people that most of us do not' (Brockington 2014, 113). An unofficial biography in the *New York Social Diary* gives us insight into her close connections with powerful people 'who wield all kinds of creative, financial and political influence' (Colombia n.d.). LeFrak's artistic work, however, has tended to focus on different expressions of injustice such as women in prison, sexual assault, and complex family dynamics. Her films have been shown at many of the most prestigious international film festivals, including Cannes, London, and Sundance.

For the purpose of this chapter, it is interesting to note that LeFrak does not define herself as a feminist in a radical sense; however, she is quite adamant in her attempt to bring attention to global gender inequalities. Her self-description is that of a person who has been inspired by her father's ambitions and, as such, possesses what might be commonly perceived as certain 'masculine' personal traits. Whether this is a conscious attempt to blur gender boundaries so as to assume that masculinity is something that can be worn quite comfortably by women and men is difficult to know. However, her own interpretation of masculinity carries features of stereotypical assumptions about men's power rather than adhering to a more fluid masculine gender identity. This is interesting because, while the public Francine LeFrak persona could be described as an expression of the values usually associated with feminism, feminism is not a label that she often assigns to her activism. At least not quite in the same way as Beyonce, Angelina Jolie, and Emma Watson have recently done (Bergman Rosamond 2016).

LeFrak's own life history and gender(ed) self-identity are powerfully recounted in an article entitled 'How I Became my Father: Generations of Visions'. Like other famous people, she possesses a private and public self, with the latter being a 'staged activity, in which the human actor presents a front or a face to others while keeping a significant portion of the self in reserve' (Rojek 2001, 11). LeFrak does not seem to problematise her particular front or face as situated within class and racial privileges, but rather visibly highlights the virtues of the entrepreneurial traits she believes to share with her late father: 'fearless, self-willed, a go-getter, and so on . . . ' Her father enriched himself while carrying through safe and affordable housing projects for the New York middle classes. LeFrak (2012a) now states, 'I now use all the traits that my father passed on to me towards my dream for global gender equality'. Unproblematically, but not uncommonly (Fraser 2009), she derives her contributions to global gender equality invoking masculine traits and practices associated with the quintessential neoliberal subject – the competitive, individual entrepreneur (Cf. Venn 2009).

Echoing the story of fair trade pioneer Edna Ruth Byler, but also that of many affluent women celebrity travellers who have discovered poverty and conflict in faraway lands, including Mia Farrow, Madonna, Jane Fonda, Angelina Jolie, and others, LeFrak seeks to use her power and status to bring attention and empower distant other women (Mostafanezhad 2015; Bergman Rosamond 2016). She discovered Rwanda (and Rwandan women) during the eight years she spent filming *100 Days of Darkness*. Although the film was never completed, LeFrak was left with a keen desire to assist in the process of women reclaiming peace and rebuilding their lives (Same Sky n.d.). Influenced by the writings of Harvard Professor Swanee Hunt's *This Was Not Our War* and of Muhammad Yunus' *Banker to the Poor* but also her self-proclaimed 'love affair' with art and objects of beauty and gift-giving that embodies 'human connections and positive energy', in 2008 she founded the company Same Sky with an ancillary foundation by the same name. Relations with Fair Winds Trading founder Willa Shalit, a fair trade businesswoman, and Mary Fisher, activist, artist, and philanthropist, enabled LeFrak to identify the Rwandan business with which she would partner, Gahaya Links. This also helped her to decide what product she would select in seeking to empower the Rwandan women that had been left without a livelihood after the 1994 genocide. She opted for beaded jewellery, such as the bracelets we show in the photograph below.

The story of how Same Sky was founded is mainly an autobiography in which the distant other woman is largely epiphenomenal. LeFrak's salvific efforts, as recounted in the Same Sky website, seem to owe little to sustained encounters or conversations directly with the genocide survivors and HIV-positive women she wants to employ. This is commonplace amongst celebrity well-doers who dedicate themselves to a particular cause without actively engaging with or listening to the desires, wishes, aspiration, and knowledge of women and men themselves (Chouliaraki 2013; Kapoor 2013). As Catia Gregoratti found during her fieldwork in Rwanda, the recruitment of the artisans is carried out, primarily Gahaya Links under the assumption that assembling jewellery is women want to do and can do best.

Figure 7.1   Beaded bracelets Photo taken by Catia Gregoratti, Gahaya Links, Kigali, Rwanda, August 2014.

In the following letter to the supporters of the Same Sky, there are deep auto-biographical references to LeFrak's individual life journey and the emotional connections she seeks to establish between herself, her celebrity supporters, and women living a world away.

> Dear Same Sky Supporter,
> Never did I think that my life's journey would bring me to own a company based in Rwanda. But sometimes life's plans are taken on a different course simply because of the people that you meet and the stories that they tell you. If you allow people to touch your earth in a certain way it changes you forever. Nine years ago this happened to me, I was so deeply affected by the lives and stories of the HIV+ women who had survived the Rwandan Genocide. I felt so compelled to offer them a hand-up not a handout, and to shed light on their powerful journey towards reconciliation.
> With your help women are now lifting themselves out of poverty. Each piece of jewelry acts as a ribbon to the courageous artisans who made it. When you wear the jewelry you are promoting change, alleviating poverty and empowering women living a world away. Not only will you look beautiful, you will also be connected to other likeminded people who want to change the world by the way they shop.
> On behalf of the artisans and the artisans and the Same Sky team, we thank you and welcome you to the Same Sky family where we are all agents for hope and change. . . .
> (Same Sky website snapshot taken in 2013, on file with the authors)

There is a clear tendency on the part of LeFrak to couch the story of her business venture within her emotions and past encounters, enrolling each individual supporter to buy a piece of jewellery to lift out of poverty a disempowered Rwandan woman. These pieces of jewellery – which we previously defined as empowering commodities – carry symbolic, aesthetic, material, and gendered attributes. Simply by wearing a bracelet, one can make a difference to the women producers' lives by 'promoting change, alleviating poverty and empowering women living a world away', even if they live in the same but deeply unequal world. This in turn will make the consumers of the products feel 'great' since it enables each one of us to 'give back' (People 2011). This resonates with Chouliaraki's (2013, 5–6) notion of 'post-humanitarianism' that 'manages to turn the ever-expanding economic exchange into a realm of private emotion (. . .) by commodifying "private emotion and philanthropic obligation". The post-humanitarian turn is "self-focused not other-focused"' (Brockington 2014, 23). The Same Sky initiative rests on such emotional identification that supports a neoliberal rendering of development, agency, and empowerment.

Ethical trade and empowerment à la Same Sky

After having investigated how Same Sky came into being and how wedded the initiative is to the life story, emotional connections, and gendered life projects articulated by its founding celebrity filmmaker and entrepreneur, we now move on to a discussion of the Same Sky ethical business model. Aside from being a producer/filmmaker activist, LeFrak defines herself as a 'good marketer' who is in the business of giving Rwandan women employment and 'the opportunity to sell their products' and, as such, promoting their empowerment (UNAIDS 2011). What is more is that she seems to have a preference for 'the celebration of a neoliberal lifestyle of feel good altruism' (Chouliaraki 2013, 4). However, this venture also mirrors colonial trading patterns where the glass bead was used as a lucrative currency for the exchange of slaves and other products. The Same Sky glass beads travel from the global North to Rwanda, where they are assembled by the women employed by the initiative, to be shipped back to the marketplace in New York and sold in luxury shops and online retail spaces. Ironically, however, the empowerment of Rwandan women seems to come at a cost to the environment. Closer to home and mirroring LeFrak's filmography,[4] in 2013 Same Sky started to pilot a jewellery-making scheme in a halfway home for former women prisoners in Jersey City to enable formerly incarcerated women to find employment and regain the confidence to rebuild their lives.

Same Sky is adamant that it is not in the business of providing gifts or aid, or what LeFrak terms a 'hand-out'. The founder's catchphrase here is 'hand-up' empowerment, materialised through the provision of jobs and sustainable wages. The ethics of women's empowerment promoted within the Same Sky trading scheme is firmly rooted in market mechanisms and the wage relation rather than questioning the transformative qualities of consumerism or the notion that poverty alleviation can come from a (piece-rate) wage (see also Hickel 2014). The discourses employed by Same Sky, on their website in particular, encourage us to turn our gaze to the income the artisans are paid, which is 15 to 20 percent higher than the average wages in Sub-Saharan African, a mantra that is continuously reiterated by LeFrak herself in various media outlets. This message has the capacity to add ethical superiority to her project and, in turn, attracts further celebrity endorsement (Wheeler 2013, 63–64). Moreover, and unlike a classical capitalist commodity chain, 100 percent of the net profits are reinvested in the provision of more training and employment directly benefiting other Rwandan women, again a message that is constantly repeated by the initiative's founder. In comparison to cause-related marketing or fair trade products, the percentage allocated to the cause of women's empowerment is astounding (Hawkins 2012). By reinvesting 100 percent of the net profits, LeFrak can escape the common criticism of celebrity philanthropists that they 'and their sponsors get much more out of support for charities and causes than they give, given the enormous commercial value of the increased visibility' (Van Krieken 2012, 115). Yet the nature and channels of redistribution are more opaque and largely piecemeal.

This is ethically problematic and raises interesting questions about the collective agency and knowledge of the producers themselves. Like Angelina Jolie's many attempts to bring attention to the victims of sexual violence in conflict (Bergman Rosamond 2016) and George Clooney's efforts in the South of Sudan (Daley 2013; Bergman Rosamond 2014), the Same Sky project rests on a fair measure of self-assuredness and assumed knowledge regarding the conditions and agency of local women, and lack thereof. What is more, there appears to be a tendency to speak on the behalf of a cosmopolitan moral order (we all live under the same sky after all) in which cultural difference and intersectional attributes have no real significance, a discourse that is omnipresent within celebrity diplomacy (Cooper 2008) and humanitarianism more broadly (Bergman Rosamond 2015).

Empowerment à la Same Sky is not only consonant with the functioning and deepening of a transnational market for empowering commodities but also with a hegemonic conception of empowerment as enabled through consumerism. Empowerment qua economic empowerment has gained much traction within contemporary neoliberal development discourses and intervention, which casts poverty as being determined by the lack of access to markets (Utting 2012), and states not allowing markets to function smoothly. LeFrak's activism is situated within neoliberalism more broadly, but it is also an outflow of contemporary celebrity culture, which 'is a central mechanism in structuring the market of human sentiments' (Rojek 2001, 14). Moreover, 'celebrities are commodities in the sense that consumers desire to possess them' (Rojek 2001, 14). The celebrity endorsement of the Same Sky project and its products is part of that 'market of human sentiments' since by buying a bracelet, one can get to be a little bit more like one's favourite celebrity activist while feeling good about one's ethical selfhood. Indeed '(c)onsumers are not merely part of a market of commodities, they are also part of a market of sentiments' (Rojek 2001, 14). In this transaction, the significance of the women producers vanishes.

With the privileging of the economic over the political, the nurturing of the industrious, entrepreneurial women over conscientisation and collective agency (Mohanty 1997; Batliwala 2007; Cornwall and Edwards 2014) comes an understanding that some inequalities will be levelled out, at least for the women chosen to work for Same Sky. Same Sky makes us see and narrates empowerment only through the (small) economic progress and the reinvestment of women's wages in housing, health, or children's education. A number of questions do not feature under Same Sky's rubric of empowerment such as how or if women organise within and beyond the workplace or whether time and spaces for collective debates and discussions are made available. Empowerment seems to be coterminous with survival rather than broader social, political, and economic transformations (cf. Wilson 2011). The celebrity supporters of Same Sky are surprisingly silent on this topic, and LeFrak herself is not in the business of much self-reflection or irony (Brassett 2009; Bergman Rosamond 2011). Likewise, magazines and newspapers do not offer much in terms of critical engagement with the Same Sky initiative, rather reporting on its virtues in an apolitical fashion.

Working black women in different 'backyards'

Discussions around so-called ethical commodities are often contextualised within the critique of commodity fetishism developed in the first volume of Karl Marx's *Capital*. Fetishism reduces commodities to things with a life of their own and works alongside the masking of social relations production and exchange. Fetishism, in late capitalism, is becoming 'pervasive and intensifying' (Hudson and Hudson 2003). Particularly in the so-called Global North, unless a major industrial disaster (e.g., Rana Plaza) forces us to read or hear about the processes by which the commodities we buy were created, most of the time, our thoughts and emotions are divorced from concerns for the lives of producers. Like other fair trade goods, Same Sky's 'empowering commodities' partially attempt to engender a process of de-fetishisation. In setting up a business model centred on caring for or, rather, economically empowering women, depicting and narrating women's work and livelihoods is a central communication strategy at the point of exchange (e.g., the website where Same Sky semi-luxurious bracelets, necklaces, and earrings are sold). We, the audience, are also being assured that its business model is sound and trustworthy. Why would it not be when the likes of Hillary and Chelsea Clinton as well as Halle Berry and Ben Affleck are wearing the bracelets proudly on the Same Sky website and in various fashion magazines?

When we virtually meet five women artisans on the Same Sky website, the first image that appears is that of black nimble fingers engaged in the deeply gendered work of crocheting tiny beads. Whether in Rwanda or in the halfway house of Jersey City, which Same Sky terms 'our own backyard', all we see are pictures of black women who crochet, smile, hug, or are being photographed next to Francine LeFrak or black women who hold or display the final products of their labour but seldom wear them. Unlike more robust ethical trade or corporate social responsibility initiatives (Richey and Ponte 2011, 172–175), we find nothing about the actual conditions of work or the dignity at work that Same Sky promises. The problem here is not a lack of information, transparency, or social accounting, but that the images and stories that (partly) unveil processes of production and daily life are part and parcel of the development fantasy the consumer buys into to reaffirm its pleasure and identity (Wright 2004; Kapoor 2013). That sense of goodness and playfulness is reinforced by celebrity endorsement (Richey and Ponte 2011).

The consumers' gaze is directed not only to images of women producers but also to oral and written biographies that reproduce a before-and-after story akin to the 'Lazarus Effect' analysed by Richey and Ponte in the context (RED) products. Before the arrival of Same Sky, artisans narrate history of rape, contraction of HIV/AIDS, and broken and insecure lives. For example, after being given employment, Solina – a Rwandan artisan – has now a home and peace of mind. She can feed her four children, and her immunity has also improved (Same Sky n.d.). Individual stories of contentment and achievement are not only imbued with gendered and stereotypical ideologies and ethical expressions of good motherhood, but also of self-improvement (i.e., the acquisition of means of subsistence) realised through nothing other than the wage relation and the commercial exchange for the empowering commodity. Moreover, in a YouTube video, we hear one of the artisans recounting, 'I hope you don't forget us' (Same Sky 2011, minute 4:27). Hence, the relationships of dependency between the hard-working woman and the Northern employer/philanthropist/celebrity/gender equality advocate are subtly revealed. Or to put it differently, what would happen to the

Rwandan and Jersey artisans if Same Sky fails to sell the semi-luxurious jewellery (cf. Mies 1998, 134–135)? Or if the celebrities endorsing the jewellery should opt for another project and exercise their ethical agency in some other way (Bergman Rosamond 2015)?

Feel-good shopping and empowerment

> Over 50% of our customers are repeat customers. In the same way that many Americans have become addicted to cheap goods, I have seen many people become addicted to quality products and the feel-good shopping that supplies our Rwandan artisans with food, medicine, mattresses and their own homes, all of which resonates with our human values.
>
> (LeFrak 2012b)

Consumption, or 'feel-good shopping', is the primary mechanism through which the empowerment of the hard-working other is achieved, and celebrities would seem to sustain this process. This is captured in another slogan used by Same Sky: 'We Employ. You Empower'. An individual act of consumption realised through the market is framed as an act setting in motion transformative changes that require little time or political efforts. The symptoms of gender inequality are seemingly addressed with the same neoliberal market-based mechanism that sustain many of these inequalities, leaving little room for progressive politics or radical transformations of such injustices. We are not invited to question the broader neoliberal forces and structures within which Same Sky operates and never questions. Rather we, and the celebrities that endorse Same Sky, help to sustain that particular economic model of development, with all its shortcomings. The political economy of gender and development is delegated to the market for Same Sky jewellery, where Same Sky and its celebrity endorsers reassure the consumer that empowerment is being delivered.

The 'you' that forms part of a virtuous circle of 'women helping women' is deeply gendered and sexualised. The employment of gendered language constructs women as shoppers caring about their own beautification and being fashionable rather than being committed to transformative practices of feminist solidarity across borders (Ferguson 2009) but also care for the distant other through shopping. These tropes are omnipresent in Same Sky's publicity and marketing. But this 'you' – a homogenous 'woman' who shops to rescue (an)other homogenous 'woman' – also needs to be problematised in terms of class and other intersectional traits. Unlike cause-related marketing or fair trade products (e.g., bottled water), which, despite having a premium price attached to them, are not completely out of reach for different classes, Same Sky bracelets are sold within a price range that goes from $40 to $400 (USD). It is a very small minority that can afford the luxury of empowering the other woman through market-based mechanisms. For Wright (2004), ethical, conscious shopping reprises an imperialist legacy of a minority that saves the majority world, concomitantly opening up questions on whether development can be achieved without a reduction in consumption or, we would add, without an overhaul in relations of production, social reproduction, and consumption.

Concluding reflections

Our account has centred on Francine LeFrak's efforts to empower women through her Same Sky initiative that provides employment to the other woman within borders (New Jersey) and beyond borders (Rwanda). We have shown, on the basis of LeFrak's own self-narratives, that her family background, her artistic experiences, mobilisation of emotive connections, and self-professed marketing skills are key to her mission. Although not an A-list celebrity, LeFrak has a global audience of sorts at her disposal, and the Same Sky founder is very well connected and figures frequently in American media. As we have shown, her products are proudly worn by mega stars, both politician celebrities and celebrity politicians (Street 2012). Her power (Marshall 1997) emerges from her privileged position within American society, her artistic achievements, and perceived authenticity, as expressed in her care for the other woman. Interestingly enough, there appears to be little attempt in American media outlets to put her achievements under scrutiny. Rather the goodness of her business initiative is accepted on face value. For example, LeFrak's dual contributions to the arts in France and the US and her humanitarianism at home and abroad were celebrated in 2013 when she received a Chevalier of the Legion of Honour by the French Ambassador to the US. The French Ambassador stated amongst other things that:

> Several years ago, in this spirit of improving the world, you courageously left a Hollywood career to start a fair-trade business in Rwanda. In 2008 you founded Same Sky, a socially conscious jewellery line that provides employment to HIV-positive women who survived the Genocide in Rwanda. This business enables the women involved to earn a sustainable income through which they provide food, education and healthcare to their families. And you are currently in the process of exporting this successful fair-trade business model to the United States. You once said: "the concept of an empowered woman changed my life." Well, you most certainly have changed these women's lives, as you give them, as you say, "a hand up and not a handout," "a trade instead of an aid." In short, you don't only provide help; rather you give them a sense of pride and dignity. . . . And through your foundation, the LeFrak Foundation, you fight to promote the full recognition of women throughout the globe. Dear Francine, tonight we honor your commitment to universal values that France holds dear. "Liberté, égalité, fraternité," as our national motto proclaims; you link these three beloved words together. . . .
>
> (Embassy of France in Washington 2013)

LeFrak's 'staged' public persona (Rojek 2001, 11) is portrayed as being angelic (almost saintly) and honourable. In other settings, she has been described as 'a born giver since she was five (as a girl she once invited an entire hat union back to her house), realized she could do more to help women on the ground' (Upbin 2013). Her generosity is thus inscribed in her private and public persona, lending credence to her ethical business venture. Little effort, to our knowledge, has been made to deconstruct the LeFrak's front or brand, as her humanitarian deeds are constructed within language of unquestionable goodness. Moreover, her situatedness within a privileged family structure, within contemporary 'celebrity culture' (Holmes and Redmond 2006) and 'celebrity society' (van Krieken 2012) as well as personal connectedness to US entertainment industry, have all enabled her as a child and as a woman to help others and has not been much debated. Yet she is part of a privileged power structure that is situated within neoliberal language and practices. The average American or global Internet consumer, in particular in times of economic crisis and unemployment, could not afford to purchase a piece of LeFrak's ethical jewellery and, as such, end up being *deprived* of the feel-good celebrity-endorsed sentiment that other more privileged consumers are free to enjoy.

Notes

1 Here we can recall the peace baskets sold by retailer Macy's but also a whole host of products sold by Walmart as part of its women's empowerment initiatives.
2 LeFrak Organization Inc. is now counted as one of the largest private real estate development companies in the world. Besides real estate, the company is also active in oil and gas exploration and financial investments.
3 Here we favour a broad notion of celebrity that captures LeFrak's privileged status and reputation, while recognising that she might not qualify as a mega star or an entertainer/activist in the same fashion as Angelina Jolie, George Clooney, or Sean Penn. Celebrities come in different shapes and forms though, with celebrity culture and digital media enabling the 'publicisation of the self' whereby our self-stories are told to 'micropublics' (Marshall 2014, 164) 'whether those that are massively large as achieved by popular artists or those that are set up by smaller players whose desires of presenting a public self and maintaining a following are much more modest' (ibid.). Against the backdrop of this discussion, it becomes less relevant whether a particular individual is a *real* celebrity or not. What matters is that person's wish to put their persona (Marshall 2013) out there for public consumption.
4 In the early 1990s, LeFrak produced for HBO the film *Prison Stories: Women on the Inside*.

References

Batliwala, S. (2007) 'Taking the Power Out of Empowerment: An Experiential Account', *Development in Practice*, 17 (4–5): 557–565.

Bergman Rosamond, A. (2011) 'The Cosmopolitan-Communitarian Divide and Celebrity Anti-War Activism', in L. Tsaliki, A. Huraliasand and C.A. Frangonikolopoulos (eds.) *Transnational Celebrity Activism in Global Politics: Changing the World?*, Chicago: Chicago University Press: 63–82.

Bergman Rosamond, A. (2013) 'Världskändisar, kosmopolitismochinternationellpolitik', *Internasjonal Politikk*, 71 (4): 561–570.

Bergman Rosamond, A. (2014) 'The Moral Agency and Surveillance of George Clooney-Celebrity Contestations of Sovereignty and Violence', paper presented at the International Studies Association 55th Annual Convention, March 26–29, Toronto.

Bergman Rosamond, A. (2015) 'Humanitarian Relief Worker Sean Penn: A Contextual Story', in L.A. Richey (ed.) *Celebrities as New Development Actors: When Does Context Matter?*, Abingdon: Routledge: 149–169.

Bergman Rosamond, A. (2016) 'The Digital Politics of Celebrity Activism Against Sexual Violence: Angelina Jolie as Global Mother', in L.J. Shepherd and C. Hamilton (eds.) *Popular Culture and World Politics in the Digital Age*, Abingdon: Routledge: 101–118.

Blair, C. (2011) 'Same Sky: Every Women, One Dream', [online] Available: http://cherieblair. org/features-videos/2010/05/same-sky-every-woman-one-dream.html [accessed 28 March 2016].

Brassett, J. (2009) 'British Irony, Global Justice: A Pragmatic Reading of Chris Brown, Banksy and Ricky Gervais', *Review of International Studies*, 35 (1): 219–245.

Brockington, D. (2009) *Celebrity and the Environment: Fame, Wealth and Power in Conservation*, London: Zed Books.

Brockington, D. (2014) *Celebrity Advocacy and International Development*, Abingdon: Routledge.

Chouliaraki, L. (2013) *The Ironic Spectator: Solidarity in the Age of Post-Humanitarianism*, Cambridge: Polity Press.

Colombia, P.D. (n.d.) 'List: Francine LeFrak', *New York Social Diary*, [online] Available: www.newyorksocialdiary.com/list/120.php [accessed 13 February 2015].

Cooper, A.F. (2008) *Celebrity Diplomacy*, London: Paradigm Publishers.

Cornwall, A. and Edwards, J. (eds.) (2014) *Feminism, Empowerment and Development*, London: Zed Books.

Daley, P. (2013) 'Rescuing African Bodies: Celebrities, Consumerism and Neoliberal Humanitarianism', *Review of African Political Economy*, 40 (137): 375–393.

Embassy of France in Washington (2013) 'Francine LeFrak Chevalier of the Legion of Honor', *Speech by Ambassador François Delattre*, New York, 26 November [online] Available: www.ambafrance-us.org/spip.php?article5095 [accessed 23 March 2016].

Ferguson, A. (2009) 'Feminist Paradigms of Solidarity and Justice', *Philosophical Topics*, 37 (2): 161–177.

Fraser, N. (2009) 'Feminism, Capitalism and the Cunning of History', *New Left Review*, 56: 97–117.

Gregoratti, C., Roberts, A. and Tornhill, S. (2018) 'Corporations, Gender Equality and Women's Empowerment: Feminism Co-opted?', in A. Nölke and C. May (eds.) *Handbook of the International Political Economy of the Corporation*, Cheltenham: Edward Elgar: 93–105.

Hansen, L. (2006) *Security as Practice: Discourse Analysis and the Bosnian War*, Abingdon: Routledge.

Hawkins, R. (2012) 'Shopping to Save Lives: Gender and Environment Theories Meet Ethical Consumption', *Geoforum*, 43: 750–759.

Hickel, J. (2014) 'The "Girl Effect": Liberalism, Empowerment and the Contradictions of Development', *Third World Quarterly*, 35 (8): 1355–1373.

Holmes, S. and Redmond, S. (2006) *Framing Celebrity-New Directions in Celebrity Culture*, Abingdon: Routledge.

Hudson, I. and Hudson, M. (2003) 'Removing the Veil? Commodity Fetishism, Fair Trade and the Environment', *Organization Environment*, 16 (4): 413–430.

InStyle (2014) 'Look Good, Do Good! Halle Berry, Jessica Alba Heart Same Sky Jewellery', [online] Available: http://news.instyle.com/2014/02/21/look-good-do-good-halle-berry-jessica-alba-heart-same-sky-jewelry/ [accessed 23 March 2016].

Kapoor, I. (2013) *Celebrity Humanitarianism: The Ideology of Global Charity*, Abingdon: Routledge.

LeFrak, F. (2012a) 'How I became My Father: Generations of Vision', *Huffington Post*, [online] Available: www.huffingtonpost.com/francine-lefrak/same-sky-lefrak-_b_1570958.html [accessed 23 March 2016].

LeFrak, F. (2012b) 'We're All in This together', *Huffington Post*, [online] Available: www.huffingtonpost.com/francine-lefrak/were-all-in-this-together_b_1823670.html [accessed 23 March 2016].

Marshall, P.D. (1997) *Celebrity and Power: Fame in Contemporary Culture*, Minneapolis: University of Minnesota Press.

Marshall, P.D. (2013) 'Personifying Agency: The Public-Persona-Place-Issue Continuum', *Celebrity Studies*, 4 (3): 369–371.

Marshall, P.D. (2014) 'Persona Studies: Mapping the Proliferation of the Public Self', *Journalism*, 14 (2): 153–170.

Mies, M. (1998) *Patriarchy and Accumulation on a World Scale*, London: Zed Books.

Mitchell, K. (2016) 'Celebrity Humanitarianism, Emotions, and the Rise of Neoliberal Citizenship', *Global Networks*, 16 (3): 288–306.

Mohanty, C.T. (1997) 'Women Workers and Capitalist Scripts: Ideologies of Domination, Common Interests and the Politics of Solidarity', in M.J. Alexander and C.T. Mohanty (eds.) *Feminist Genealogies, Colonial Legacies and Democratic Futures*, New York: Routledge.

Mostafanezhad, M. (2015) 'Angelina Jolie and the Everyday Geopolitics of Celebrity Humanitarianism in a Thailand-Burma Border Town', in L.A. Richey (ed.) *Celebrities as New Development Actors: When Does Context Matter?*, Abingdon: Routledge: 27–47.

Mubanda Rasmussen, L. (2015) 'Madonna in Malawi-Celebritized Interventions and Local Politics of Development in the South', in L.A. Richey (ed.) *Celebrities as New Development Actors: When Does Context Matter?*, Abingdon: Routledge: 48–69.

Pearson, R. (2007) 'Beyond Women Workers: Gendering CSR', *Third World Quarterly*, 28 (4): 731–749.

People (2011) 'Gifts to Give: Same Sky's Prosperity Bracelets', [online] Available: http://stylenews.peoplestylewatch.com/2011/11/30/gifts-to-give-same-skys-prosperity-bracelets/ [accessed 23 March 2016].

Prügl, E. (2015) 'Neoliberalising Feminism', *New Political Economy*, 20 (4): 614–631.

Prügl, E. and True, J. (2014) 'Equality Means Business? Governing Gender through Transnational Public-Private Partnerships', *Review of International Political Economy*, 21 (6): 1137–1169.

Richey, L.A. and Budabin, A.C. (2016) 'Celebritizing Conflict: How Ben Affleck Sells the Congo to Americans', *Humanity Journal*, 7 (1): 27–46.

Richey, L.A. and Ponte, S. (2011) *Brand Aid: Shopping Well to Save the World*, Minneapolis and London: University of Minnesota Press.

Roberts, A. (2012) 'Financial Crisis, Financial Firms. . . . And Financial Feminism? The Rise of "Transnational Business Feminism" and the Necessity of Marxist-Feminist IPE', *Socialist Studies/Étudessocialistes*, 8 (2): 85–108.

Roberts, A. (2015) 'The Political Economy of Transnational Business Feminism: Problematizing the Corporate-Led Gender Equality Agenda', *International Feminist Journal of Politics*, 17 (2): 209–231.

Rojek, C. (2001) *Celebrity*, London: Reaction Books.

Same Sky (n.d.) 'Our History', [online] Available: www.samesky.com/pages/our-history [accessed 26 March 2016].

Same Sky (n.d.) 'Solina', [online] Available: www.samesky.com/pages/solina [accessed 26 March 2016].

Same Sky (2011) 'Same Sky in Rwanda', [online] Available: www.youtube.com/watch? v=VLIqR0A6l3U [accessed 26 March 2016].

Street, J. (2004) 'Celebrity Politicians: Popular Culture and Political Representation', *The British Journal of Politics and International Relations*, 6 (4): 435–452.

Street, J. (2012) 'Do Celebrity Politics and Celebrity Politicians Matter?', *The British Journal of Politics and International Relations*, 14 (3): 346–356.

UNAIDS (2011) 'Women Under the Same Sky', *UNAIDS Featured Story*, 11 March [online] Available: www.unaids.org/en/resources/presscentre/featurestories/2011/march/ 20110310samesky/ [accessed 26 March 2016].

Upbin, B. (2013) 'Francine LeFrak: Women Can Exit Poverty Through Business', *Forbes*, 17 November [online] Available: https://web.archive.org/web/20141015130142/www. forbes.com/sites/bruceupbin/2013/11/17/francine-lefrak-one-powerful-way-lift-african-women-out-of-poverty [accessed 26 March 2016].

Utting, P. (2012) 'The Challenge of Political Empowerment', *Capacity.org: A Gateway for Capacity Development*, [online] Available: www.capacity.org/capacity/opencms/en/ topics/ chains/the-challenge-of-political-empowerment.html [accessed 26 March 2016].

Van Krieken, R. (2012) *Celebrity Society*, Abingdon: Routledge.

Venn, C. (2009) 'Neoliberal Political Economy, Politics and Colonialism: A Transcolonial Genealogy of Inequality', *Theory, Society and Culture*, 26 (6): 623–643.

Wheeler, M. (2013) *Celebrity Politics*, Cambridge: Polity Press.

Wilson, K. (2011) 'Race, Gender and Neoliberalism: Changing Visual Representations in Development', *Third World Quarterly*, 32 (2): 315–331.

Wright, C. (2004) 'Consuming Lives, Consuming Landscapes: Interpreting Advertisements for Cafédirect Coffees', *Journal of International Development*, 16 (5): 665–680.

Yrjölä, R. (2012) 'From Street into the World: Towards a Politicised Reading of Celebrity Humanitarianism', *The British Journal of Politics and International Relations*, 14 (3): 357–374.

8 Co-opting the 'Losers'

Bob Geldof and neoliberal activism after the financial crisis

Nathan Farrell

Among the more effective means of representing a celebrity's activism as the outcome of a genuine concern over social or environmental issues, and thus encouraging audiences to interpret the celebrity as authentic, are the longevity of the celebrity's activist career and the successful depiction of them as non-partisan. The first of these demonstrates the celebrity's commitment to the cause, as opposed to their activism being prompted by social trends or a particular blip in their public approval that necessitated them being seen to 'give back to the community'. The second suggests the independent nature of their politics and that they are not motivated by institutional allegiance or loyalty to a political party. Their perceived independence from centres of political and economic power helps to solidify their image as representatives of 'the people'.

However, in this chapter, I want to outline some of the deeper ways in which celebrity activism can be very closely aligned with political and economic power by demonstrating the consistencies between some of the key instances of Western celebrity activism and the overarching political-economic doctrines that governed state policy at the time. To do this, I will offer an analysis of the rock musician and political activist Bob Geldof. Geldof has enjoyed both a long career as a political activist, and has also maintained an image, within popular discourse, as an impartial political outsider and 'punk diplomat' (Cooper 2008) while organising some of the largest moments of celebrity activism: Live Aid and Live 8. In this chapter, I argue that such distinctions are quite superficial, and I demonstrate how, throughout Geldof's career, his activism is very much consistent with the form of neoliberal governance that was dominant at the time. Charting his activist career from the 1980s to the present day, I show how his work conformed to Thatcherite roll-back neoliberal in the 1980s and Blairite roll-out neoliberalism in the 1990s. I then argue that after the 2008 financial crises, Geldof has aligned himself with a group of committed business leaders and activists who are working to reinvigorate the neoliberal project. These 'conscience capitalists' accept many of the arguments levelled by neoliberalism's critics but attempt to subsume them into the project by arguing that neoliberalism accounts for social and environmental externalities and solves them through market mechanisms. As such, their efforts facilitate further neoliberal colonisation, and Geldof serves as a key celebrity champion for this. My argument in this chapter is *not* that Geldof is not genuine or that he is inauthentic in his concerns over social problems but rather that his proposed solutions have moved with the prevailing current of neoliberal thinking, which contrasts more simplistic readings of his outsider status.

Born in the Dublin suburb of Dún Laoghaire in 1951, Bob Geldof rose to fame as the lead singer of the rock group The Boomtown Rats. The group enjoyed chart success between the late 1970s and early 1980s with a number of UK hits. When the group's success began to falter in the mid-1980s, Geldof found himself struggling to publicise his band's music and, by his own admission, was at home on the night of October 23, 1984, when he ideally should have been out touring (Gerard 2005). This, however, allowed him to see BBC journalist Michael Buerk's report form the Korem refugee camp in Ethiopia in which Buerk relayed the effects of a famine of 'biblical proportions'. Like many who witnessed Buerk's report, Geldof was deeply moved and inspired to act. This marked a turning point in Geldof's life as he became increasingly involved in international development and anti-poverty activism. Using his music industry contacts, he organised the charity single 'Do They Know it's Christmas?', which reportedly raised over £150m for famine relief (Johnson 2009). He also established the Band Aid Charitable Trust to facilitate the distribution of the donations. Geldof went on to organise Live Aid: two simultaneous fundraising rock concerts held on July 13, 1985, in London and Philadelphia. While his philanthropic work made him popular with large sections of the public, this was also helped by his brash style of personal communication about important political issues, his 'no-nonsense' demeanour and his willingness to conflict with the those in political power, which Geldof credits to his problems with 'authority' and people in power (Morris 2014).

By the 2004, then-UK Prime Minister Tony Blair invited Geldof to form part of the newly formed Commission for Africa with a brief to 'define the challenges facing Africa, and to provide clear recommendations on how to support the changes needed to reduce poverty' (Commission for Africa 2005). The two's paths had crossed before when Blair formed the Band Aid cross-party Parliamentary Committee in 1985 (Bishop and Green 2008, 205). In 2005 Geldof co-organised Live 8, a series of pop concerts held simultaneously around the globe, which was aligned with the concurrent Make Poverty History (MPH) campaign. Timed to coincide with the UK's presidency of the EU and hosting of the Group of Eight (G8) summit in 2005, MPH was a coalition of more than five hundred organisations, including numerous prominent UK-based NGOs, trade unions, and faith groups that sought to mobilise large sections of the Western population around demands of the G8 governments concerning trade justice, dropping developing world debt, and providing more and better aid (Make Poverty History n.d.). More than this, MPH sought to raise the profile of global, specifically African, poverty and position it at the centre of mainstream political debate.

Throughout this period, Geldof was also actively pursuing a musical career and enjoying success as a businessman and entrepreneur within the television industry, in particular through his ownership of the production companies Planet 24 and Ten Alps.

'Punk diplomacy': the activism of the outsider

An initial reading of Geldof's political activism shows him as the archetypal out-sider. As Cooper explains, Geldof 'communicates *at*, not in conjunction *with*, other actors [. . . and so he is] not naturally *of* the diplomatic world' [original emphasis] (Cooper 2008, 52, see also Wheeler 2013, 153–156). Indeed Geldof has a stated 'poor opinion of all politicians, regardless of colour or ideology' (Blundy and Val-lely 1985, 37). For such reasons, he is labelled by Cooper as 'an antidiplomat'; a moniker that resonates quite closely with Geldof's self-appraisal as a practitioner of 'punk diplomacy' (Geldof 1986). While no concise definition of punk diplo-macy has been offered, it is exemplified by Geldof's deviation from established diplomatic protocols, set out by Cooper as including the wearing of smart attire, a 'capacity for discretion', and a 'love for the application of ambiguity'. In contrast, Geldof is a 'verbal machine, capable of pouring out torrents of declaratory state-ments' (Cooper 2008, 53). While potentially costly to his activism, Geldof's punk diplomacy affords the musician 'enormous potential for saying the unsayable and confronting those in power with problems which aid workers and even diplomats dared not raise for fear of jeopardising long-term relationships' (Geldof 1986, 311). Geldof's outsider status is reflected in corporate media representations of his altercations with Thatcher (Geldof 1986, 292–293; see also Young 1985) and the EEC – the progenitor of the EU – (Merritt 1985) during the Band Aid/Live Aid campaign and declarations within the press during Live 8 that '[n]o leader of a government that didn't put the plight of Africa high up on its agenda escaped a tongue-lashing from the out-spoken former rocker' (Clancy 2005, 8).

However, Geldof's position outside elite political institutions does not automat-ically align him with that of traditional grass-roots lobby groups and non-profit organisations. Indeed, he derides the 'marches and other kinds of protest politics' that such groups use as 'a waste of time' (Geldof 1986, 199). Moreover, Geldof's outsider status places him frequently at odds with what he calls 'the posturings of those who styled themselves as political activists' (Geldof 1986, 165). That Geldof declares no affinity with either Western governments or the established non-profit organisations who often oppose state policy suggests a certain non-partisan nature to his political activism. This is consistent with his oft-repeated phrase, 'I will shake hands with the devil on my left and the devil on my right to get to the people who need help' (Geldof 1986, 398; James 2005). From his per-ceived impartiality and apparent transcendence of the political spectrum, at least as it is understood in popular discourse, Geldof is able to derive a certain amount of social capital. Moreover, that he maintains a reputation as an outsider to the political elite generates solidarity capital as a specific form of social capital for Geldof (see Campanella in this volume), as he represents 'no constituency but a moral one' (Geldof 1986, 397). This includes solidarity with 'ordinary people' in the developed world against political hierarchies, demonstrated by Geldof's role as 'a representative of all the people who made donations to the Band Aid funds' and a 'latterday Everyman' during a Band Aid delegation to Saharan Africa in 1986 (Blundy and Vallely 1985, 66). Moreover, he is able to generate solidarity capital through his connection with 'the poorest of the poor', to whom he is 'totally committed' (Clancy 2005, 8).

Bob Geldof as neoliberal celebrity activist

However, read more deeply, the political activity of Geldof can be seen in a manner, not so much as an outsider, but largely consistent with the overarching ideological orthodoxy of Western political establishments: neoliberalism. Within this chapter, neoliberalism is understood as a political-economic project, which broadly advocates a strong market economic system unhindered by and, in fact, facilitated by the state and the use of the market as a model for other areas of political/social life. In its general sense, neoliberalism concerns 'the capture and reuse of the state in the interests of shaping a pro-corporate, freer-trading "market order"' (Peck 2010, 9). It is important, as some critiques have noted (see McCarthy 2005), to consider neoliberalism not as a monolithic doctrine but as 'an adaptive, mutating and contradictory mode of governance' (Peck 2010, xiii) that is historically and geographically contingent. In the US/UK setting, Jamie Peck and Adam Tickell go some way to charting these different modes of neoliberal governance. They describe the 'roll-back neoliberalism' of the 1980s, marked by 'the active *destruction and discreditation* of Keynesian-welfarist and social-collectivist institutions' [original emphasis] (Peck and Tickell 2002, 384). With an emphasis on private individuals in distinction to collective groupings, its basic principles were to 'minimize the size of government, make space for competitive forces [and] enlarge the scope and reach of the private sector' (Tickell and Peck 2003, 173). Additionally they outline the 'roll-out neoliberalism' of the 1990s and beyond as the phase in which the project 'focused on the purposeful *construction and consolidation* of neoliberalised state forms, modes of governance, and regulatory relations' [original emphasis] (Peck and Tickell 2002, 384). Here the 'neoliberal state is a facilitative, market-managerial presence in matters of capital regulation' (Tickell and Peck 2003, 175). It assists in expanding the reach of markets by opening up to it key economic areas through the normalisation of market-like practices.

Seen through a neoliberal lens, Geldof's activism very much conforms to the dominant forms of neoliberalism found throughout his career as a political activist, as his methods and goals shift along with the evolution of the larger neoliberal project. For example, during the Live Aid campaign of the 1980s, a process of roll-back neoliberalisation was an established influence on UK state policy. Accordingly, Live Aid had a highly visible corporate presence as Pepsi and Kodak ranked among the event's sponsors and British Airways flew musician Phil Collins with much fanfare from the London to Philadelphia concert via Concorde. Additionally these events were articulated in terms of the appropriateness and efficiency of private philanthropic initiatives. For example, Thatcher's Overseas Development minister, Timothy Raison, opined, 'I think that to have people mobilised in this way is magnificent [. . .] The idea that you leave everything to the Government seems to me to be wrong' (quoted in Ezard 1985, 1). Despite much commentary at the time relating Live Aid to the countercultural and anti-corporate spirit of the 1960s and noting how many of the concert's performers were of the baby-boomer generation (see, for example, Shearer 1985; Turner 1986), policy elites were able to frame a mass outpouring of public charity in terms of the proficiency of the rolling back of the state. *The Times*, in its appraisal of Live Aid, surmised that the campaign's supporters were

> responding against institutional inadequacies when they took up Bob Geldof's challenge [. . .] The success of his fund-raising campaign for the sick and starving in Africa is a sign that men and women everywhere felt let down by those great bodies which exist to deal with such disasters. It took a private individual with millions of individuals behind him to break through the red tape of bureaucracy that ensured much-needed relief.
>
> (The Times 1985)

Consistent with this is Geldof's own distrust of the EEC and its member states, which represent for him 'the epitome of wasteful bureaucracy, governmental bungling and, Western arrogance' (Blundy and Vallely 1985, 16).

Geldof's position in this campaign can be aligned with a form of romanticism in which, according to Chouliaraki, the rock star acts as 'the signifier of a true, primordial self against societal constraints' and their music 'glorifies the will of the individual in its heroic [. . .] opposition against structures of power' (Chouliaraki 2013, 119). Crucially, however, this romanticism overlaps with roll-back neoliberal ideas of the rugged, self-reliant individual and provides a culturally potent framework in which the retreat of the state from areas of famine relief and poverty reduction, in favour of the activities of commercial agents, can be legitimised. This process of legitimisation rests, for Chouliaraki, on a discourse of 'romanticist corporatism' that combines the romantic notions of the rock musician with the perceived 'getting things done' ethic of commercial enterprise (Chouliaraki 2013, 120). The two decades that separate Geldof's Live Aid of 1985 and Live 8 of 2005 are marked by what Chouliaraki describes as a 'shift from a romanticist corporatism to an entrepreneurial corporatism', for which the two concerts serve as noticeable examples. Unlike romantic corporatism, entrepreneurial corporatism 'intensifies the market links between the music-media industry complex and the humanitarian field' (Chouliaraki 2013, 132), as the non-profit sector becomes increasingly marketised and individual organisations adopt a more commercial orientation (Wright 2012). This shift can also be observed through a neoliberal lens.

By the 1990s and 2000s, a process of roll-out neoliberalisation was underway. Accordingly, there was a shift away from delegitimizing of the role of the state in aid provision and towards opening up the non-profit sector as a more commercial area that necessitates the influence of the market, facilitated by the state. The ethos of 2005's Live 8 concerts was very much consistent with this. Unlike Live Aid, Live 8 was not aimed at eliciting charitable donations from the public as part of an enterprise outside the state. Instead it sought to mobilise Northern populations to demand action from the G8 regarding African poverty (Make Poverty

History n.d.). In contrast to the at least superficial antagonism between Geldof and the UK political establishment in the 1980s, the relationship between Geldof and then-UK Prime Minister Tony Blair was represented as one of shared goals between two committed campaigners for justice (see, for example, Vallely, Geldof *et al*. 2005, 14). The two men, according to this narrative, began to work closely towards alleviating poverty in Africa. This is also consistent with Geldof's assertion that 'in order to affect change you must engage with the agents of change' (quoted in Lawson 2013), in this case, politicians. As such, UK government officials were seen alongside Geldof and Live 8's key figures, sharing press conferences to articulate their mutual goals of combating poverty by establishing a freer global market order.

Following suit, many media and political commentators saw Live 8 as a clear opportunity to promote the virtues of the market, representing it as the optimal solution to poverty in sub-Saharan Africa, while simultaneously obscuring any role it might have historically played in the creation or exacerbation of poverty. Poverty in Africa was instead understood as largely the outcome of poor leadership or environmental factors in 'a continent still stricken by corruption and conflict' (Baldwin 2005, 9) whose governments were described as 'corrupt' and 'kleptocratic' (Swain 2005, 20). The influences of policies imposed by Northern transnational institutions upon the developing world, which may have facilitated the transfer of wealth from the South to the North, were omitted from much of the coverage within the corporate media at the time – with some exceptions (for example, Lucas and Siva 2005, 27; Monbiot 2005, 21). Instead it was assumed that Africa's politicians 'abhor the accountability that market economics brings' (Times 2005, 17), and the G8 leaders were urged to 'not be distracted from their initial instincts that the best means to secure those noble ends [of poverty reduction] are to promote free trade, free markets and free societies'. Among MPH's celebrity organisers, the rhetoric was much the same; for scriptwriter and MPH co-founder Richard Curtis, 'bad government and poverty go together' (Curtis 2005, 20–21).

However, interviews with representatives of a range of MPH's member organisations paint a picture of a deeply divided movement (see Atkins 2009). For example, John Hilary, then of War on Want, and Benedict Southworth, then of the World Development Movement, argue that the Live 8 concerts took vital media attention away from discussion of poverty and focussed it instead on coverage of celebrity activity. In addition, Hilary expressed frustration that Live 8 concerts were scheduled in such a way that they clashed with prearranged MPH events. First the concerts in London and elsewhere clashed with the MPH march Edinburgh, and second, a further concert in Murrayfield clashed with the MPH march to the G8 summit in Gleneagles. This highlights the tensions between different factions within the MPH coalition and suggests, as Biccum has argued, that the spectacle of Live 8 attempted 'to negate the critiques of various global protesters by stage-managing "democracy-at-work"' (Biccum 2007, 1120, see also, Nash 2008). Consequently, the space in which meaningful critiques of the G8's policies might have occurred was replaced with celebratory images of roll-out neoliberal solutions to poverty.

These tensions were further entrenched when the G8 eventually released its communique, outlining the summit's agreements and establishing future development policies. Divisions immediately emerged between MPH's celebrity spokespeople and many of the NGOs that comprised the coalition. For Geldof, speaking at press conference to mark the communique, it was clear that 'Africa and the poor of that continent have got more from the last three days than they have ever got at any previous summit'. He continued to score the G8 '[o]n aid, 10 out of 10. On debt, eight out of 10' (quoted in Hodkinson 2005, 13, see also Shabi 2005). In terms of trade, Geldof commented that 'this summit, uniquely, decided that enforced liberalisation must no longer take place', allowing him to declare 'mission accomplished' to spontaneous applause from journalists and campaigners (Hodkinson 2005). However, as Brockington amply demonstrates, the post-summit press conference became the point when underlying tensions between the more '"radical outsiders" who felt most comfortable lobbying oppositionally' and the '"moderate insiders" who wanted a more intimate relationship with authority' erupted (Brockington 2014, 65). Crucially, and in contrast, to the 'Punk Diplomat' representations outlined above, Geldof was situated squarely in the latter camp, and he sought in a later op-ed piece to deflect criticisms of him and the G8 as distracting 'side arguments or internal squabbling' (Geldof 2005, 33).

However, by that point it was clear that, despite Geldof's pronouncement that debt cancellation had been cleaved from neoliberal policy enforcement, only eighteen countries would receive 100 percent multilateral debt cancellation. Moreover, the beneficiary nations had just completed nine years of IMF/World Bank neoliberal structural adjustment policies as part of the Heavily Indebted Poor Country (HIPC) scheme (Hodkinson 2005). One such nation that been subjected to the structural adjustment policies is Ethiopia, the nation whose 1984–1985 famine proved a pivotal moment in Geldof's political activism. By 2001, the IMF decided in favour of the Ethiopia 'becoming the 24th country to qualify for debt relief under the Initiative's enhanced framework' (International Monetary Fund 2001). The Ethiopian government had since the early 1990s embarked on a privatisation programme under the auspices of the Ethiopian Privatization Agency (EPA).[1] The programme began by selling off smaller assets such as retail outlets before progressing to the privatisation of larger state initiatives, often within agriculture and largely in partnership with foreign agents.

The scheme is, in all likelihood, a lucrative business opportunity for the numerous foreign – read, developed world – investors. One such group is the private equity firm '8 Miles'. The company is comprised of an investment team with prior experience in a range of financial and private-equity institutions such as Lehman Brothers, Morgan Stanley, Credit Suisse, HSBC, and the Egyptian stock exchange. The company's current chair is its co-founder, Bob Geldof KBE. As the above arguments suggest, Geldof's conversion to, in his own words 'a private equity whore' (quoted in Scott 2012), should come as no surprise, aligning as it does with the prevailing neoliberal common sense of using the (in this case, Ethiopian) state to open up and facilitate business opportunities for private investors. Within 8 Miles' portfolio is a 81 percent interest in the previously state-owned Awash Wine Share Company. 8 Miles have also invested in elini, a private, Kenyan-based company that establishes commodity exchanges in different African nations. Among their achievements is the establishment of the Ethiopian Commodities Exchange (ECX), which has worked to transform the Ethiopian economy into one more ready for direct engagement with foreign investors and integration into the global capitalist system.

As can be seen, while Geldof's representation within popular discourse tends towards him being an anti-authoritarian outsider and 'punk diplomat', such renderings are only superficial in nature. Below the surface, Geldof's activism – leaving aside its successes or failures – has evolved in tandem with the overarching dominant neoliberal ideology. During the 1980s consistencies between Geldof's activism and Thatcherite roll-back neoliberalism can be observed. In the 1990s as the neoliberal project shifted, so too does Geldof's political motivations and modes of operations. In the next section, the consistencies between Geldof's political activism and the broader neoliberal environments in which it occurs are drawn out more fully. They are used to establish a set of expectations about Geldof's politics that can be tested against more recent developments in Western neoliberalism.

Co-opting 'the Losers'

The rifts that developed in the MPH coalition, outlined above, were mirrored by a similar divide between the anti-poverty protesters who took part in MPH-branded marches and attended the Live 8 concerts, on the one hand, and protesters who 'aimed at disrupting the G8, through unlawful civil disobedience' (Biccum 2007, 1121), on the other. The former group targeted the abstract concept of poverty. The 'anti-poverty' protests featured a wide demographic that included the public, entertainment celebrities and members of the political elite, including then-UK Chancellor of the Exchequer, Gordon Brown. The latter group, though also of a varied demographic, did not seem to contain members of the entertainment, political, or economic elites. This group was comprised of coalitions such as 'Dissent!' and 'G8 Alternatives', organisations serving as 'a mechanism for communication and co-ordination [. . .] of resistance to the G8, and capitalism in general' (Dissent! n.d.).

For the corporate media, the anti-G8 protesters – in fact, any of the protesters not demonstrating under the MPH umbrella – were consistently articulated with terms such as 'threat', 'fear', 'anger', 'militant', and 'cynical'. They were described by *The Times*'s David Lister as 'frustrated extremists' and 'a hotchpotch of anarchists and radicals' (Lister 2005, 7). They were also discursively isolated from mainstream society and popular sentiment through representations of them as 'revolutionaries, with their zeal, pleasurable anger and contempt for ordinary folk' (Aaronovitch 2005, 4), who were 'lacking the tacit support of their generation' (Baldwin 2005, 9). For supporting evidence, the press turned to the police, who 'praised the behaviour of' the 'trouble-free' MPH protesters (Lister 2005, 7), but were 'stunned by the level of violence' exhibited by the anti-G8 protesters (Lane 2005, 4–5).

Crucially, Geldof himself derided the anti-G8 protestors as 'a bunch of losers' (quoted in Cramb 2005, 8). 'Losers' is hardly a surprising label for Geldof to use as it fits neatly with the appraisal of protest politics he expressed some two decades earlier. In fact, throughout his career as a political spokesperson and activist, Geldof has displayed some remarkable consistencies in his modes of operation. As such, it could be expected that aspects of his political views would remain unchanged. Drawing on the commentary of Geldof's major campaign activities above, his approach to activism can be loosely summarised as:

1. Deal foremost with the individuals at the top of commercial and non-profit organisations and government departments.
2. Where possible, rely on commercial enterprise and financial investment to get things done.
    This is represented as a 'common sense' and pragmatic method. Contrasting approaches are generally considered unnecessarily bureaucratic or ideologically motivated and therefore suspect.
3. Avoid protests and marches as these are less effective
4. Use the 'proper channels' and do not embarrass (Western) government ministers, unless it is unavoidable or conflicts with point 2.

These points are not always present in Geldof's work, but they do serve as an overarching guide to his political activity. So, for example, while Geldof had some public disagreements with Thatcher and her government, these tended to concern more superficial aspects of his political work that left the deeper ideological convergences between Thatcher and Geldof intact. Geldof's dispute with Thatcher concerning UK tax exemption for the Band Aid charitable single can be distilled down to his entrepreneurial activism being hindered by a specific government bureaucracy. However, philosophically, antagonism to much of state bureaucracy was a position shared by Thatcherism, and so a common ground between the two can be seen. During the 1980s, more of Geldof's ire was directed towards the EEC than the UK state, as the EEC was responsible for more of the 'undergrowth of bureaucracy', which comprised 'the main obstacle in the aid jungle' (Blundy and Vallely 1985, 16) that hindered Geldof's entrepreneurial approach to poverty relief and international development. Such scepticism of Europe, framed in terms of its rather un-neoliberal bureaucracy, permeated much of the Thatcher regime and the discourses with which it is associated (Aitken 2013).

Geldof's approach led him to work exclusively with the most commercially powerful enterprises as corporate sponsors and internationally famous celebrities in an attempt to maximise income for his cause. Consequently, when a minister of Burkina Faso enquired about the possibility of a Burkinian version of Live Aid with local Burkinian musicians, Geldof instructed him – perhaps half-heartedly – to 'scrap the ethnic crap' and instead 'get in some of the American superstars like Michael Jackson and Lionel Richie [. . .] You make a lot of money, they make a lot of money. Got it?' (Blundy and Vallely 1985, 46–48). Importantly, throughout this part of Geldof's campaign, he 'worked through all the proper channels [and . . .] deliberately refrained from attacking the government publically' (Geldof 1986, 395). This policy was adhered to twenty years later when, in 2005, Geldof instructed performers at Live 8 to avoid mentioning the Iraq War and publicly attacking or embarrassing Tony Blair and George Bush (Davies 2005, 2).

The common features of Geldof's approach to political activity, outlined above, have changed little in over thirty years. As such, they can be used to determine Geldof's expected response to a range of emerging political issues and causes. For example, by 2008, the economic landscape had changed significantly since Geldof's Live 8 concerts three years before. Much of the global economy was in a significant state of crisis. As Ivashina and Scharfstein (2010) describe, a credit boom that peaked in 2007 was followed by 'the meltdown of [US] subprime mortgages and all types of securitized products [. . . which] in turn, raised concerns about the solvency and liquidity of financial institutions, becoming a full-blown banking panic'. While governments were quick to intervene in order to 'promote the liquidity and solvency of the financial sector [. . .] cost of corporate and bank borrowing rose substantially, and financial market volatility rose to levels that have rarely, if ever, been seen' (Ivashina and Scharfstein 2010, 319, see also Kotz 2009). A substantial and well-documented global and financial crisis and recession ensued. The significant tax-funded state bailouts provided to some of the larger financial institutions, combined with the implementation of austerity programmes for other sections of society, contributed to an emerging discourse in which a disparate range of protests began to emerge throughout the world. One key vehicle of protest was the Occupy Movement.

For many commentators, the Occupy Wall Street movement began on September 17, 2011, when a group of activists occupied the Zuccotti Park in New York City. The movement took its inspiration from 'the global protest wave' that spread across the Middle East, North Africa, Greece, and Spain (Costanza-Chock 2012, 376). The actions of Occupy Wall Street inspired others, in places such as London, as it was argued that '[o]rdinary people and communities around the world are being devastated by a crisis we did not cause. Our political elites have chosen to protect corporations, financial institutions and the rich at the expense of the majority' (Occupy London n.d.). To many commentators, as Pickerill and Krinsky suggest, Occupy represented 'the moment when resistance to the inequalities of capitalism finally emerged: a tipping point in which the unfairness of bank bailouts juxtaposed against rising personal poverty triggered a moment of clarity of the absurdity of the current economic and political system' (Pickerill and Krinsky 2012, 279).

A protest such as Occupy shares many of its structures, practices, and ideological underpinnings with the anti-G8 protests experienced by Geldof in 2005. Accordingly, it might be expected that Geldof would repeat his critical condemnation, and it would be unsurprising if the self-proclaimed 'private equity whore' would offer a scathing appraisal of a largely anti-capitalist movement that eschews much of his normal modes of operation. Curiously, however, this is not the case. In an interview with journalist Emma Alberici (Alberici 2013), Geldof was asked for his opinion on the movement.

EMMA ALBERICI: So how do you explain the disaster of the Occupy movement
which was –
BOB GELDOF: I don't think it was a disaster. I think it was a fantastic thing.
EMMA ALBERICI: But what did it achieve?
BOB GELDOF: It achieved a lot.

Geldof's stated admiration for Occupy stems from the simplicity of their message, which he paraphrases as "'fuck off, everything, just fuck off, it's crap" [. . . and] "We resist. We say no." What do you say no about? "The lot. Everything. It's just not working"' (Alberici 2013).

At first glance, this could be mistaken for an about-turn, an abandonment by Geldof of an entrepreneurial style of activism that has shifted in form with the prevailing neoliberal orthodoxy or an embracing of the punk-diplomacy popularly bound up with his persona. This, however, is not quite the case. A more convincing understanding takes account of the man seated next to Geldof during the ABC interview, the businessman David Jones. As a very successful advertising executive, Jones enjoyed high-profile positions at PR and advertising agencies such as Havas and Euro RSCG Worldwide and has led an advisory team for then-Conservative Party Leader David Cameron.

Jones is an active advocate of ethical business practises, and he sets out many of these principles in his book *Who Cares Wins* (Jones 2012). It is Jones's contention that 'consumers, customers, employees and now shareholders expect business to be more socially responsible' (Jones 2012, xiii) at a time when social media provides a powerful platform to help them realise these expectations. For Jones, this is a key feature of 'The Age of Damage', the name he gives the current phase in the history of business in order to emphasise the potential negative outcomes for companies that fail to meet consumers' moral standards. The target audience for his work is clearly members of the business sector, whom he advises to 'out-behave' the competition (Jones 2012, xiv). It is perhaps because of this audience that Jones frames his arguments in a way that invokes an archetypal rationale actor. For example, much of his book is given to explaining that '[t]he danger of being one of the companies punished by empowered consumers for failing to do the right thing far outweighs the downsides of changing to be a better business' (Jones 2012, xiv).

Leaving aside Jones's emphasis on the new power of social media, his arguments in favour of ethical business practices are not entirely unique. In fact, his belief that '[d]oing the right thing does not mean sacrificing profit' but, on the contrary, 'will protect companies in the future' (Jones 2012, 22) aligns Jones squarely with a small cluster of business leaders, entrepreneurs, and activists who have elsewhere been labelled as 'conscience capitalists' (Farrell 2015). Although conscience capitalists predate the financial crisis, their public visibility and the veracity of their arguments have heightened since the economic downturn. Spanning both the for- and non-profit sectors, conscience capitalists argue in different ways that 'market capitalism and areas of conscience (concern for social and environmental problems) should be linked' (Farrell 2015, 258). Those emerging from the for-profit sector 'often argue for the transformation of free-market capitalism to account for social/environmental externalities' (Farrell 2015, 258). They appropriate some of the criticisms of neoliberal capitalism that emerged in the aftermath of the crisis, claiming that capitalism has failed and so must be replaced by a new type of capitalism. This, they argue, requires a more thorough integration of conscience into business practice, in a manner distinct from traditional corporate social responsibility initiatives that often append conscience to the essential core of profit-seeking.

Their equivalents in the non-profit sector often assert that 'when applied to social and environmental causes, some combination of private (corporate) philanthropy, market principles, and commercial thinking will prove more effective than state aid and charity' (Farrell 2015, 258, for an example see Bishop and Green 2008). Charity and state aid, it is argued, have failed to effectively curb environmental degradation or alleviate suffering in the world (Frances 2008). They argue that it is time for business to take the lead in solving the world's problems and 'business people, because of the success they have enjoyed in private ventures, are well suited to bring their skills to the non-profit sector' (Farrell 2015, 258, for an example, see Mackey 2009). As such, the non-profit variant of conscience capitalism asserts that the solution to the world's problems is a more commercialised and business-oriented non-profit organisation that frames both problems and solutions in market-like terms. One of the formulations that receives substantial praise from conscience capitalists is the social enterprise, 'an organisation that attacks [social and environmental] problems through a business format, even if it is not legally structured as a profit-seeking entity' (Bornstein and Davis 2010, xv). David Jones's argument that the for- and non-profit sectors 'can learn a lot from each other' is consistent with this variant of conscience capitalism.

Elsewhere it has been shown (Farrell 2015) that rather than offering a critique of neoliberalism, conscience capitalism actually provides a way to *advance* neoliberalism's political-economic project by offering it new environments in which to grow, such as areas of conscience. Rather than providing an alternative to neoliberal doctrines, conscience capitalism represents a new variant in the evolution of the neoliberalism that leaves intact the essential neoliberal predilection for entrepreneurialism and unfettered markets. In addition, conscience capitalism takes account of, and attempts to subsume, the arguments popularised after the financial crisis by movements such as Occupy. It does this by arguing for a 'new' form of capitalism. However, this new capitalism leaves many of the tenets of neoliberalism in place. For example, most conscience capitalist literature is written for business leaders and speaks largely to a self-interested individual that needs to be convinced of the potential personal benefits of altruism. For example, Kotler and Lee rhetorically ask, 'why should we care about the poor?' The answer is because, first, there is something to gain from it in the form of lucrative new markets and, second, global poverty can create other problems that might, in turn, affect the global rich. For example, the hopelessness of the poor makes them susceptible to political and religious extremists who might target the global rich (Kotler and Lee 2009, 14–15). On a related note, Jones's essential lesson for business leaders is that, when it comes to doing good, it is better to act 'before somebody acts on your behalf' (Jones 2012, 16). That is to say, the potential loss in revenue due to bad publicity is greater than the cost of doing good.

While such conscience capitalist sentiments act as a key refrain for both Jones and Geldof in media interviews (Alberici 2013; see also Bennett 2014), they also form the core values of the charity organisation One Young World, with which the two are deeply involved. One Young World is UK-based charity established in 2009 by Jones together with Kate Robinson, who is also of the Havas advertising company. The main function of the organisation is to convene an annual summit, hosted in a different global city each year, that brings together a select group of 'the most valuable young [18–30 years old] talent from global and national companies, NGOs, universities and other forward-thinking organisations' (One Young World n.d.). The summit provides a forum for the young people, referred to as delegates, to network with each other and to 'debate, formulate and share innovative solutions for the pressing issues the world faces'. Attendance at the summit is restricted, and delegates must apply to take part. Successful applicants will likely already

> have demonstrated leadership ability and a commitment to effecting positive change. Many have already had an impact in their home countries on a range of issues, including the role of business in society, transparency in business and government, the impact of climate change, global health and hunger relief.
>
> (One Young World n.d.)

Attendance at the One Young World Summit is not free, and to enjoy the benefits offered by the event, delegates must pay a substantial fee. For the 2016 summit, this fee was £2,975 (plus VAT). However, it is possible for those with the financial means to sponsor a delegate from within their own organisation and/or pay to send delegates from other organisations. Typically, sponsors are from the corporate sector, and companies such as Accenture, Adidas, Barclays, BP, Coca-Cola, KPMG, Pepsico, and Unilever are listed as having sent delegates.

One Young World encourages its delegates – who after they have attended the summit are branded as 'One Young World Ambassadors' – to work together to create 'initiatives' that provide 'solutions for the pressing issues the world faces'. However, it seemingly encourages them to do so exclusively through business methods. The organisation and its summits are structured in such a way as to promote the idea that ambassadors start social enterprises and make a 'social return on investment'. To facilitate this, the organisation has created the 'One Young World Social Business Accelerator' that provides loans (£2,000 – £20,000) or grants (£500 – £2,000) to help ambassadors start social enterprises. Moreover, the organisation's impact report uses a model devised in partnership with PricewaterhouseCooper to clearly demonstrate the social impact on investment of the ambassador's initiatives and thus prove the worth of One Young World to its corporate sponsors (One Young World 2015).

It is beyond the remit of this chapter to assess the worth or value of the initiatives inspired by One Young World or to appraise the social and environmental benefits they may have produced. What is important, though, is to note the extent to which One Young World espouses the version of conscience capitalism adhered to by Jones. The young people involved with the organisation are encouraged to reformulate society or the environment as things relatable to the market and to consider social or environmental problems as requiring solutions that can demonstrate a 'social return on investment'. In this way, the ambassadors help to make businesses more ethical, but do so in a manner that facilitates further processes of neoliberalisation. One Young World says of its delegates that 'many return to their companies and set about creating change from within, energising their corporate environment (One Young World n.d.).

One Young World Ambassadors are not alone in their efforts as they are joined by a range of established world leaders, referred to by the organisation as 'counsellors'. These counsellors meet with the delegates over the course of the summit and address the cohort with inspiring speeches. Previous counsellors include a range of entrepreneurs, business leaders, celebrities, political elites, and activists. These include Carl-Henric Svanberg, chair or BP and Volvo; former UN Secretary-General Kofi Annan; Muhammad Yunus, micro-finance specialist; businessman Richard Branson; Archbishop Desmond Tutu; and Bob Geldof.

Unlike many other counsellors, Geldof has addressed the One Young World summit in each year. His performances on each occasion play to his established 'punk diplomat' image. Accordingly, while many of his fellow counsellors are smartly dressed, Geldof is noticeably more casual in his appearance. His speeches are delivered in his established caustic style that works to provoke those around him. Most notably, in 2015 Geldof remarked to his audience that 'your generation is already stained with blood. Your age group are the killers of Syria' (Geldof 2015). Also in 2010, Geldof cites the estimated amount of finance needed to mitigate climate change and compares this to the amounts spent each year on cosmetics, fashion, and consumer technology. He implies that global priorities are misdirected and levels this accusation squarely at his young audience.

However, he also castigates his own generation for its political, economic, social, and environmental failures. These failures, Geldof contends, are the result of the dominant political paradigm of the twentieth century, competition. By contrast, the political paradigm of the twenty-first century is, for Geldof, cooperation (Geldof 2010). In his address to the 2011 One Young World Summit, Geldof continues his narrative on the failures of the twentieth century's dominant political paradigms. Among the key hindrances to effective political change is that '[f]ormal power still resides with the nation state at the precise moment that the nation state in incapable of dealing with the issues it encounters', such as climate change. He notes global protest movements and concedes that they have emerged because 'the commercial class has failed, the political class has failed, the fourth estate – the media – has utterly failed, the churches have nothing to say that recognises anything'. Geldof then finishes with a prediction that 'a new politics is coming because a new economics demands it' (Geldof 2011). The task for his audience of One Young World delegates is to devise that new politics.

Geldof's succession of addresses to the One Young World summits perfectly encapsulate the main characteristics of his political persona. Aesthetically, he displays all the hallmarks of the punk diplomat identified by Cooper (2008), as evidenced by Geldof's appearance. His appearance contrasts that of the other counsellors, and his pessimistic tone and profanity-laden rhetoric also speak to his punk image and work to distance him from those around him. Moreover, he disrupts some of the main marketing identifiers of One Young World. The organisation targets the young delegates as the leaders of the future. However, for Geldof, the delegates are the 'thinking present, not the future', and he asks of them to 'spare me the young stuff' (Geldof 2011). Geldof routinely rails against the political and commercial establishments and distances himself from them by highlighting their failures. In addition, he goes on to offer a clear criticism of the concept of competition that has dominated Western political thinking throughout the twentieth century.

However, despite Geldof's protestations against the dominant political order and its institutions, as well as his efforts to position himself as antagonistic to authority, his political pronouncements within the One Young World forum still align closely with the neoliberal project. More specifically, Geldof's position is consistent with a type of conscience capitalism that accounts for the failures of the neoliberal project and acknowledges the problems this has created, but which argues for a new, invigorated form of neoliberalism to solve those very problems. This 'new economics' – which accounts for social and environmental externalities and attempts to subsume within a market system in order to extract value from them while ostensibly 'solving' them – demands a 'new politics'. Geldof's role within One Young World is to inspire and guide the delegates to realise this new market paradigm.

Conclusion

The longevity of Geldof's career as a political activist offers a unique insight into the evolving nature of celebrity activism and its relationship with the political-economic environments in which it operates. Geldof's distinctiveness automatically limits the extent to which his example can be extrapolated to account for celebrity activism in general. Also the myriad external factors that influence the shape of specific instances of celebrity activism render such a task difficult.

In each phase of Geldof's political career, he has been represented as a 'punk' outsider to authority who dismisses the protocols of diplomacy in an effort to get things done. This has helped align him with populations in both the global North and South for whom he is represented as being above party politics and ideology. However, underneath the surface of Geldof's outsider persona, his activism is closely aligned with the dominant form of neoliberalism and has shifted in its nature in a manner synchronous with the broader neoliberal project. Geldof's activism and its popular representation in the 1980s closely matched the key tenets of Thatcherite roll-back neoliberalism; by the 1990s, Geldof's politics was more akin to Blairite roll-out neoliberalism. In the aftermath of the 2008 global financial crises, Geldof's political activity shifted again to support an emerging group of conscience capitalists who want the neoliberal project to account for previously disregarded externalities in order to ostensibly make the world a better place. However, in the process, they want to realise untold financial benefits of doing good and sustain the neoliberal project by offering new geographical and social arenas to colonise. The historical shifts in Geldof's activism serve to highlight the potential disjuncture between a celebrity activist's performances – both aesthetically and rhetorically – and the persona they help to craft, on the one hand, and the underlying political-economic structures in which the celebrity system operates, on the other.

Note

1 This was merged with the Public Enterprises Supervising Agency (PESA) to form the Privatisation and Public Enterprises Supervising Agency (PPESA) in 2004.

References

Aaronovitch, D. (2005) 'This Was a Strange and Wonderful Day', *The Times T2 Supplement*, 4 July: 4.

Aitken, J. (2013) *Margaret Thatcher: Power and Personality*, New York: Bloomsbury.

Alberici, E. (2013) 'Jones and Geldof Say Business Must "Do Good"', *ABC Lateline*, [online] Available: www.abc.net.au/lateline/content/2013/s3724453.htm. [accessed 21 January 2015].

Atkins, C. (2009) *Starsuckers* [DVD]. United Kingdom.

Baldwin, T. (2005) 'Tony and Gordon Are on Song, But the Backing Band's Off-Key', *The Times*, 4 July: 9.

Bennett, A. (2014) 'Bob Geldof Backs Russell Brand's Revolution in Call for New Politics', *The Huffington Post*, [online] Available: www.huffingtonpost.co.uk/2014/01/18/bob-geldof-russell-brand_n_4622761.html [accessed 21 January 2015].

Biccum, A. (2007) 'Marketing Development: Live 8 and the Production of the Global Citizen', *Development and Change*, 38 (6): 1111–1126.

Bishop, M. and Green, M. (2008) *Philanthrocapitalism*, London: A&C Black.

Blundy, D. and Vallely, P. (1985) *With Geldof in Africa: Confronting the Crisis*, London: Times Books.

Bornstein, D. and Davis, S. (2010) *Social Entrepreneurship: What Everyone Needs to Know*, New York: Oxford University Press.

Brockington, D. (2014) *Celebrity Advocacy and International Development*, Oxon: Routledge.

Chouliaraki, L. (2013) *The Ironic Spectator: Solidarity in the Age of Post-Humanitarianism*, Cambridge: Polity Press.

Clancy, P. (2005) 'Go Ahead Punk, You Make Our Day', *The Sun*, 6 July: 8.

Commission for Africa (2005) "Report of the Commission for Africa", [online] Available: www.commissionforafrica.info/wp-content/uploads/2005-report/11-03-05_cr_report.pdf [accessed 15 October 2010].

Cooper, A.F. (2008) *Celebrity Diplomacy*, New York: Paradigm Publishers.

Costanza-Chock, S. (2012) 'Mic Check! Media Cultures and the Occupy Movement', *Social Movement Studies*, 11 (3–4): 375–385.

Cramb, A. (2005) 'You're a Bunch of Losers, Geldof Tells Violent Protesters', *The Daily Telegraph*, 6 July: 8.

Curtis, R. (2005) 'How Live 8 Can Save Lives', *The Mirror*, 2 July: 20–21.

Davies, H. (2005) 'Leave Bush Alone, Geldof Warns Stars', *The Daily Telegraph*, 21 June: 2.

Dissent! (n.d.) *Introduction to the Dissent! Network*, [online] Available: http://dissent-archive.ucrony.net/dissent-uk-2005/content/view/62/52/ [accessed 21 February, 2015].

Ezard, J. (1985) 'Band Aid Gears Up for Action after "Ultimate Day"/Marathon Rock Concert to Aid the African Famine Appeal', *The Guardian*, 16 July: 1.

Farrell, N. (2015) '"Conscience Capitalism" and the Neoliberalisation of the Non-Profit Sector', *New Political Economy*, 20 (2): 254–272.

Frances, N. (2008) *The End of Charity: Time for Social Enterprise*, New South Wales: Allen & Unwin.

Geldof, B. (1986) *Is That It?*, Middlesex: Penguin.

Geldof, B. (2005) 'Our Fight Goes on to Make Poverty History', *The Independent*, 14 September: 33.

Geldof, B. (2010) 'Bob Geldof Addresses One Young World', *One Young World*, [online] Available: www.youtube.com/watch?v=LaoNCrf938E [accessed Retrieved 21 January 2015].

Geldof, B. (2011) 'Bob Geldof Speaking at the Opening Ceremony of One Young World', *One Young World*, [online] Available: www.youtube.com/watch?v=dlyk951rGtg [accessed 21 January 2015].

Geldof, B. (2015) 'You Have Blood on Your Hands', *One Young World*, [online] Available: www.youtube.com/watch?v=jKA6x-eR_Xo [accessed 15 February 2016].

Gerard, J. (2005) 'Handbuilt for the Driven Man', *Sunday Times*, 26 June: 3.

Hodkinson, S. (2005) 'Do Stars Really Aid the Cause? You Bought the Wristband, Went to the Concert, Joined the March and Rejoiced When a Deal Was Struck to Save Africa: But Don't Be Fooled: Nothing has Changed', *The Independent*, 26 October [online] Available: www.independent.co.uk/news/world/politics/do-stars-really-aid-the-cause-512618.html [accessed 1 July 2011].

International Monetary Fund (2001) 'IMF and World Bank Support US$1.9 Billion in Debt Service Relief for Ethiopia Under Enhanced HIPC Initiative', *IMF*, [online] Available: www.imf.org/external/np/sec/pr/2001/pr0145.htm [accessed 15 December 2015].

Ivashina, V. and Scharfstein, D. (2010) 'Bank Lending during the Financial Crisis of 2008', *Journal of Financial Economics*, 97 (3): 319–338.

James, G. (2005) 'Geldof: I'll Criticise Tories If They Refuse to Listen', *The Telegraph*, 29 December [online] Available: www.telegraph.co.uk/news/uknews/1506511/Geldof-Ill-criticise-Tories-if-they-refuse-to-listen.html [accessed 21 January 2016].

Johnson, A. (2009) 'Feed the World? Band Aid 25 Years On', *The Independent*, 22 November [online] Available: www.independent.co.uk/news/world/africa/feed-the-world-band-aid-25-years-on-1825385.html [accessed 10 September].

Jones, D. (2012) *Who Cares Wins*, Harlow: Pearson Education.

Kotler, P. and Lee, N. R. (2009) *Up and Out of Poverty: The Social Marketing Solution*, New Jersey: Pearson Education.

Kotz, D. M. (2009) 'The Financial and Economic Crisis of 2008: A Systemic Crisis of Neoliberal Capitalism', *Review of Radical Political Economics*, 41 (3): 305–317.

Lane, D. (2005) 'Demo Shame: Attack of the Losers: Anarchists Riot as Leaders Haggle on Debt', *The Mirror*, 7 July: 4–5.

Lawson, M. (2013) 'Mark Lawson Talks to . . . Bob Geldof', *Mark Lawson Talks to . . .,* *BBC 4*, 6 October: 21:00.

Lister, D. (2005) 'Anarchists Threats Put City on Alert', *The Times*, 4 July: 7.

Lucas, C. and V. Siva (2005) 'G8's Free Trade Project Is Here to Stay: Along with World Poverty', *The Guardian*, 4 July: 27.

Mackey, J. (2009) 'Foreword', in M. Strong, *Be the Solution: How Entrepreneurs and Conscious Capitalists Can Solve All the World's Problems*, Hoboken, NJ: John Wiley & Sons: xi–xv.

Make Poverty History (n.d.) *What Do We Want?*, [online] Available: www.makepoverty history.org/whatwewant/index.shtml [accessed 21 September 2012].

McCarthy, J. (2005) 'Devolution in the Woods: Community Forestry as Hybrid Neoliberalism', *Environment and Planning A*, 37 (6): 995–1014.

Merritt, G. (1985) 'An Answer (of Sorts) to Bob Geldof/EEC's Response to Live Aid Organiser on Issue of Surplus Food Stocks', *The Sunday Times*, 27 October.

Monbiot, G. (2005) 'Africa's New Best Friends: The US and Britain Are Putting the Multinational Corporations that Created Poverty in Charge of Its Relief', *The Guardian*, 5 July: 21.

Morris, E. (2014) 'Bob Geldof: The Moment', [online] Available: www.youtube.com/watch?v=-IJ-sQE_WT8 [accessed 21 January 2015].

Nash, K. (2008) 'Global Citizenship as Show Business: The Cultural Politics of Make Poverty History', *Media, Culture and Society*, 30: 167–180.

Occupy London (n.d.) 'About', [online] Available: http://occupylondon.org.uk/about-2/ [accessed 21 February 2015].

One Young World (2015) *Impact Report: How Far Have We Come?*, London: One Young World.

One Young World (n.d.) 'About Us', [online] Available: www.oneyoungworld.com/about-us [accessed 21 January 2015].

Peck, J. (2010) *Constructions of Neoliberal Reason*, Oxford: Oxford University Press.

Peck, J. and Tickell, A. (2002) 'Neoliberalizing Space', *Antipode*, 34 (3): 380–404.

Pickerill, J. and Krinsky, J. (2012) 'Why Does Occupy Matter?', *Social Movement Studies*, 11 (3–4): 279–287.

Scott, P. (2012) 'How Saint Bob became (in His Own Words) a "Private Equity Whore" by Launching £125m Fund', *Daily Mail*, [online] Available: www.dailymail.co.uk/news/article-2150195/How-Saint-Bob-words-private-equity-whore-launching-125m-investment-fund.html [accessed 26 May 2014].

Shabi, R. (2005) 'Was Africa Short Changed? The Gleneagles Aid Package May Have Hit the Right Notes with Bob Geldof: But Others Are Not So Sure', *The Guardian*, 13 July: 13.

Shearer, A. (1985) 'Bob and Old Nick', *The Guardian*: unknown page.

Swain, J. (2005) 'The Truth Is That There Will Be No Fundamental Change in Africa Until There Is a Great Change in the Attitude and Thinking of African Leaders', *Sunday Times Magazine*, 2 July: 20.

Tickell, A. and Peck, J. (2003) 'Making Global Rules: Globalization or Neoliberalization', in J. Peck and H. Wai-Chung Yueng (eds.) *Remaking the Global Economy*, London: Sage: 163–181.

The Times (1985) '1985: Main Events of the Year', *The Times*, 31 December: unknown page.

Times, T. (2005) 'The Better Tune', *The Times*, 4 July: 17.

Turner, S. (1986) 'Spectrum: From Protest to Participation/Impact of the Post-War Generation', *The Times* [London]: unknown page.

Vallely, P. *et al.* (2005) *Live 8: The Official Book*, London: Century.

Wheeler, M. (2013) *Celebrity Politics*, Cambridge: Polity Press.

Wright, G.W. (2012) 'NGOs and Western Hegemony: Causes for Concern and Ideas for Change', *Development in Practice*, 22 (1): 123–134.

Young, H. (1985) 'A Message from the Prince of Darkness/the Live Aid Famine Appeal and Government Responsibility', *The Guardian*, 18 July: unknown page.

9   Authentic activism
Challenges of an environmental celebrity

Jackie Raphael

Concerns regarding the effects of environmental degradation and anthropogenic climate change, as well as the need for more sustainable societies, have been a recurring feature of public discourse for decades. In line with other activist causes, environmentalism has included celebrities among its most passionate supporters for decades, such as Robert Redford's work in the 1970s (Lifset 2014). More recently, as celebrity and political cultures have become increasingly entangled and as entertainment celebrities have been more readily accepted into elite political institutions, environmentalism has witnessed high-profile celebrities fronting campaigns for non-government organisations and engaging with governments and agencies such as the United Nations. One such high-profile celebrity, who often speaks on behalf of the environment, is Leonardo DiCaprio. Famed as an Oscar-winning, A-list Hollywood actor, renowned for dating glamorous fashion models, DiCaprio has more recently been positioned at the forefront of many environmental campaigns by using his celebrity to publicly speak about environmental causes. In addition, he often fills his social media feeds with posts relating to protecting nature, and he endorses various green companies.

DiCaprio's fame provides a vehicle for him to raise public awareness about environmental causes. Concurrently, however, his fame has been developed within a system of media production not known for its environmental credentials. Equally, the celebrity system perpetuates and individual celebrity fame is maintained through an economic system of commercial endorsements in which the persona of glamour and luxurious lifestyles in the form of commodities circulate freely. This has the possibility to create tension in the public image of A-list celebrities who, on the one hand, wish to speak against environmental degradation while acknowledging the causal role of Western industrial capitalism in such environmental damage and, on the other hand, are dependent on that system to maintain their celebrity status.

This chapter argues that a celebrity's success in both their professional and activist fields is dependent on their audience's perception of a consistency between these two aspects of the celebrity's public persona. This results in the need for a detailed brand management plan for the celebrity and their handlers to facilitate successful 'meaning transfer' (McCracken 1989) between the different facets of the celebrity's brand and the brands of their media, corporate, and activist partners. The chapter uses the case study of Leonardo DiCaprio, a celebrity who it is argued is attempting to carefully negotiate the implicit tensions between his professional and activist careers, to explore some of the means by which the overarching economic structures of the system of celebrity production can shape celebrity activism.

Through an analysis of DiCaprio's public persona, the chapter draws out the means by which the actor has attempted to fashion a consistent brand. It explores the potential damage created when discrepancies between the constituent elements of DiCaprio's brand come to light and poses questions about what this might mean for the perception of DiCaprio and, by extrapolation, political celebrities more broadly as authentic activists.

Celebrity as commodity: branding, authenticity, and capital

Daniel Boorstin's often quoted adage that a 'celebrity is a person who is known for his [or her] well-knownness' (Boorstin 1963, 67) is overly simplified and somewhat inaccurate. Celebrities, as Graeme Turner (2013, 3) suggests, often emerge from the entertainment and sports industries and consequently are 'well-known' for their work as entertainers or entertaining athletes, and their success in these fields. Scholarship in celebrity studies over the past few decades has demonstrated that, as the phenomenon of celebrity has proliferated in Western societies, those labelled celebrities can emerge from broader locations, such as the political or the scientific. This is part of how celebrity, as Marshall contends, is but one aspect of the greater centralisation of the individual within contemporary societies and the increasing importance attached to the 'the publicisation of the self' (Marshall 2014, 154). While celebrity culture has become more diverse, one aspect that spans many social fields is the function of the celebrity as a commodity. As Turner (2013) explains, celebrities 'are developed to make money'. While they are 'cultural workers [. . .] paid for their labour', they are also 'a financial asset to those who stand to gain from their commercialisation' (Turner 2013, 36–37). Celebrities generate economic capital through cultural labour, such as DiCaprio's films, and their wider media appearances and commercial endorsements. The level of economic capital and the period over which it accumulates are dependent on the celebrity's ongoing career choices and the linked development of their public persona. As with any commodity, the marketing value and success is dependent on the brand strategy. Hence, a celebrity's identity functions as their brand.

Branding, as Banet-Weiser (2012) outlines, is based on a perception of 'the series of images, themes, morals, values, feelings, and sense of authenticity conjured by the product itself' (Banet-Weiser 2012, 4). Such a definition is equally applicable when discussing celebrities as commodities. The celebrities are products sold to fans but are also used to help promote other products and services. The celebrity's value as a commodity is based upon the audience perception of their persona. A celebrity's brand is influenced by elements including their ethnicity, gender, and sexual orientation and the interaction of these factors with their appearance, fashion, and tone of voice. This, in turn, informs their career choices, media appearances, marketing, commercial endorsements, and connection to social causes. Equally, a career choice can send a celebrity along a trajectory perhaps unintended but quickly adapted to for their benefit.

A key aspect of successful celebrity branding – that is, one that generates sufficient economic capital – is consistency. Film stars, Richard Dyer argues, are ideologically constructed in the sense that the social meanings of stars are generated through a combination of the repeated representation of their performances and the relationship between the types of individuality the star represents and society as a whole. In this instance, Dyer was considering the typecast film star in the Hollywood system, such as John Wayne's association with the Western genre (Dyer 1998 [1979], 63–64). However, one might extrapolate for celebrity culture more generally and consider the necessity of repeated, consistent performances that span numerous media platforms and encompass multiple aspects of the celebrity's professional as well as their personal life, as reported in the media. Such consistency, in this light, can be seen as a fundamentally important aspect of an audience's affective response to a celebrity and an indication of their underlying authenticity.

While Boorstin intended his argument to demonstrate the fabricated and inauthentic nature of celebrity culture rather than outline the conditions of modern fame, it is clear that concepts of in/authenticity are strikingly more complicated than the value judgements implicit in Boorstin's prose. 'Authenticity' is often derived from the public perception of someone or something seeming genuine, credible, or believable. In the case of celebrity, this rests on the identification of consistencies between the celebrity's private and public personas, the different aspects of their public activities, and their stated beliefs and observable actions. To some extent, a celebrity's success in being recognised by an audience as 'authentic' is a product of how the celebrity industry 'encourages us to think in terms of "really"; what is the celebrity 'really' like? (Dyer 2004 [1986], 2). Drawing on Dyer's work, Su Holmes observes that audiences are 'perpetually encouraged to search the persona for elements of the real and [therefore] authentic' even though they 'may be aware of the constructed nature of this framework' (Holmes 2005, 24). The public cannot judge whether a celebrity is accurately portraying their 'true' selves. However, they can choose to accept the image being conveyed and perceive the celebrity as authentic. Such a decision can occur in spite of the construction of a celebrity's brand, which blurs the view of a celebrity as 'authentic'. Authenticity, it seems, is not only viewed 'as residing inside the self, but also is demonstrated by allowing the outside world access to one's inner self' (Banet-Weiser 2012, 60). This is somewhat dependent on the celebrity presenting a convincing view of what they are 'really' like. In this way, a celebrity's ability to create an 'authentic' brand can be seen to make a contribution to their career and their capacity to generate economic capital.

More than this, a celebrity's brand is intertwined with their ability to generate 'social capital'. Understood as the assets possessed by an individual derived from what the person means to those in the surrounding social field, Bourdieu's arguments concerning social capital demonstrate the opportunities for an individual generated through 'the acquisition of a reputation for competence and an image of respectability and honourability' or, one might add, authenticity (Bourdieu 1984, 291). Bourdieu's work on social capital explores the inherent value in an individual's social networks, the circles in which an individual moves. The social capital of celebrities can be seen in their 'greater presence and a wider scope of activity and agency than [. . .] those who make up the rest of the population . . . [and their ability] to move on the public stage while the rest of us watch' (Marshall 2001, ix). As the features of celebrity culture and the institutions of formal politics become more closely aligned (see Wheeler 2013), the social networks in which celebrities move are increasingly political in nature. This is evident in the political activism of Angelina Jolie – in particular, her work with the UN Refugee Agency – and Bono, who has met with G8 leaders (Cooper 2016). The development of this type of what could be referred to as 'political capital' (French 2011) can also be seen with DiCaprio, particularly in his role as UN Messenger of Peace for Climate Change (Zennie 2014).

Ultimately a celebrity's public persona can be viewed as, among other things, a commodity that generates economic capital for both the celebrity and those who seek to profit from the commercialisation of the individual. The increasing economic capital of the celebrity also escalates their social capital, which might be put to political use in the form of activism. However, the success of all these endeavours is influenced by the continued audience perception of the celebrity as being in some way authentic. This authenticity is, to some degree, influenced by the observation of consistencies between the celebrity's public life and the glimpses of their private life that the public are able to see. It is also influenced by the consistencies between the celebrity's cultural labour and the types of commercial and non-profit endorsements they perform. In this regard, consistency correlates to successful 'meaning transfer'. As McCracken (1989) explains, 'meaning transfer' describes the process whereby the celebrity's image is transferred to the product or service they are endorsing through the advertisement and then on to the end user of the product or service. This transfer can work in both directions, where not only does the celebrity's brand impact the brand being sold, but the celebrity can be affected by the brand they have chosen to support. Through this process, the celebrity's brand is not only altered by what they endorse, but the brand they support also borrows from their image, and the consumer then reads the meaning transferred. McCracken's ideas have been an important feature of research on advertising (see, for example, Tripp, Jensen and Carlson 1994, 535; Choi and Rifon 2007). This concept is applied to the case study of DiCaprio to explore the features of his brand and how meaning is transferred between his identity and the brands of the products he endorses. The chapter also includes an analysis of how DiCaprio is able to develop an 'authentic' brand and considers how inconsistencies in his persona can potentially damage his brand.

Leonardo DiCaprio: the man and the brand

Born in Los Angeles on November 11, 1974, A-list actor Leonardo DiCaprio is perhaps best known as one of the leads in the blockbuster *Titanic* (1997) and his subsequent film work with acclaimed director Martin Scorsese. However, DiCaprio is also associated with the trappings of a glamorous lifestyle, such as his frequent dating of fashion models. In addition, DiCaprio owns the film company Appian Way Productions. He is also an environmental activist and founded his own non-profit organisation in 1998, the Leonardo DiCaprio Foundation. Until recent years, traditional media shaped DiCaprio's brand; however, he has adapted and embraced social media, using it to promote his environmentalism.

DiCaprio has sustained a Hollywood career for more almost three decades. In that time, his brand has developed with maturity and professional experience. Compared to many of his contemporaries, DiCaprio is very private, which means his public image is more reliant on his film appearances and other professional work than on media portrayals of his life outside of his professional activities. To date, there have been five distinct stages in DiCaprio's brand development. DiCaprio's first big role was in *Growing Pains* (1991), which launched his brand as a cute teenager. DiCaprio then showed greater acting range through his appearance as a disabled young man in *What's Eating Gilbert Grape* (1993) and a drug addict in *Basketball Diaries* (1995). *What's Eating Gilbert Grape* (1993) also led to DiCaprio's first Oscar nomination, moving his brand towards being an upcoming star. DiCaprio's aesthetic appearance and romantic roles in the films *Romeo and Juliet* (1996) and *Titanic* (1997) led him to become a teenage heartthrob. This brand began to align with images more commonly understood as 'masculine' and 'serious' with roles in *Gangs of New York* and *Catch Me If You Can* in 2002. Following these films, he had more Oscar nominations for *The Aviator* (2004) and *Blood Diamond* (2006), which helped his image grow from 'pretty boy' to A-list actor. Overall, the five stages of DiCaprio's brand development can be summarised as cute teenager, young talent, pin-up boy, rise as a serious actor, and A-list environmental activist. Understanding these phases of DiCaprio's brand development helps identify two key factors: first, the facets of his media representation and the nature of his celebrity; and second, how his image is used to represent other brands through endorsements.

DiCaprio has developed a reputation as a political activist and describes himself on his Twitter profile as an 'Actor and Environmentalist'. His activity in this regard is demonstrated by publicly raising awareness about the environment with comments such as '[w]e simply cannot allow the corporate greed of the coal, oil and gas industries to determine the future of humanity' (Associated Press 2016a) and a much-publicised meeting with the pope in which they reportedly spoke about the environment (Associated Press 2016b). DiCaprio's environmentalist image became more prominently intertwined with his professional film work with the release of the 2007 climate change documentary, *The 11th Hour*, and with his personal life through the frequent photographs of him riding a bicycle (White and Duram 2013).

The representation of DiCaprio within the traditional, corporate media can be considered generally positive. Among the conventional media coverage of DiCaprio during his film promotions, the media often acknowledges his prowess as an A-lister. This can be seen in frequent coverage discussing DiCaprio in relation to the Oscars that suggested he very much deserved the overdue accolade (for example, Hooton 2016). Indeed, when DiCaprio eventually won an Oscar, the media reported on the world record of 'the most tweeted moment in Oscar history', reaching '440,000 tweets per minute' (Jarvey 2016).

More common are media reports that attempt to tie DiCaprio into celebrity culture more generally by highlighting his links and friendships with other high-profile celebrities and providing a journalistic analysis of his observable social networks. For example, media coverage is generated each time DiCaprio and his *Titanic* and *Revolutionary Road* (2008) co-star, Kate Winslet, are seen together, highlighting their enduring friendship, much to the delight of their fans (Mullins 2016; Takeda 2016; Yandoli 2016). In addition, there was media commentary suggesting DiCaprio as a 'good sport' after James Cordon and Jennifer Lopez pranked him on the *Late Late Show* in 2016. Cordon had messaged DiCaprio from Lopez's phone stating, 'Hey baby, I'm kind of feeling like I need to cut loose. Any suggestions?', to which DiCaprio wrote back, 'You mean tonight booboo, clubwise?' (McClendon 2016). Despite his response to her text message reinforcing his reputation as a partygoer, the focus in the media was more about the unexpected friendship between DiCaprio and Lopez (Ganney 2016). Similarly, articles spread when Britney Spears posted a 'throw back Thursday' photo of her and DiCaprio together on Instagram (Marcus 2016; Prakash 2016). The media expressed excitement for this nostalgic image of a moment that was unknown to the public and therefore offered potential glimpses of what DiCaprio is 'really' like. The media has also shown interest in the support DiCaprio has gained by other celebrities, such as Kanye West, Oprah Winfrey, and Ellen DeGeneres who congratulated him on his Oscar win (Jang 2016). This type of focus on DiCaprio highlights the social networks in which he circulates and, by extension, demonstrates his social capital.

Importantly, however, DiCaprio openly expresses apathy towards certain types of media coverage. For instance, during the 2016 Hollywood awards season, considerable media attention was given to DiCaprio's reaction to Lady Gaga bumping into him as she walked by at the Golden Globes. His response when shown the video was 'that's trending, huh?' (Yapalater 2016). These types of statements by DiCaprio, which publicly distance him from what might be considered by social commentators as the trivialities of celebrity culture, help position him as more serious. This paves the way for DiCaprio to use his celebrity to promote political issues. The primary example of this is DiCaprio's Oscar acceptance speech in which he stated that climate change is 'the most urgent threat facing our entire species' and which, predictably, the media discussed heavily (Lenker 2016; Mooney 2016; Chow 2016; Lewis 2016; Strause 2016). DiCaprio's use of his Oscar speech to spark a discussion about climate change demonstrates his intentions to use his celebrity status to promote his environmentalism as he was, no doubt, aware his speech would be among the most covered moments of his career.

As a social media user, DiCaprio tweeted two messages on the night of his Oscar win. The first was a thankful message to the Academy; the second was a message about climate change, the topic to which he devoted his acceptance speech. In doing so, he demonstrated a consistency between his use of traditional and social media. This consistency helps generate a sense of authenticity. In addition, fellow celebrities followed DiCaprio's lead. For example, *Inception* (2010) co-star, Joseph Gordon-Levitt, reposted DiCaprio's environmental message on Facebook and stated, 'This is definitely the baller thing to be tweeting about the night you win an Oscar. Congrats pal!'. This is a significant moment in terms of furthering any understanding of DiCaprio. It is here that he demonstrates the social capital he garners and how this can be converted into political capital, demonstrated through his ability to drive discussions about climate change among fellow celebrities, the media, and wider audiences.

DiCaprio's social media presence is not restricted to Twitter as he is also involved in Facebook, Instagram and, mostly indirectly, on YouTube. His activities on each platform, together with audience-created content, contribute to how his brand is perceived online. Twitter, Instagram and Facebook have 'verified ticks' as a system to identify official celebrity profiles from those generated by others. Within DiCaprio's official social media profiles, he can control the visuals, language, and content released. Frequently DiCaprio includes links to his self-titled main website on his social media accounts. This demonstrates a consistency among his platforms and helps create a coherent brand. Surveying DiCaprio's social media presence, it is evident that his use of social media is generally consistent with his attempts to publicly distance himself from many trappings of celebrity culture. His posts tend to concern endangered animals and sustainability. In addition, he has a more informative and concerned tone, using statistics, videos, and photos to promote environmental causes and urge environmentally friendly activity. While there is content relating to DiCaprio's professional activity such as film-related behind-the-scenes photographs and posters that might make fans feel part of a community, these posts are often formal and lack candidness. While many celebrities do not directly use YouTube to interact with fans, it is still a pivotal part of their brand. Predictably, there are thousands of videos that appear when searching for DiCaprio. The majority are fan dedications, media interviews, paparazzi footage, old commercials he did before he was famous, clips from his films, and rare videos of his teenage years. These were uploaded by fans wanting to interact globally, and some were from interviewers promoting themselves. Either way, DiCaprio does not have direct control of the resources spread online, yet they can affect people's perceptions of his brand. In contrast, DiCaprio's only direct use of YouTube formed part of the promotion for *The 11th Hour*. Generally, DiCaprio's profile pictures are professional headshots that are rarely changed. The backgrounds often consist of screenshots from films, working as online billboards for his movies, or an environmentally themed image.

While one can only speculate as to the reasons for DiCaprio's reserved online approach, one outcome is to protect him from ridicule and maintain privacy by avoiding being overly accessible to fans. Even with DiCaprio's lack of online candidness, his number of Twitter and Facebook followers has grown from approximately 4 million in January 2013 to 14 million in January 2016. His first post on Instagram was in September 2014 and it has now become his most popular social media presence with 32 million followers (as of June 2019). Hence, constant endorsement posts regarding his charities and films do not seem to affect his online popularity. His website has been redesigned multiple times in the past five years, but always maintains a modern, clean, and professional appearance. It focuses on his charity and films, rather than his personal life. The website overall reflects a controlled and conservative approach to a celebrity brand. This further reinforces his own identity as a leader and activist.

The consistency that can be observed between DiCaprio's professional work in film and his activities as an environmentalist are demonstrated in his efforts as an endorser. Frequently, DiCaprio's endorsements aid in the representation of his environmental image. DiCaprio has endorsed several commercial companies and non-profit organisations, and in recent years, the majority support and augment his environmentalism. In terms of the commercial organisations with which DiCaprio has worked, he has previously been part of an advertising campaign for Tag Heuer, a luxury watch brand. In 2009, the two parties signed an agreement that royalties would go towards the environmental charities Natural Resources Defense Council (NRDC) and Green Cross International (TAG Heuer 2009). In early 2012, DiCaprio teamed up with coffee company, La Colombe, to create new environmentally sustainable coffee beans from mountains in Haiti, Ethiopia, Brazil, and Peru, with profits from the Lyon brand invested into sustainability (Schrodt 2012; Leonardo DiCaprio Foundation 2016). On July 3, 2012, DiCaprio announced a deal with Fisker Automotive to promote new environmentally friendly vehicles that ranged from luxury sports cars to a more affordable range (Leonardo DiCaprio Foundation 2016). On November 11, 2015, DiCaprio announced on Facebook he invested in Diamond Foundry, 'a company that is reducing the human and environmental toll of the diamond industry – by sustainably culturing diamonds without the destructive use of mining'. This particular venture drew upon DiCaprio's association with the film *Blood Diamond* (2006), a fictional rendition of the very real concerns regarding the ethical sourcing of precious stones. This investment allowed DiCaprio to demonstrate a consistency between his role, in what might be considered as a conscientious film with a message about the ethical concerns about the diamond industry, and his life outside of his acting career. The two mutually reinforce the representation of DiCaprio as a man of conscience, legitimising his activism and potentially establishing his authenticity in this regard.

The link between DiCaprio and the film characters he has portrayed is also used in his commercial endorsements. Indeed he is not alone in this regard, as this is a technique used by various actors to lend their characters, rather than themselves, to sell products. DiCaprio did this for an overseas advertisement, where he relied on his character from *Inception* to sell the product. This works as a strong cross-promotion. The campaign was titled *Find Me* and was used to promote a Chinese phone called OPPO Mobile (*DeMélopée 2011*). The advertisement was designed to replicate the style of the film, depicting DiCaprio as a heroic character searching for a mysterious woman. The meaning transferred from DiCaprio's fictional character to the product was futuristic excitement and innovation. While it does not strengthen or negatively impact his environmentalist image, it does help to reach an international audience and reinforce his A-list image and economic capital. Maintaining this status is the key to having the ability to be a celebrity activist.

In another double promotion for his film *Inception*, DiCaprio posted pictures of a Pure Power Distribution solar panel on Facebook on November 7, 2009, and wrote about the ethical choice to use them on set. 'These solar panels power all of the base on the "Inception" set except for 2 trailers. They produce 600 amps of power, which could power 8 houses!'. Ultimately DiCaprio is using this online environment to endorse the use of solar panels while also helping promote his film. Photos such as these can encourage discussion about sustainability and help promote the company and film. This post also reinforces his active use of environmentally sustainable products and adds credibility to his image.

In terms of non-profit organisations, DiCaprio is on the board of organisations such as the International Fund for Animal Welfare, World Wildlife Fund, The Natural Resources Defence Council, and Global Green USA (Leonardo DiCaprio Foundation 2016). He established the Leonardo DiCaprio Foundation (LDF) in 1998, an organisation that focuses on protecting endangered animals and building a sustainable future (Leonardo DiCaprio Foundation 2016). 'Through grantmaking, public campaigns and media initiatives, LDF brings attention and needed funding to four focus areas – protecting biodiversity, oceans conservation, wildlands conservation, and climate change' (Leonardo DiCaprio Foundation 2016). Through LDF, DiCaprio has specifically supported projects such as Protecting Wild Tigers in Nepal, World's Largest Marine Reserve, Restoring Brazil's Atlantic Coastal Forest, and Protecting Indigenous Lands of the Amazon (Leonardo DiCaprio Foundation 2016).

DiCaprio has also been involved in activities relating to the US presidential elections in 2008 and 2012, through the *5 Friends* and *Vote 4 Stuff* campaigns, respectively. Both campaigns relied on viral marketing and media hype. To help gain attention, DiCaprio recruited other high-profile celebrities. Those appearing in the *5 Friends* campaign include Kevin Bacon, Julia Roberts, Halle Berry, and Tom Cruise. However, the *Vote 4 Stuff* campaign specifically targeted a younger audience, and thus the celebrities that participated include Joseph Gordon-Levitt, Jonah Hill, Selena Gomez, and Zac Efron. The advertisements maintained the same tone of voice, humour, and similar directing style to encourage people to vote. The first asked people to register to vote and then send the video to five friends to create a chain effect. The second campaign became even more interactive by asking the public to send in videos about things they believed were worth voting for. One day after the election, it was announced on the *Vote 4 Stuff* Facebook page that '[w]e are so proud & excited to announce that youth vote share was up this year, and young people have once again played a critical role in electing a president'. These campaigns further reinforced DiCaprio's serious leadership side in his concern for politics and sustainability.

In both his endorsements for commercially available products and for non-profit causes, DiCaprio displays the same noticeable consistency. His commercial endorsements frequently tie together the prestige, glamour, and sophistication of his celebrity status – such as luxury watches and sports cars – with consumer commodities. At the same time, however, the nature of his commercial partnerships also augments DiCaprio's image as an environmentalist; he engages in commercial endorsements, but he does so in a manner that helps to promote environmentally friendly ideals. This, therefore, provides a successful meaning transfer between both DiCaprio's brand and those of the brands he is endorsing, the latter being able to draw upon DiCaprio's environmentalist image to enhance the credibility of their products. The environmentally friendly nature of DiCaprio's commercial endorsements also helps legitimise his position as an environmental activist. The consistencies between his activities in the two areas demonstrate not only that DiCaprio is willing to lend his name to good causes, as so many celebrities are, but he is also willing to integrate the ideals that stem from his activism into his professional practices. This aids the perception of him as an authentic environmental activist. Due to his perceived authenticity, DiCaprio is of use to commercial companies that want to advertise their sustainable principles, while avoiding accusations of 'greenwash'. As such, DiCaprio is able to convert his social capital into economic capital. In addition, his authenticity helps DiCaprio convert the social capital as a high-profile celebrity – as evidenced by his connections with people such as Kevin Bacon, Julia Roberts, Zac Efron, and Selena Gomez – into political capital by recruiting them into the *5 Friends* and *Vote 4 Stuff* campaigns and, presumably, promoting the message not only to his fans, but also to theirs.

Controlling DiCaprio's brand

As established, there is a relatively strong consistency in DiCaprio's brand as his professional film work, commercial endorsements, and activism mutually reinforce his authenticity as an environmental activist. However, there are numerous incidents that include DiCaprio's endorsements and how he is represented in traditional and social media that are inconsistent with DiCaprio's brand. These have the potential to undermine his status as an authentic activist and demonstrate the inherent problems for an individual seeking to convert economic and social capital into political capital for an environmental cause within the structures of celebrity culture.

While *Vote 4 Stuff* and *5 Friends* were campaigns targeted at US citizens, the videos were viewed globally online. This is, of course, unsurprising when the global nature of the Internet it considered. However, while YouTube can facilitate a celebrity's global online presence, it can also pose problems for a celebrity's brand. In common with many celebrities, DiCaprio has done some overseas advertisements that do not directly cohere with his brand in Hollywood. While this was less of an issue prior to social media, it has likely become a branding concern for celebrities, as YouTube and other sites offer a global sharing platform for such material. The increasing difficulties in regionalising advertising suggest the priority for celebrities to maintain a coherent international brand identity.

An example of one of DiCaprio's earlier endorsements in Japan, which can be found on YouTube, is for the Orico Card in the late 1990s. This shows DiCaprio overacting a heroic action scene and is somewhat stylistically at odds with his usual brand (Tanaka2192, 2006). A more recent example is DiCaprio's endorsement for Jim Beam in Japan, which showed him playing with ice to create a drink (Stampler 2013). While the music and style of the advertisement clashed with the professional tone he usually portrays in the media, it did somewhat relate to his 'party boy' image often leaked through paparazzi photos. Most of DiCaprio's overseas endorsements have been strongly tied to his environmentalist image, such as his endorsement of Toyota's hybrid car in Japan (Leonardo DiCaprio 2016). However, his work with Jim Beam and Orico allowed both brands to draw from DiCaprio's image, while giving him further visibility in Japan, but did not have a strong return in building DiCaprio's brand.

Overall. DiCaprio has been relatively consistent in his endorsements and online presence, reinforcing his environmentalist image and creating a stronger meaning transfer process. This generally occurs when public messages like films, endorsements, and statements are within his control. The global dissemination of regional commercial endorsements suggests problems for celebrities such as DiCaprio when direct control over their image is taken away. This can equally be seen in some of the ways in which the traditional corporate media portray DiCaprio. While some praise his activism, others question his authenticity. In such instances, DiCaprio's strategically planned persona is brought into question by representations of him that are very much inconsistent with his activist image.

For many media commentators, a key focus in their coverage of DiCaprio is the apparent discrepancies between the expected nature of a high-profile celebrity lifestyle and the perceived principles of a committed environmentalist. For DiCaprio, this comes in the form of reports about his partying with models on expensive yachts and a reported penchant for private jets, which is in contrast to his position on climate change. For example, the media reported, '[a]ccording to newly leaked Sony emails, the actor happily availed himself of more than $200,000 worth of private jet travel in just six weeks in 2014' (Cronin 2015). While DiCaprio's decision may be typical behaviour for an A-lister, some might describe it as an unequivocal 'hypocrisy' when considered in conjunction with his environmental message. For example, writing for the *Toronto Sun*, Lorrie Goldstein (2014) argues,

> [t]o be fair, DiCaprio has had his own environmental foundation since 1998. But he also rented the world's fifth-largest yacht so he could watch the World Cup in Brazil in the lap of luxury, making it clear he doesn't understand the issue he presumes to lecture the rest of us about.

More than this, Goldstein points to a fundamental incompatibility between the economic structures of celebrity and environmental activism because celebrities

> work for an industry dedicated to conspicuous consumption, from the designer gowns and jewellery they constantly promote on the red carpets of

the world, to the countless product placements in endless movies encouraging us to buy, buy, buy.

Equally, while commenting on a speech made by DiCaprio at the United Nations, Michael Zennie (2014) opined that the event 'cemented his reputation as one of the world's highest-profile activists on climate change'. Having the support of the UN certainly adds authenticity to DiCaprio's environmental image but equally raises the stakes. This is because the meaning transfer between the UN and DiCaprio, while allowing the UN to acquire the celebrity-driven pop-cultural appeal of DiCaprio, equally allows DiCaprio to acquire the UN's position as a globally central institution. As DiCaprio's image is augmented in this way, it has the potential to increase the amount of damage negative press can create. This makes the additional comments by Zennie (2014) that DiCaprio 'spent his World Cup vacation on the fifth largest yacht in the world, a 482-foot behemoth owned by Mansour bin Zayed Al Nahyan – a billionaire oil tycoon from the UAE' all the more troublesome for DiCaprio's brand. This is further exacerbated by DiCaprio's comments about the greed of oil companies, cited above. As previously noted, the inherent structure of social media makes it potentially difficult to control how brands are portrayed.

It is equally the case that, as traditional media move online and facilitate platforms for reader comments, the possibility for discussion of celebrity brands in a way not controllable by celebrities increases. This can be seen in a video clip entitled 'Leonardo DiCaprio Owns 5 Luxury Homes, Rented World's 5th Largest Yacht, Now Marches to Save Climate' uploaded by PJ Media (2014). While there are many online forums critically discussing DiCaprio's environmentalism, PJTV's is significant in that it shows DiCaprio outside the organised comfort of a studio, in which he and his media handlers would have some control, and places him in an awkward public setting with a camera shoved in his face, being asked direct questions by journalist Michelle Fields about the inconsistencies in DiCaprio's environmentalist image.

The footage shows DiCaprio dressed casually and walking among the public. There are no screaming fans and the people surrounding him seem unfazed by his presence. Fields begins by asking DiCaprio what he hopes to achieve through the march. He responds with, 'We want to create 100 per cent clean energy. We need to make a transition in this country. We need to show leadership and that's what we are here to represent'. As they continue walking, fellow actor and renowned activist Mark Ruffalo appears next to DiCaprio. Field follows up with, 'What do you say to critics who say you go on yachts, you're travelling and then here you are trying to get climate change'? DiCaprio ignores the question while a man jumps past Ruffalo and in between DiCaprio and Field stating, 'We have to get the climate march going. Sorry'. It can be assumed the man who interrupted works with DiCaprio's publicity team or security. Regardless, DiCaprio does not answer the question, and the video cuts away to an interview with Senator Bernie Sanders.

DiCaprio's avoidance of the question of his lifestyle choices can have a negative impact on his brand. He is usually somewhat protected by his publicity team and strong brand strategy to promote an environmental image, as is evident in the many endorsements discussed; however, his lack of candidness on the topic does create media ridicule. Another example of the media responding to DiCaprio's inconsistencies is a *Sydney Morning Herald* article by Andrew Hornery, which came out after DiCaprio's Oscar speech. Hornery (2016) wrote, 'when it comes to individual "big polluters", they don't come much bigger than DiCaprio'. Hornery (2016) went on to explain. 'On New Year's Eve 2012, DiCaprio, along with a posse of party pals, chartered a private 747 to fly from Sydney to Las Vegas so the actor could see in the New Year . . . for the second time'. While this certainly adds to his Hollywood status, it has a negative reflection on his environmental image. The article also discusses DiCaprio's claims to be carbon neutral and thus offsetting his pollution by planting a forest. Yet, Hornery argues this is not enough to account for the amount of yachts and private jets used by DiCaprio.

There is certainly a discrepancy in what DiCaprio says and does. As a result, it leaves the media and the public questioning his authenticity, which can impact on the meaning transfer process. Fortunately for DiCaprio, his consistency in his endorsement campaigns and publicity surrounding his charitable side seem to maintain his brand as an environmental activist. Ultimately, DiCaprio's success is simultaneously dependent on his authenticity as an environmentalist and his status within a system of celebrity. That system is not particularly environmental, and hence, a tension is created within his brand. Like many other celebrities, DiCaprio must find a balance between the limitations placed on him as an activist and as a celebrity.

Conclusion

As has been shown, Leonardo DiCaprio's brand identity is determined by a series of professional choices in terms of the films in which he appears, the commercial and non-profit endorsements he undertakes, his social media presence, and his activist endeavours. In addition, however, the success of his brand identity is dependent on the acceptance of his public persona by his audience. This acceptance is shaped, in part, by the perception of a continuity between the different aspects of his persona. For the large part, DiCaprio has been successful in creating a coherent brand in which the constituent elements of his identity each reinforce the representation of him as a conscientious and environmentally aware individual. It is through this means that DiCaprio can be said, by some, to be authentic in his environmental concerns. This authenticity helps DiCaprio to generate social capital, and as has been shown, this can be transferred into both economic and political capital. DiCaprio's social capital is demonstrated by his access to institutions such as the UN and the personal social networks of other A-list celebrities. The distinct nature of these two types of social fields exemplifies some of the inherent tensions between the political economic nature of contemporary celebrity culture on the one hand and its mobilisation for political, social, and environmental goals on the other. That is to say, DiCaprio's position as a promi-nent Hollywood celebrity is bound up with associations with the iconography of elite celebrity culture: luxury goods, private jets, and parties on exclusive yachts. It is this aspect of celebrity culture that drives interest for some members of the audience and, therefore, to some extent, perpetuates celebrity culture. However, this can be seen to be at odds with DiCaprio's sometimes anti-corporate, environ-mental proclamations. While DiCaprio has had considerable success in negotiat-ing these two aspects of his persona, challenges still arise when public attention is drawn to the perceived conflicts between what he says and what he does. This has the potential to undermine DiCaprio's brand identity by questioning his authen-ticity, which can also impact the meaning transfer process of his endorsements.

It is important to note that DiCaprio is not emblematic of all celebrity activ-ists and it is possible for celebrities to promote environmental sustainability and conservation while leading a life consistent with these ideals. In other words, celebrity and environmentalism are not mutually exclusive. However, DiCaprio provides a useful case study to tease out the inherent tensions between the con-dition of Western celebrity culture, which is tied to practices of commodifica-tion and carbon-intensive activities, and an environmentalism that questions this. Moreover, it suggests that while celebrities are given 'greater presence and a wider scope of activity and agency than [. . .] those who make up the rest of the population' (Marshall 2001, ix), there might be structural limitations to the extent of that agency that curb the progressive potential of celebrity activism *in some instances* and its perception as genuinely authentic.

References

Associated Press (2016a) 'Leonardo DiCaprio Rips Big Oil During Davos Remarks', *Hollywood Reporter*, [online] Available: www.hollywoodreporter.com/news/leonardo-dicaprio-rips-big-oil-857185 [accessed 3 February 2016].

Associated Press (2016b) 'Leonardo DiCaprio Meets with Pope, Discusses Environment', *Hollywood Reporter*, 28 January [online] Available: www.hollywoodreporter.com/news/leonardo-dicaprio-meets-pope-discusses-860075 [accessed 2 February 2016].

Banet-Weiser, S. (2012) *Authentic TM: The Politics of Ambivalence in a Brand Culture*, New York: New York University Press.

Boorstin, D.J. (1963) *The Image: A Guide to Pseudo-Events in America*, Harmondsworth: Pelican Books.

Bourdieu, P. (1984) *Distinction: A Social Critique of the Judgement of Taste*, London: Routledge.

Choi, S.M. and Rifon, N.J. (2007) 'Who Is the Celebrity in Advertising? Understanding Dimensions of Celebrity Images', *The Journal of Popular Culture*, 40: 304–324.

Chow, L. (2016) 'Leonardo DiCaprio Devotes Oscars Speech to Climate Change', *EcoWatch*, [online] Available: http://ecowatch.com/2016/02/29/dicaprio-oscar-speech-climate-change/ [accessed 25 April 2016].

Cooper, A.F. (2016) 'Celebrity Diplomats: Differentiation, Recognition, and Contesta-tion', in P.D. Marshall and S. Redmond (eds.) *A Companion to Celebrity*, Oxford: Wiley Blackwell: 258–272.

Cronin, M. (2015) '"Hypocrite!" Leonardo DiCaprio Took 6 Private Jet Flights in 6 Weeks Sony Emails Reveal: Despite Climate Change Advocacy Work', *Radar Online*, [online] Available: http://radaronline.com/exclusives/2015/04/leonardo-dicaprio-climate-change-hypocrite-sony-emails-wikileaks/ [accessed 7 January 2016].

De Mélopée, M. (2011) 'OPPO Mobile Campaign: Starring Leonardo DiCaprio', [online] Available: www.youtube.com/watch?v=TWIJHmTr1t0 [accessed 10 May 2016].

Dyer, R. (1998 [1979]) *Stars*, London: BFI.

Dyer, R. (2004 [1986]) *Heavenly Bodies*, London: Routledge.

French, R.D. (2011) 'Political Capital', *Representation*, 47 (2): 215–230.

Ganney, M. (2016) 'Jennifer Lopez Reveals What Leonardo DiCaprio REALLY Thought about James Corden's Flirty Message', *Daily Mail*, [online] Available: www.dailymail.co.uk/tvshowbiz/article-3519498/Do-want-Jennifer-Lopez-reveals-Leonardo-DiCaprio-really-thought-flirty-message-James-Corden-sent.html [accessed 5 April 2016].

Goldstein, L. (2014) 'Why Leonardo DiCaprio is a Poor Role Model for Saving the Planet', *Toronto Sun*, [online] Available: www.torontosun.com/2014/09/27/why-leonardo-dicaprio-is-a-poor-role-model-for-saving-the-planet [accessed 7 January 2016].

Holmes, S. (2005) '"Off-guard, Unkempt, Unready"? Deconstructing Contemporary Celebrity in heat Magazine', *Continuum*, 19 (1): 21–38.

Hooton, C. (2016) 'Oscars 2016: It Looks Like It's Finally Leonardo DiCaprio's Year', *The Independent*, [online] Available: www.independent.co.uk/arts-entertainment/films/news/oscars-2016-it-looks-like-it-s-finally-leonardo-dicaprio-s-year-a6812646.html [accessed 15 January 2016].

Hornery, A. (2016) 'Oscars 2016: Leonardo DiCaprio's Climate Speech at Odds with His Huge Carbon Footprint', *The Sydney Morning Herald*, [online] Available: www.smh.com.au/lifestyle/celebrity/private-sydney/oscars-2016-leonardo-dicaprios-climate-speech-at-odds-with-his-huge-carbon-footprint-20160301-gn81iw.html [accessed 25 April 2016].

Jang, M. (2016) 'Oscars: Kanye West, Oprah Winfrey, More Stars Congratulate Leonardo DiCaprio on First Win', *Hollywood Reporter*, [online] Available: www.hollywoodreporter.com/news/kanye-west-oprah-winfrey-celebs-871470 [accessed 4 April 2016].

Jarvey, N. (2016) 'How Twitter Topped TV on Oscar Night', *Hollywood Reporter*, [online] Available: www.hollywoodreporter.com/news/how-twitter-topped-tv-oscar-871975?facebook_20160302 [accessed 29 March 2016].

Lenker, M. (2016) 'Leonardo DiCaprio Uses Oscar Speech to Speak Out on Climate Change', *Variety*, [online] Available: http://variety.com/2016/film/news/leonardo-dicaprio-oscar-speech-climate-change-1201717970/ [accessed 4 April 2016].

Leonardo DiCaprio Foundation (2016) 'Projects', *Leonardo DiCaprio Foundation*, [online] Available: https://www.leonardodicaprio.org/ [accessed 25 April 2016].

Lewis, T. (2016) '"The Revenant" Production Crew Had to Move "Just to Find Snow": Leonardo DiCaprio gave an Oscars Climate-Change Speech That Will Give You Chills', *Business Insider*, [online] Available: www.businessinsider.com.au/leonardo-dicaprio-climate-change-speech-oscars-2016-2 [accessed 15 April 2016].

Lifset, R.D. (2014) *Power on the Hudson: Storm King Mountain and the Emergence of Modern American Environmentalism*, Pittsburgh: University of Pittsburgh Press.

Marcus, S. (2016) 'Britney Spears and Leonardo DiCaprio are the Embodiment of the Early 2000s in Throwback Pic', [online] Available: www.huffingtonpost.com.au/entry/britney-spears-leonardo-dicaprio_us_56fe6627e4b0a06d58056793?section=australia [accessed 4 April 2016].

Marshall, P.D. (2001) *Celebrity and Power*, Minneapolis: University of Minnesota Press.

Marshall, P.D. (2014) 'Persona Studies: Mapping the Proliferation of the Public Self', *Journalism*, 15 (2): 153–170.

McClendon, L. (2016) 'Watch: Jennifer Lopez, James Corden Prank-Text Leonardo DiCaprio on "Carpool Karaoke"', *Variety*, [online] Available: http://variety.com/2016/tv/news/jennifer-lopez-james-corden-leonardo-dicaprio-carpool-karaoke-1201742079/ [accessed 5 April 2016].

McCracken, G. (1989) 'Who Is the Celebrity Endorser? Cultural Foundations of the Endorsement Process', *The Journal of Consumer Research*, 16 (3): 310–321.

Mooney, C. (2016) 'Leonardo DiCaprio's Oscars Speech Was about Climate Change, Which Could Be Worse Than We Thought', *The Washington Post*, [online] Available: www.washingtonpost.com/news/energy-environment/wp/2016/02/29/leonardo-dicaprios-oscar-speech-was-about-climate-change-which-could-be-worse-than-we-thought/ [accessed 25 April 2016].

Mullins, J. (2016) 'Leonardo DiCaprio and Kate Winslet Were So Cute together at the 2016 SAG Awards It Was Actually Ridiculous', *E Online*, [online] Available: www.eonline.com/news/735587/leonardo-dicaprio-and-kate-winslet-were-so-cute-together-at-the-2016-sag-awards-it-was-actually-ridiculous [accessed 8 February 2016].

PJ Media (2014) 'Leonardo DiCaprio Owns 5 Luxury Homes, Rented World's 5th Largest Yacht, Now Marches to Save Climate', [online] Available: www.youtube.com/watch?v=wQxia_M-NkU [accessed 10 May 2016].

Prakash, N. (2016) 'Britney Spears TBT with Leonardo DiCaprio is the Best Unseen Moment of the '00s', *Mashable UK*, 1 April [online] Available: http://mashable.com/2016/04/01/britney-spears-leo-dicaprio-tbt/#BOIePSRXvGqw [accessed 2 April 2016].

Schrodt, P. (2012) 'Leo DiCaprio and Coffee That Helps', *Esquire*, [online] Available: www.esquire.com/food-drink/food/a12561/leo-dicaprio-coffee-6649727/ [accessed 25 April 2016].

Stampler, L. (2013) 'Leonardo DiCaprio Made This Really Strange Whiskey Ad in Japan', [online] Available: www.businessinsider.com.au/leonardo-dicaprio-made-strange-japanese-jim-beam-ad-2013-2?op=1-sean-connery-for-biogurt-5 [accessed 8 November 2013].

Strause, J. (2016) 'Leonardo DiCaprio Wins First Oscar, Says "Climate Change Is Real"', *The Hollywood Reporter*, [online] Available: www.hollywoodreporter.com/news/2016-oscars-leonardo-dicaprio-wins-869238 [accessed 15 April 2016].

Tag Heuer (2009) 'Leonardo DiCaprio and TAG Heuer Partner to Help the Environment: Two Join Forces to Support NRDC and Green Cross International', [online] Available: www.facebook.com/note.php?note_id=54818767719&comments [accessed 3 March 2011].

Takeda, A. (2016) 'Leonardo DiCaprio Hugs Kate Winslet after First SAG Awards Win for "The Revenant"', *US Magazine*, [online] Available: www.usmagazine.com/entertainment/news/leonardo-dicaprio-hugs-kate-winslet-after-first-sag-awards-win-w163073 [accessed 5 February 2016].

TANAKA2192 (2006) 'Leonardo DiCaprio Orico Card OK?', [online] Available: www.youtube.com/watch?v=3Qfe-8iNLR4 [accessed 10 May 2016].

Tripp, C., Jensen, T.D. and Carlson, L. (1994) 'The Effects of Multiple Product Endorsements by Celebrities on Consumers' Attitudes and Intentions', *Journal of Consumer Research*, 20 (4): 535–547.

Turner, G. (2013) *Understanding Celebrity*, London: Sage.

United Nations (2014) 'Secretary General Designates Leonardo DiCaprio UN Messenger of Peace', [Online] Available: www.un.org/climatechange/summit/2014/09/secretary-general-designates-leonardo-di-caprio-un-messenger-peace/ [accessed 25 April 2016].

Wheeler, M. (2013) *Celebrity Politics*, Cambridge: Polity.

White, K.K. and Duram, L.A. (eds.) (2013) *America Goes Green: An Encyclopedia of Eco-Friendly Culture in the United States*, Santa Barbara: ABC-CLIO.

Yandoli, K.L. (2016) 'Oh My God, Look at How Cute Leonardo DiCaprio and Kate Winslet Are', *Buzzfeed*, [online] Available: www.buzzfeed.com/krystieyandoli/leonardo-dicaprio-and-kate-winslet-looked-perfect-together-a-.tueBjG9vY0 [accessed 8 February 2016].

Yapalater, L. (2016) 'Leonardo DiCaprio Blushed Real Hard When He Watched Himself Make That Face at Lady Gaga', *Buzzfeed*, [online] Available: www.buzzfeed.com/lyapalater/thats-trending-huh-leonardo-dicaprio?bftw&utm_term=.jwDaQ219gz-.jxlVB8PA0X [accessed 2 February 2016].

Zennie, M. (2014) '"You Can Either Make History or Be Vilified by It": Leo DiCaprio Lectures UN on Climate Change (But No Mention of His Four Homes, Private Jets and Renting the FIFTH Biggest Yacht in the World from an OIL Billionaire)', *Daily Mail*, [online] Available: www.dailymail.co.uk/news/article-2766871/Leonardo-DiCaprio-s-climate-change-hypocrisy-As-Hollywood-star-lectures-U-N-MailOnline-reveals-jetset-lifestyle-includes-19-flights-world-year-borrowing-mega-yacht-owned-oil-billionaire.html [accessed 5 January 2016].

10 Celebrity activism and revolution

The problem of truth and the limits of performativity

Panos Kompatsiaris

The British actor and comedian Russell Brand has recently turned into a celebrity propagating anti-capitalist values and preaching against exploitation and economic inequality. With tens of millions of views on his YouTube videos and equally high numbers of followers in his Facebook and Twitter accounts, in the span of around three years, roughly from 2012 to 2015, Brand grew to a spokesperson and symbolic representative of the anti-austerity movement by British mainstream media, a movement culminating in the massive rallies and student dissent of 2010 and 2011 as well as in numerous protests against the first Tory government. In November 2013, Brand gave an interview to the journalist Jeremy Paxman for the BBC show *Newsnight* where he advocated, among other things, a 'revolution' and a 'massive redistribution of wealth' (2014). The clip became viral (currently more than 11 million views on YouTube) with Brand gaining widespread popularity and raising debate in left-wing and anarchist circles and the press. In 2014, he urged for a non-violent insurrection against the current political system in his eloquently titled book *Revolution*, citing Gandhi, Jesus Christ, and Che Guevara as his sources of inspiration. The same year, he founded a daily online show on his YouTube channel called *The Trews* (from the words 'true news'), taking a militant position on a variety of everyday social issues. From these platforms, as well as from his participation in anti-austerity demonstrations and anti-gentrification protests, Brand launched critiques against corporations, the political establishment, and the media industry, encouraging and making public, as the Marxist commentator Mark Fisher puts it, 'a call to arms' across the British society (2013).

Brand became a regular target of the conservative press with newspapers such as *The Daily News* and *The Sun* running smear and character assassination campaigns against him. Due to such defamation efforts, his overall flamboyant style, and scandalous past that involved promiscuity and drug addiction, he is thought to be a controversial figure, adding, what Mills et al. call 'public drama' to his reputation as a celebrity (2015, 602). His revolutionary manifestoes are grounded on a type of social constructionism,[1] fused by a belief in the endless possibilities of human beings for immanent transformation and a transcendental faith to a God-like, superior being with which humanity should connect in order to follow virtuous spiritual paths. Themes such as union, awakening, oneness, transcendence, and the idea that earth is a symbiotic, interrelated organism are usual references in his discourse (Brand 2014, 17). Brand argues that the capitalist system is preserved by the immorality and greed of wealthy bankers and politicians with dramatic consequences on the lives of all the rest (2014, 80). Against this greed, Brand advocates a peaceful revolution and propels his audiences to work on 'dismantling the machinery of capitalism', not by armed struggle but by 'winning over the military with our flower-power clap-trap and distributing all their wealth' (2014, 116). The instigation to a non-violent revolt and Brand's often invocation of Gandhi's motto 'be the change you want to see in the world' resonate with the politics of the Occupy and square movements that rose in several countries around the world in and after 2011 (Taylor 2013).[2] Occupy's prefigurative politics are the kind of politics that practice in the 'here' and 'now' the qualities of the ideal future society, for example, in the form of self-organised communities of equals, ethical consumption, or rejection of authoritarianism in everyday life (Taylor 2013, 735). In these ways, Brand's political persona rose to fame in the context of a generalised discontent against capitalism and the dogma of austerity that dominated Europe's mainstream political agenda after 2009.

Despite these radical declarations, there is a striking distance between Brand's anti-capitalist statements and his actual celebrity status. Taking on board Brand's constitution as a figure of resistance against capitalism or even his self-constitution as a revolutionary, this chapter employs the case of Brand in order to look at how the most fundamental antinomies of this type of celebrity activism put in tension some prevalent theoretical frameworks around the field. On the one hand, the activist celebrity propagates a change in the economic system or, in Brand's case, even 'total disobedience' (Kellaway 2014). And on the other, they are key in asserting the most essential values of that system by way of their professional practice. Caught in this double-bind, the anti-capitalist celebrity is constantly suspect of lacking the quality of parrhesia, what Michel Foucault, via an exploration of ancient Greek and Roman texts, names as a modality of truth-telling in which the speaking subject takes a risk that is subsequently reflected in the subject's way of life (2011, 2012). Contrary to previous cases, for example, the music band Rage Against the Machine, what seems remarkably unique in Brand's case, a celebrity whose net value is currently calculated to $15 million,[3] is both his extreme mainstream popularity as well as a clearly noticeable and largely unashamed gap between his pro-activist statements and fully commoditised professional career.

Since a distinction between theory and practice or between what one 'says' and what one 'does' is hard to maintain in ontological terms, one may protest that addressing this gap is a futile process and that we should focus on what his discourse 'enacts' to the world. I hold, however, that keeping this gap exposed, a gap consisting on one hand of Brand's public appearances and on the other his more general way of life, helps bring to the surface critical issues around celebrity activism as well as the state of revolutionary politics today and their entanglement with processes of assimilation, commoditization, and spectacularisation. Far from advocating a purist position where words need to perfectly reflect actions (something anyway untenable), this questioning wishes to underscore the value of sustained negation in the practice of revolutionary politics, a negation that rejects as much as expresses modalities of being in discordance with normative actualities. After discussing Foucault's historization of the concept of parrhesia and its capacity to provide an effective supplement and critique to theories of performance in the examination of celebrity politics, I explore how the devotion to the revolutionary cause was embodied in the ethos of anarchist and Marxist revolutionaries of the past. This discussion leads to an outline of the inverted figure of the committed revolutionary, the creative celebrity. The creative celebrity is constituted by capitalizing on those lifestyle aspects indexing anti-conformism and anti-normativity. Brand's identity both as a superstar of creative Britain and a revolutionary agent of anti-austerity movements displays the in-built conflicts, tensions, and discrepancies that the figure of the activist celebrity embodies today. Here, rather than as representative of all celebrity activism, the persona of Russell Brand serves a case study for exploring the potential of perspectives and approaches used for registering and qualifying anti-capitalist discourse and practice. In this sense, this article is predominantly concerned with the theoretical implications that the phenomenon of Brand entails for broadly conceived emancipatory politics and research.

Parrhesia, truth, and performance

There is an age old dilemma in activist politics of whether to risk co-optation by engaging with media spectacles and other capitalist institutions or remain 'pure' within small political formations, risking, however, political isolation (Graeber 2013; Ruiz 2005). In turn, following the rise of postmodern thought, the distinction between mainstream and activist media in the socially engaged theory of the recent decades is fraught with uneasy tensions. Contemporary theory displays an unreserved disdain against practices of political purity (the designation of someone's politics as 'purist' usually implies naïveté or fascist tendencies) in favour of multidimensional forms of resistance and diffused tactics of subversion. Along these lines, the idea that individuals or institutions who enjoy mainstream visibility can be the carriers of subversive politics, injecting seeds of discontent to the masses, is carried through a post-Marxist, social constructionist framework and 'non-essentialist' concepts like 'potentiality', 'contingency', and 'performance', stressing the ability of these actors to reach wide audiences and thus advance progressive causes (Mouffe 2013). In particular, the notion of performativity, understood as the capacity of subjects, objects, or events to 'do' things in the world by means of 'language, gesture, and all manner of symbolic social sign' (Butler 1998, 519) has been crucial in assigning a potentially transformative value to celebrities' political articulations. Celebrity politics are conceived as performative (Street 2004; Wheeler 2012; Brassett 2016; Andrews, Lopes and Jackson 2013), in the sense of being able to enact symbolic identifications with this or that cause and thus reshape social subjectivities. Thus, in recent scholarship around the phenomenon of Russell Brand, it is argued that the 'performance' in Paxman 'can be regarded as an act intended to disrupt the normative repetitive depictions of the dutiful citizen' (2014, 144). Or that Brand's 'performances' generate 'a sophisticated (form of) critique of market life that reaches a large audience in a manner that is potentially democratizing' (Brassett 2016, 3). Here, his 'performances' have the capacity to do things, to act, to disrupt, and to generate. In platforms with anarchist orientations, such as libcom.org, and comments by eponymous radical scholars, we can find an echoing approach. To refer to one example among many others, for Mark Fisher and Jeremy Gilbert, Brand's performance is 'already an act of seizure ("I'm taking it") of a mainstream media terrain which had seemed almost entirely colonised by the imperatives of communicative capitalism'. Within this framework, 'celebrity performances' have the potential to give rise to previously marginalised debates, invent new forms of political representation, and can generally shape 'new forms of political engagement' (Wheeler 2012, 1).

While the above viewpoint is powerful for doing away with the false separation between words and actions (by showing that words are also actions), it often leaves unaddressed questions surrounding the possible effectiveness and appeal of values related with fidelity, dedication, and commitment in political ideals. Especially in the case of Brand and given that his declarations are conceived as mirroring some sort of truth (e.g., that he speaks truth to power), a discussion on the sincerity of his intentions, however banal it may sound, cannot be avoided and is anyway always present in relevant discussions. Stemming from this fact, it is productive to conceive an analysis of Brand's performance by qualifying and exploring his presumed challenge to power in relation to his role as someone who purports to tell the truth, an aspiring 'truth-teller', and through what Foucault calls the 'dramatics of true discourse' (2011, 70). This dramatics, according to Foucault, refers to the manners in which an enunciator of 'truth' constitutes a subjectivity that is bound by that truth. In other words, the dramatics of truth is the process in which the act of truth-telling modifies the enunciator in a way that their subsequent way of living is expressed by it. The parrhesiastic utterance, speaking truth to power and accepting the possible consequences of it, is, according to Foucault, a form of such dramatics (2011, 70). Offering among others the Cynic philosophers as an example, Foucault argues that the person practicing parrhesia is bound to the statement of truth, as in the act of asserting the truth 'one constitutes oneself as the person who tells the truth, who has hold the truth, and who recognises oneself in and as the person who has told the truth' (2011, 70). Rather than seeking to discover truth in an axiomatic sense, Foucault encourages us to focus on the interplay between the statements that purport to challenge power and their binding force in modifying the enunciator's way of live.

Given these observations, the aim of this article is twofold.

First, it wishes to act as a corrective and complement on approaches on politics (and celebrity politics in particular), which seem to emphasise the power that certain performances might have in transforming political debate. Turning the idea of the performative on its head, one can argue that Russell Brand, simultaneously with his anti-capitalist critique, performs a totally recuperated and narcissistic lifestyle, which may be equally influential in constructing public attitudes. The concept of the parrhesiastic utterance, as the act of speaking truth to power and allowing oneself to be modified by it, can then provide an alternative entry point for looking at Brand's politics. Through it, we can read the anti-capitalist celebrity as lacking the quality of parrhesia, the virtue of setting one's life as an example in supporting and magnifying the scope of one's linguistic utterance. It is in the above sense that Foucault opposes the parrhesiastic with the performative utterance (2010, 61–63).[4] In Foucault's view of parhessia, the radicality of a statement that claims to be true does not only lie in its capacity to 'do' things in the world, but equally in the ways it transforms the enunciator as a bearer of that truth and, in turn, mobilises across the public sphere values of consistency, devotion, and commitment to a cause. The power of a performance, in this regard, cannot be solely understood as lying within the singular moment of an interview, a speech, a theatrical play, or a symbolic gesture, but has to be traced across the speaking subject's overall communicative affects, social position, professional background, and general way of life, elements that are also transmitted in one's formation as a truth-teller.[5] In long-term studies of the celebrity, the above reading can encourage approaches to celebrity politics attuned to critical anthropological and ethnographic methodologies (for instance by 'following the celebrity') where such contradictions can be observed in a more apparent way and be addressed in larger detail.

Second, this chapter wishes to argue for the significance of preserving a version of (commodity and ideology) critique against capitalism when grappling with activist celebrity politics. Unless one has a very broad understanding of performance, as the sum of discourses, affects, and materialities enacted by a person (which in practice may be intractable to entirety locate), the insistence on the capacity of certain performances to challenge the capitalist narrative includes the danger of doing away with some of the actualities that the celebrity, as the quintessence of consumer culture, unleashes. The preservation of critique, as an act that denaturalises what is given, is here needed not for single-mindedly denying the very real effects that a celebrity's words or actions may have in the world, but for emphasizing the danger of succumbing to a defeatist narrative in which the celebrity may become the flagship of revolution, one that may, intentionally or not, legitimise the market ideology and the 'genius' of the creative persona. Thus, while condoning to idea that resistance is multidirectional and that '[t]here is never a pure point of resistance, but always a reciprocal play of resistances that form clusters or sequences of resistance and counter-resistance responding to each other' (Caygill 2013, 5), I would also argue against the festishisation of the performative act in favour of a reading that pays attention to the multimodal actualities of the activist celebrity. Joel Olson's idea of the 'zealotry' as the 'extraordinary political mobilisation of the refusal to compromise' (2014) or Benjamin Noys's conception of courage 'as a non-heroic political virtue' in the name of negativity (2010, 153) may be some alternative paths to think through the figure of militant resistance today.

Before moving on, a note should also be made on celebrities and populism. As celebrities employ an immediate relationship with the public, celebrity politics are often thought to be blatantly populist, in the sense that they speak a language relying on simplistic dichotomies so as to be understood and appreciated by 'common' people and fans. Indeed Brand, who makes extensive use of the category of the 'people' as the subject to which his revolutionary discourse is addressed, is branded as an anarcho-populist (Gerbuado 2013) and his political position as an outsider populism (Nolan and Brookes 2015, 353). Here, I find it useful to avoid seeing populism as a de facto condescending term and, following an approach attuned to Jacques Ranciere, to focus on the categories that the celebrity's utterances and lifestyle suggest within a given regime of sense perception (2004). A regime of sense perception, according to Ranciere, refers to the distribution of practices, discourses, and aesthetic facts that make themselves available within a particular social and temporal setting (2004). A fruitful debate currently takes place in relevant literature concerning the meaning, uses, and misuses of the word 'populism' (a label often given to parties and social groups by political opponents in order to delegitimise their standpoints), advancing an effort to unhinge what we may call 'populist politics' from its exclusively negative connotations and uncover its possible progressive forms (see Stavrakakis 2014). In discussing celebrity populism, Nolan and Brookes (2015) argue that the charge of 'populism' against celebrities often implies a latently undemocratic dichotomy between the experts and the masses, those who 'know' what politics are and are entitled to practice it and those who do not. Rather the examination of politics that rely on the category of the people, as in the case of Brand, can seek to identify 'the conditions, nature, and consequences of populist appeals in determinate historical circumstances' (2014, 350). In the same spirit, it will also be useful to break away from the debate around celebrity and political representation (e.g., found in Street 2004). The activist celebrity does not simply represent a part of the population that is unable to find representation through formal political channels. It rather unleashes affective and cognitive modalities of thinking and being that interweave or at cases rupture with the available facts of sense perception. The tensions that the activist celebrity enables (that can take a progressive direction or not) may renegotiate dominant regimes of understanding by offering visibility to new vocabularies around social concerns without necessarily being perceived as a reaction against available electoral politics.

Revolution and truth as a style of life

From the standpoint of revolutionary politics operating around Marxist political economy, a celebrity can hardly be seen as a revolutionary agent or legitimate militant figure. Occupied by the figure of the proletarian or generally the dispossessed as the true carrier of radical politics, Marxist theory has been unsympathetic and suspicious not only against celebrities and media personas preaching radical social change but generally against individuals in the possession of enormous amounts of fame or material wealth claiming to be against the capitalist system. In terms of Marxist political economy, the abstract antithesis between labour and capital is concretely expressed in the antithetical interests between the proletariat and the bourgeoisie, where the latter, as a class, is determined to strive for preserving the capitalist mode of production upon which its privilege rests. In an antagonistic class society then, the bourgeois class, as an objective position and independently of a person's intentions, *de facto* conflicts with the interests of the working class.

Historically, the suspicion against members of the capitalist class who wished to practice radical egalitarian politics was revoked through the demonstration of some 'true' commitment to revolutionary causes. Archetypical figures of Marxism and anarchism, like Friedrich Engels or Pierre Kropotkin,[6] were born to affluent and very privileged backgrounds. In order to legitimise themselves as revolutionaries, however, they had to either sacrifice these backgrounds or offer their fortunes to the cause of revolution. From the nineteenth century onward, in a tradition spanning from Russian and American anarchism, the Paris Commune and Latin American guerilla fighters, and figures such as Louis Blanqui, Henry David Thoreau, and Che Guevara, revolutionary life came strongly to be connected with a devoted lifestyle and generally to what Foucault calls the 'style of existence' (2012, 185), that is to say, the 'manifestation of truth' in the militancy of one's life itself (2012, 185). This manifestation of truth renounces luxurious possessions in favour of the commitment to the prospect of a classless society, implying that there is a performative contradiction in advancing a society without exploitation while at the same time enjoying the luxuries of the privileged class. Indicatively, the Russian anarchist Mikhail Bakunin denounced luxurious lives, noting that '[f]or the privileged classes a life of luxurious idleness gradually leads to moral and intellectual degeneration' and that a high-born aspiring revolutionary should be 'ashamed of his aristocratic lineage and renounce privileges of birth' (1980, 91). Ron Taber describes the ethos of Bolsheviks as being consisted of 'personal dedication and single-mindedness', involving 'a kind of asceticism, a pride in being able to do without luxuries and things most people take for granted' (1988, 38–39). Rosa Luxemburg notes how 'sacrifices are part of a socialist's work in life, that they are simply a matter of course' (2011, 923), and Simone de Beauvoir famously predicts that 'every *revolution*, demands the *sacrifice* of a generation, of a collectivity, by those who undertake it' (1996, 99). Similarly, although she anecdotally protested against a danceless revolution, Emma Goldman's devotion to the revolutionary cause was firmly established, and for her and her comrades in New York at the turn of the twentieth century, the '[r]evolution was who they were and what they did' (Gornick 2011, 24).[7] For these iconic figures, the truthfulness and convincing power of the revolutionary statement is not simply a matter of how many people it manages to reach, but becomes an issue intimately connected to lifestyle choices, reflecting (or not) some real commitment through present time sacrifices. More concretely, in the life of the revolutionary as a devotee to a higher egalitarian cause, there is a strong emphasis on sacrifice, the sacrifice of one's conformism towards a greater purpose, the revolution. Stemming from the appraisal of values of fidelity and sincerity in revolutionary politics, the validation of revolutionary life required consistency between one's preaching and ways of being as a 'form of life', as Foucault puts it, 'which, breaking with all accepted life, reveals the truth and bears witness to it' (2012, 186). A deteriorated offshoot of this perception, especially within post-war

Stalinist parties, was that the militant whose life was often self-characterised by 'heroic fidelity to the revolution' became the one with the 'correct revolutionary line and authentic revolutionary will' (ENDNOTES 2015).

In a similar ethos, the writings of intellectuals working around Marxism and critical theory conceive the media star or the celebrity (although often without naming it as such) as a commodified actuality with little revolutionary potential on its own. For instance, in his *The Work of Art in the Age of Mechanical Reproduction*, Walter Benjamin, after praising the potentially democratizing process that film can bring as a technical medium, sketches an early critique of the celebrity, 'the cult of the movie star, fostered by the money of the film industry, preserves not the unique aura of the person but the "spell of the personality," the phony spell of a commodity' (1968, 11). Likewise, and more poignantly, for Adorno and Horkheimer, the culture industry functions as 'mass deception' as the '*the cult of celebrities (film stars) has a* built-in social mechanism to level down everyone who stands out in any way' (1997, 236). The counter-capitalist ethic, as was understood by these writers, advances a critique of the commodity based on the latter's form and the commoditised actualities that installs into the world (rather than its content and future potentials), being at odds to what we now think of as a celebrity and its connotations.

A gradual breakdown of this so-called purist position in radical left politics came from and with the rise of the New Left and its academic branches as well as from the gradual loss in credibility of the project of Soviet Union (where self-declared revolutionaries lived the lives of bureaucrats) in the post-war world. From a theoretical and epistemological standpoint, the idea of the revolutionary as a hero who lives up to what they preach came also to be seriously challenged. While there is no space to review all of these positions here, we can indicatively mention a few: the withdrawal of class as a legitimate marker of resistance politics; the questioning of the unified subject by post-structuralist theory; the emergence of cultural studies and the focus on the 'uses' of the commodity rather than its form within a system of production; the popularity of Foucault's idea that 'power is everywhere' and thus resistance can be found anywhere; the rise of a Gramscian post-Marxism and the validation of the idea that engaging with, or 'marching through', institutions of power is an effective path towards left-wing hegemony; the concept of 'social labour' that transforms everyone to a worker (and thus a potential revolutionary agent) whose intellectual and affective abilities (or 'labour power') are exploited by capital; and the idea that the task of liberating desire is an effective modality of resistance, associated with the thought of Gilles Deleuze, are some of these developments. In the broadly conceived left-wing thought, these ideas put pressure on a conception of the revolutionary as a figure whose statements need to embody and reflect a life of heroic fidelity to a cause. For instance, since the subject is split and one's subjectivity can never be consistent and unified, the sacrificial demand becomes obsolete, and the sacrificial act can be seen as a mere 'performance' of sacrifice. Or since social change can be more effectively performed from within platforms of visibility, the commodity critique can be seen as paralyzing, secondary, and even backward practice in relation to how the commodity is 'performed' within complex matrixes of power. After all, Marx's *Capital* is sold as a commodity.

The creative celebrity as a style of life

In the emerging field of celebrity studies, some of the particularities of this shift are evident in the influential work of John Street that suggests an equal move away from ideology and commodity critique so as to focus on celebrity performances (2003, 2004, 2012). The focus on how celebrities produce politics through their performances challenges the (elitist) dismissal of celebrities on the basis of their tendency to dump down the political debate (Street 2004; Tyler and Bennett 2010). It does so by emphasizing how celebrity politics have the ability to reshuffle political debate by putting in motion relationships of recognizability and trust (Street 2004). This is pertinent in the case of Brand since, as we shall see, the symbols he manipulates in his revolutionary campaigns aim to speak to the 'heart' of the people and generally instigate intimacy. The tendency to stylize politics, as Street comments (2012), was brought in the mainstream of political life during the government of New Labour in Britain where celebrities were employed to deliver policy or use their symbolic capital to positively shape the government's image. In the turn-of-the-millennium years of 'Cool Britannia', the Brit-Pop musicians, the young British artists, and film stars came to be regarded not only as emblematic of the British's society talent and creativity but also its main exporting good in the context of post-industrial restructuring. The milieu around the creative industries of Britain gave rise to what we can name as the 'creative celebrity'. Street's approach is thus partly useful for demonstrating how the dimension of style (and generally of aesthetics) is becoming increasingly influential in shaping the sphere of traditional political representation (Street 2004). By employing stylistic conventions in the exercise of politics, the activist celebrity wishes to construct a humane, caring, and informed image regarding pressing social issues. Celebrity activism can be then seen as part of this larger tendency of stylizing of politics. As an instrument and marketing tool, it can offer increased symbolic and social capital as well as craft a progressive outlook that can possibly lead to higher market value and thus economic capital.

In the context of critical celebrity studies scholarship, the negligence of the dimension of political economy and the actualities that installs in the world can lead to a defeatist and already recuperated position, an 'always-already co-optation' (Christopher Connery quoted in Noys 2010, 70). It is in this sense that we can turn to ideology critique and insist on the significance that a parrhesiastic 'style of life' can have in effectuating alternative modalities of being and inspiring struggles against normative hierarchies. In contrast to these outcomes, the creative celebrity propagates the implicit normativity of creative economy and commoditization, including the promotion of values of entrepreneurialism, innovation, flexibility, mobility, and multitasking as pillars of a successful personality. The principal arena where this 'creativity dispositif', as Angela McRobbie calls the neoliberal world of work that promotes the ideology of the 'uniquely personal creative capacities' (2015), is enacted and seeks legitimation is the market. The marketplace in the context of liberal governmental practice is, for Foucault, a place of truth and justice, a place where ability and worth assume validity (2010, 32). In the context of the economic capital of a creative celebrity, the narrative of a person's alternative unconventionality that opposes the mainstream (the 'outlaw narrative') is a potential 'asset', often providing the founding stone in crafting a self-mythologizing biography and the cultivation of a controversial yet 'genius' status. For instance, the multi-billionaire artist Damien Hirst frequently poses as an ex-drug user and alcoholic and a former enfant terrible within the so-called legendary milieu of late 1980s Goldsmiths. Such a rule-breaker storyline was attached to a larger or lesser degree to countless celebrities of this generation, from the fellow YBA artist Tracey Emin to the Oasis guitarist Noel Gallaher.

Here, one's 'deviant' biographical traits are potential assets in the celebrity marketplace and 'revolutionary life' is turned to a potential exchange value. By capitalizing on the outlaw narrative, the creative celebrity becomes the inverted figure of the committed ideologue. In contrast to the ideologue who remains faithful to the subversive discourse they pronounce and are bound by it, the creative celebrity mobilises this discourse for advancing one's own career. In the case of the celebrity who claims to speak truth to power then, we need to take into consideration, along with the calls for revolution, the ways that dominant hierarchies, ideologies, and power relations are arranged and distributed through this persona within society at large. The communicative affects that Brand unleashes, rather than being neutral or indifferent, are closely bound to dominant creative economy discourses of self-actualization by means of self-stylization and entrepreneurialism (Wittel 2004; Kompatsiaris 2014).

Brand, who grew to an enfant terrible of the British showbiz during the same era of the mid-2000s, can be seen as an exemplary creative celebrity. He appears as a multitalented, witty, and charming persona with a rags-to-riches narrative and a past life carved by drug, alcohol, and sex addiction (Mills, Patterson and Quinn 2015, 606). His overall performance, rather than a call to arms, recites an entrepreneurial marketing logic, according to which the 'deviance from the norm' is exploited for accumulating increased social and symbolic capital. The capitalisation on his disadvantaged youth status, for instance, according to which the one child from working-class background becomes multi-billionaire, mirrors the quintessence of an entrepreneurialist narrative and the basic outlines of the ideology of the American dream. If the child of a single mother in benefits growing up in a suburban English town can make it to the top, everyone can. Rather than protesting against the journalists and the press for exploiting his personal story, Brand regularly inflates this self-mythologization. In a chapter from his book *Revolution*, tellingly titled 'Hero's Journey', he recounts how he broke away from the misery of his hometown by following an unconventional path leading to money, success, and worldwide fame, which, in turn, he (unconventionally) denounces as pointless. The 'heroism' promoted in this case is not that of some committed radical sacrificing convenience for some project of social transformation but of a self-made (white) man rising to stardom. As there is no actual denouncement of the celebrity status in material terms, this denouncement ends up being a rhetorical and highly privileged exercise followed by a pedantic advice to the young ('been there, done that') that further mythologises his persona. The celebrity identity is here crafted as rebellious, experienced, and authentic, having the capacity to escape and transform one's own circumstances by mobilising the power of will. In their renowned work *The New Spirit of Capitalism*, Luc Boltanski and Eve Chiapello (2005) describe very acutely how the figure of this type of free-spirited, rebellious, and self-made individual provides both the ideological alibi and horizon of new economistic social subjectivities.

In line with this practice, there is a more general cultivation of a personality cult in Brand's activities. This is again at odds with an effort to challenge existing power relations, as it reasserts the canonical narrative of a charismatic and exceptional creative persona worthy of admiration. Street argues (2004, 441) that the rise of the cult of personally has its root at the transformation of the mode of communication and does not coincide with the advent of mass media and celebrity culture. However, this should not discourage a critique against it; the production of this cult is regressive as it generates fictions of 'gifted individuals' who are bold, risk-taking, unique, and deserve to be loved. In Brand's case, the production of this cult does not seem to be an accidental fact but a consciously performed practice. Brand puts a sole photograph of his face in the cover of his book under the title *Revolution*, reminds the audience in each and every *Trews* video to *subscribe now* in his YouTube channel, and posts the line *RBnews* before his tweets. His 2013 show *Messiah Complex* tries to be ironic with his 'leader syndrome', but through the conscious display of wit and self-reflexivity, it proposes a further constitution of the celebrity as a resourceful and sharp individual who happens to be a Che Guevara and Malcom X endorser. These tactics cannot be seen as irrelevant as to what Brand performs but as another aspect of his performance that asserts a blatantly self-promotional ethos. Even a 'chav celebrity' like Brand then (Tyler and Bennett 2010) cannot be exempt from the general features of the industry of celebrity-making and the actualities it foregrounds in social life.

In a recent article, Mills et al. conceive, in a condescending way, Brand's revolutionary articulations as another marketing technique, a scam aiming to preserve the scandalous and controversial nature of his public persona (Mills, Patterson and Quinn 2015). One might protest to this position by arguing that even if his rhetoric is a marketing scam, it can still contribute to building some resistant consciousness by exposing the public and communities of fans to these radical ideas and personalities. Despite the fact that this latter argument holds water, it can be further challenged, not by insisting on the 'deceitful' character of his performances (in fact, we cannot know if his revolutionary rhetoric is a marketing scam or not, but even if this were the case what matters is less what it 'really' is but what the public makes out of it), but by pointing to the affective states unleashed on the grounds of his celebrity status. True, through Brand the idea of a revolution becomes mainstream and more people are interpellated by it. But then again one should ask: how does it reshuffle the existing power relations and distribution of the sensible? What kind of idea of revolution is he propagating, and for whom?

Performing the celebrity?

The tendency to put faith in the power of statements for challenging capitalist normativity is expressive of what Benjamin Noys describes as the predominance of 'affirmationism' in contemporary left politics (2010). Affirmationism, according to Noys, is a form of thought that mistrusts the negative dimension of political antagonism, asserting the creative potential of the subject and the belief in the transformative power of an action or event (2010). For Noys, this model is predicated on defending the 'inexuastile value creating powers of novelty, production and creativity' as well as an idea of resistance as a potentiality or as a 'perpetually occluded actuality', which makes it 'all too vulnerable to the cunning of capitalist reason' (2010, xi). Leaving little room for ideology critique, the embracing of the immanent activist possibilities of the celebrity constitutes the latter as a legitimate protesting subject and even semi-shamanistic figure, contributing to its political-economic valorisation. The production of forms of critique 'dulled by resonance with business discourse and a concomitant weakening of the left as a project of social transformation' is thus an alarming possibility for Brand who represents a version of neo-anarchist politics very prone in such forms of capitalist recuperation (Taylor 2013, 733). As a case in point, Brand was mobilised by the 2015 Labour leader Ed Miliband in order to promote an open, inclusive image of the Labour party before the latest British elections. In the interview Brand conducted with Ed Miliband before the elections, one can observe the limits of Brand's critique when faced with the rationalizing tendencies of mainstream politics. Shifting his earlier 'immovable' thesis that all voting is fruitless and politicians are corrupt, Brand supported voting the Labour party in 2015 British elections. From the perspective of critical political economy, we can observe the possible or, in this case, the actual recuperation of a celebrity's 'radical voice' within mainstream political discourse.

By exploring the figure of Brand and his (lack of) parrhesia, this chapter questions and complicates the idea that the activity of a (self-proclaimed) anti-capitalist celebrity is a de facto beneficial phenomenon to resistant politics. It wishes to problematise the often-singular focus on how a performance, as the singular moment of a speech or other symbolic act, enacts progressive politics. While the idea of the performative is helpful for blurring the binary between words and actions, its insisting focus on the act, linguistic or otherwise, whose utterances open up a space of possibility for contesting normativities (of class, race, gender, and sexuality), manifests its limits in the figure of the anti-capitalist celebrity. The case of Russell Brand is exemplary, as his revolutionary persona is framed by the idea that he speaks truth to power. The focus on the function of parrhesia can, in this regard, provide an alternative entry point in examining the celebrity's political economic role. Yet one needs to consider, as Samuel Burgum argues (2015), that much of the criticism against Brand from a left-wing perspective is characterized by a kind of cynicism and a desire on the part of the critic to affirm one's authenticity as the real revolutionary. Much of the criticism also comes from the conservative press. In response to conservative and self-affirming responses, one can encourage a deeper understanding of the phenomenon by intensifying a multimodal questioning of statements coming from positions of privilege and power (Burgum 2015, 310). Once more, non-heroic political positions characterized by courage, fidelity, consistency, and self-sacrifice can be thought through as supplementary models of inspiration and horizons for the prospect of egalitarian politics.

Notes

1 For instance, in his book *Revolution*, Brand mentions, 'I was taught that my reality, including the whole concept of "a self", is a construct and that I can alter it if it isn't conductive to my well-being' (Brand 2014, 70).
2 'I like the idea of creating autonomous organizations to perform necessary social functions that re not motivated by profit. This, along with the principles of equality, non-violence and ecological responsibility are necessary pillars of Revolution' (Brand 2014, 98).
3 This data is provided by the website *The Richest* www.therichest.com/celebnetworth/celeb/actors/russell-brand-net-worth/
4 That said, Foucault's understanding of the performative utterance mostly responds to Austin's idea of a linguistic statement that operates within certain, mainly ritualistic, contexts without taking into account the more expanded understanding of the term that conceives every linguistic utterance, independently of its context, as being able to do things in the world associated with post-structuralism and authors such as Judith Butler.
5 In this sense, to this we can add those elements that are absent in one's performance, what one does not say (Farrell 2012, 395).
6 Kropotkin questioned, 'What right had I to these higher joys?' and 'whatsoever I should spend to enable me to live in that world of higher emotions must needs be taken from the very mouths of those who grew the wheat and had not bread enough for their children?' (Kropotkin quoted in Gornick 2011, 63).
7 Berkman writes in his prison memoirs, 'Could anything be nobler than to die for a grand, a sublime Cause? Why, the very life of a true revolutionist has no other purpose, no significance whatever, save to sacrifice it on the altar of the beloved People. And what could be higher in life than to be a true revolutionist?' (2011, 8).

References

Adorno, T. and Horkheimer, M. (1997) *Dialectic of Enlightenment*, London and New York: Verso.

Andrews, L., Lopes, V. and Jackson, S. (2013) 'Neymar: Sport Celebrity and Performative Cultural Politics', in P. D. Marshall and S. Redmond (eds.) *A Companion to Celebrity*, Sussex: Wiley: 421–439.

Bakunin, M. (1980) *Bakunin on Anarchism*, Quebec: Black Rose Books.

Benjamin, W. (1968) *The Work of Art in the Age of Mechanical Reproduction*, New York: Shocken Books.

Berkman, A. (2011) *Life of an Anarchist: The Alexander Berkman Reader*, New York: Seven Stories Press.

Boltanski, L. and Chiapello, E. (2005) *The New Spirit of Capitalism*, London: Verso.

Brand, R. (2014) *Revolution*, London: Arrow Books.

Brassett, J. (2016) 'British Comedy, Global Resistance: Russell Brand, Charlie Brooker and Stewart Lee', *European Journal of International Relations*, 22 (1): 1168–1191.

Burgum, S. (2015) 'The Branding of the Left: Between Spectacle and Passivity in an Era of Cynicism', *Journal for Cultural Research*, 19 (3): 306–320.

Butler, J. (1998) 'Performative Acts and Gender Constitution: An Essay in Phenomenology and Feminist Theory', *Theatre Journal*, 40 (4): 519–531.

Caygill, H. (2013) *On Resistance: A Philosophy of Defiance*, London and New York: Bloomsbury.

De Beauvoir, S. (1996) *The Ethics of Ambiguity*, New York: Citadel Press.

Endnotes (2015) 'A History of Separation: The Rise and Fall of the Workers' Movement, 1883–1982', *Endnotes*, [online] Available: http://endnotes.org.uk/en/endnotes-a-history-of-separation [accessed 19 February 2016].

Farrell, N. (2012) 'Celebrity Politics: Bono, Product (RED) and the Legitimising of Philanthrocapitalism', *The British Journal of Politics and International Relations*, 14 (3): 392–406.

Fisher, M. (2013) 'Exiting the Vampire Castle', *The North Star*, [online] Available: www.thenorthstar.info/?p=11299 [accessed 19 February 2016].

Foucault, M. (2010) *The Government of Self and Others*, Basingstoke: Palgrave.

Foucault, M. (2012) *The Courage of Truth: The Government of Self and Others II*, Basingstoke: Palgrave.

Gerbuado, P. (2013) 'When Anarchism Goes Pop', *Open Democracy*, [online] Available: www.opendemocracy.net/paolo-gerbaudo/when-anarchism-goes-pop/ [accessed 19 February 2016].

Gornick, V. (2011) *Emma Goldman: Revolution as a Way of Life*, Yale: Yale University Press.

Graeber, D. (2013) *The Democracy Project: A History, a Crisis, a Movement*, New York: Spiegel and Grau.

Kellaway, L. (2014) 'Lunch with the FT: Russell Brand', *Financial Times*, [online] Available: www.ft.com/intl/cms/s/2/64206eb2-583f-11e4-a31b-00144feab7de.html/ [accessed 19 February 2016].

Kompatsiaris, P. (2014) '"To See and Be See": Ethnographic Notes on Cultural Work in Contemporary Art in Greece', *European Journal of Cultural Studies*, 17 (5): 507–524.

Luxemburg, R. (2011) *The Letters of Rosa Luxemburg*, London and New York: Verso Books.

McRobbie, A. (2015) 'Is Passionate Work a Neoliberal Delusion?', *Open Democracy*, [online] Available: www.opendemocracy.net/transformation/angela-mcrobbie/is-passionate-work-neoliberal-delusion [accessed 19 February 2016].

Mills, S., Patterson, A. and Quinn, L. (2015) 'Fabricating Celebrity Brands via Scandalous Narrative: Crafting, Capering and Commodifying the Comedian, Russell Brand', *Journal of Marketing Management*, 31 (5–6): 599–615.

Mouffe, C. (2013) *Agonistics: Thinking the World Politically*, London and New York: Verso Books.

Nolan, D. and Brookes, S. (2015) 'The Problems of Populism: Celebrity Politics and Citizenship', *Communication Research and Practice*, 1 (4): 349–361.

Noys, B. (2010) *The Persistence of the Negative: A Critique of Contemporary Continental Theory*, Edinburgh: Edinburgh University Press.

Olson, J. (2014) 'Rethinking the Unreasonable Act', *Theory & Event*, 17 (2).

Ranciere, J. (2004) *The Politics of Aesthetics*, London and New York: Continuum.

Ruiz, P. (2005) 'Bridging the Gap: From the Margins to the Mainstream', in W. de Jong, M. Shaw and N. Stammers (eds.) *Global Activism, Global Media*, London: Pluto Press: 194–207.

Stavrakakis, Y. (2014) 'The Return of "the People": Populism and Anti-Populism in the Shadow of the European Crisis', *Constellations*, 21 (4): 505–517.

Street, J. (2003) 'The Celebrity Politician: Political Style and Popular Culture', in J. Corner and D. Pels (eds.) *Media and the Restyling of Politics*, London: Sage.

Street, J. (2004) 'Celebrity Politicians: Popular Culture and Political Representation', *The British Journal of Politics & International Relations*, 6 (4): 435–452.

Street, J. (2012) 'Do Celebrity Politics and Celebrity Politicians Matter?', *The British Journal of Politics & International Relations*, 14 (3): 346–356.

Taber, R. (1988) *A Look at Leninism*, New York: Aspect Foundation.

Taylor, B. (2013) 'From Alterglobalization to Occupy Wall Street: Neoanarchism and the New Spirit of the Left', *City*, 17 (6): 729–747.

Tyler, I. and Bennet, B. (2010) '"Celebrity Chav": Fame, Femininity and Social Class', *European Journal of Cultural Studies*, 13 (3): 375–393.

Wheeler, M. (2012) 'The Democratic Worth of Celebrity Politics in an Era of Late Modernity', *The British Journal of Politics & International Relations*, 14 (3): 407–422.

Wittel, A. (2004) 'Culture, Labour and Subjectivity: For a Political Economy from Below', *Capital and Class*, 28 (3): 11–30.

Index